Cognitive Psychology
A Neural-Network Approach

Cognitive Psychology
A Neural-Network Approach

Colin Martindale
University of Maine

Brooks/Cole Publishing Company
Pacific Grove, California

Brooks/Cole Publishing Company
A Division of Wadsworth, Inc.

Printed in the United States of America

10 9 8 7 6 5 4 3 2

Library of Congress Cataloging-in-Publication Data

Martindale, Colin.
    Cognitive psychology: a neural-network approach/Colin Martindale.
        p.   cm.
    Includes bibliographical references and index.
    ISBN 0-534-14130-7
    1. Cognitive psychology. 2. Neural circuitry. I. Title.
    BF311.M417   1990
    153—dc20   90-34255
                                                                  CIP

Sponsoring Editor: *Vicki Knight*
Editorial Assistant: *Heather Riedl*
Production Editor: *Timothy A. Phillips*
Manuscript Editor: *Molly Kyle*
Permissions Editor: *Carline Haga*
Interior and Cover Design: *Roy R. Neuhaus*
Cover Illustration: *Roy R. Neuhaus*
Art Coordinator: *Cloyce J. Wall*
Interior Illustration: *Precision Graphics*
Typesetting: *Dayton Typographic Service*
Cover Printing and Binding: *Malloy Lithographing, Inc.*

Preface

Cognitive Psychology: A Neural-Network Approach is an introductory level textbook that covers the basic topics and findings of cognitive psychology in a new and exciting way. Whereas other introductory cognition texts follow an information-processing approach (the mind works like a computer), I have used the new neural-network or connectionist approach (the mind works like a brain). There has recently been a veritable explosion of interest in the neural-network or parallel-distributed-processing approach to cognition. *Cognitive Psychology: A Neural-Network Approach* is intended as a basic and nontechnical text that covers this new approach. Although there is massive interest in the neural-network approach, there has been no satisfactory entry-level text. There are many good books on the topic, but none were intended to be textbooks, and all of them get quite quickly into mathematics that beginning students, whether graduate or undergraduate, cannot readily understand. This book explains what neural networks can do in a completely qualitative way. After reading it, a student will be prepared to tackle and understand much of the literature on neural networks. When one has an overall grasp of what the neural-network approach is trying to accomplish, one quickly discovers that a lot of the mathematics is not really so difficult after all.

Neural-network or connectionist models deal with nodes representing features or "atoms" of knowledge and the connections among these nodes. These connections store our long-term memory of what goes with what. Nodes can take on varying levels of activation, and connections can be strengthened or weakened. This concept sounds simple enough, but it gets complicated rather quickly when one considers a large set of nodes all simultaneously interacting with one another. It gets very complicated, indeed, when one delves into the equations describing exactly how these nodes interact. Because this is an introductory book, I don't deal with these equations. My aim is to give a completely nonquantitative overview. To keep things understandable, I have, of course, had to oversimplify some aspects of the neural-network approach. The biggest oversimplification is that I usually designate one node as representing one thing, whereas most connectionist theorists—for good reason—usually have a whole set of nodes distributed across a field as representing any one thing (your grandmother, for example). This many-nodes-standing-for-one-item approach becomes crucial only when one field of nodes begins to send activation to and receive activation from another field of nodes. The crucial feature is that the nodes have nonlinear input and output functions. (If you understand the last several sentences, you are clearly not a beginner and don't need to read this book.) In short, I deviate somewhat from the "distributed" part of parallel-distributed processing models because most beginning students find it confusing, and it only becomes crucial when one gets into advanced topics and the mathematics of neural networks.

This book has several intended uses. It can be used as the main text for cognition courses in which the instructor wants to approach the topic from a consistent neural-network perspective. The book is also short enough to use as a supplementary text by either undergraduate or graduate instructors who prefer to use an information-processing text as their main one, but want to give their students some exposure to the neural-network explanations. With such a use in mind, I have included discussions of how neural-network explanations complement—or occasionally clash with—information-processing explanations. For those already well versed in cognitive psychology, the book may be useful as a very basic primer on neural-networks; it will give some idea of what all the excitement is about.

In writing this book, I have assumed no specialized background beyond an introductory course in psychology. A more extensive background could not hurt, though. The chapters are in the order usually covered in cognition courses. The first four chapters should be read first and in order, as they lay the foundation for all that follows. Later chapters do not necessarily need to be read in order, as each is fairly self-contained.

A number of colleagues and reviewers have provided helpful comments on portions of this book. I especially want to thank Ms. Audrey Dailey, University of Maine; Dr. William Johnston, University of Utah; Dr. Timothy McNamara, Vanderbilt University; Dr. Robert Mathews, Louisiana State University; Dr. Guy Van Orden, Arizona State University; Dr. Charles Richman, Wake Forest University; Dr. Steven M. Smith, Texas A & M University; Dr. Richard Wagner, Florida State University; and Dr. John Lindsay, Jr., who provided extremely detailed and useful comments on the manuscript. Of course, any errors and infelicities of phrasing are my fault rather than theirs. Ms. Vicki Knight, of Brooks/Cole, deserves my special thanks for help and encouragement throughout the writing and production of the book. Finally, I want to thank Eva Benson, Kathy McAuliffe, and Marian Perry, who deciphered what I call handwriting and patiently typed— or whatever it is one does with word processors—and retyped successive drafts of the manuscript.

Colin Martindale

Contents

C H A P T E R   T W O

Pattern Recognition
19

CHAPTER THREE

Mental Modules and Mental Contents
45

C H A P T E R   F I V E

Attention
95

C H A P T E R   S I X

Primary Memory
119

C H A P T E R   S E V E N

Learning and Forgetting
147

LEARNING   147

C H A P T E R   E I G H T

Long-Term Memory
171

C H A P T E R   N I N E

Language
201

C H A P T E R   T E N

Thinking
225

Introduction

WHAT IS COGNITIVE PSYCHOLOGY?

Cognitive psychology deals with questions about how people learn, store, and use information. Cognitive psychologists are interested not only in specialized knowledge, such as how to fix a car or how to play chess, but in knowledge in the broadest possible sense of the term. How do you understand the meaning of words? How do you recognize a friend's face? How do you remember how to climb stairs? All these activities involve knowledge of one kind or another. All of us have a vast amount of knowledge. The questions cognitive psychology focuses on include how we get this information, how it is stored, and how it is used.

Knowledge is stored in the form of mental representations that stand for or symbolize external objects or relationships. These mental representations are based upon our perception of the external world. Perception does not, however, give us *direct* knowledge of the world. We shall see that perception is an active process that involves constructing a model of the world rather than a passive reception of an exact copy of external reality. Perception itself is a mental representation; it corresponds to patterns of firing of neurons in the brain rather than to a copy of reality that somehow finds its way into the brain. Our perceptions, we shall see, are determined as much by the way our mind works as by what is really out there.

PARADIGMS IN PSYCHOLOGY

STRUCTURALISM

There have been three dominant paradigms, or schools of thought, in 20th-century American psychology: structuralism, behaviorism, and cognitive psychology. At the beginning of the century, psychology was dominated by the structuralist approach. Structuralists such as E. B. Titchener (1910) asserted that the proper subject matter of psychology is the study of the mind. Many of the theories and methods the structuralists used were quite similar to those that cognitive psychologists use today. Some of their methods were subjective, however, and caused them difficulty. Introspection for example, was an attempt to observe one's mental processes as they occur. Of course, we pay attention to our mental activities all the time, but the structuralists felt that such casual observation was of little value. They argued that to obtain useful data, observers must be systematically trained in introspective methods. That training, though, opened the possibility that people were actually being trained to observe whatever a theorist expected they ought to find. Titchener (1910) believed that all mental events are composed of simple sensations, or "psychical elements," such as redness, roughness, and so on. Külpe (1912) said this is not true, and that there are "imageless thoughts," such as intentions or acts of will, that are not composed of simple sensations. Both Külpe and Titchener produced introspective data to support their positions. But because no one can look into another's mind, there was no way to resolve the controversy, and the argument came down to Titchener's word against Külpe's. Because it was so subjective, introspection was inherently unreliable and unscientific.

BEHAVIORISM

The behaviorists, led by J. B. Watson (1913), criticized the subjective nature of introspection. They argued that any observer can objectively measure overt behavior because, unlike mental events, which are private, behavior is public. There is thus no problem in obtaining reliable observations. Two people can observe the same behavior—for example, a rat's turning right or left at a given point in a maze—and agree upon what they have seen. The behaviorist criticism of introspection went much further than this. Watson (1913) argued that the proper subject matter of psychology should be behavior rather than the mind. He even argued that there is no evidence that mental events are of any use in predicting behavior. He did not deny that mental events occur, but he did deny that they can be studied scientifically. Although only a minority of structuralist experiments involved introspection, Watson said that all of structuralist psychology should be discarded because of this one faulty method—a classic case of throwing out the baby with the bathwater.

The behaviorist notion was that mental events are merely by-products; whatever causes behavior may also incidentally cause mental events (Skinner, 1975). This approach may make some sense in the case of simple behaviors—recall, for example, Pavlov's (1927) conditioning experiments with dogs. After a few trials in which a bell is sounded and meat powder is put into a dog's mouth, the dog is conditioned to salivate whenever it hears the bell, so it is reasonable enough to say that the stimulus (the bell) automatically elicits the response (salivation). It would not seem to add anything to the explanation to speculate about the dog's thoughts concerning the situation. Behaviorism was initially successful at explaining the behavior of lower animals, but ran into difficulties when confronted with the problem of explaining complex human abilities such as language (Chomsky, 1959). It has been calculated, for example, that if the behaviorist theory of language learning were correct, people would grow old and die before they learned to utter anything beyond pitifully simple grammatical sentences (Miller, 1965). The failure to offer adequate explanations for phenomena such as language opened the way for cognitive psychology.

COGNITIVE PSYCHOLOGY

Cognitive psychology represents a return to the historical subject matter of psychology in that it asks questions concerning the nature of the mind. Cognitive psychologists fully agree with the structuralists that the proper subject matter of psychology is mind rather than behavior. As Paivio (1975) points out, though, cognitive psychology uses objective rather than subjective methods: overt behavior is observed to *infer* mental events. The behaviorist is interested in behavior for its own sake, whereas the cognitive psychologist is interested in behavior only to the extent that it tells him or her something about the mind.

To clarify this point, let's consider a classic experiment. Collins and Quillian (1969) asked subjects a number of seemingly ridiculous questions, such as "Does a duck quack?" and "Does a duck have eyes?" Of course,

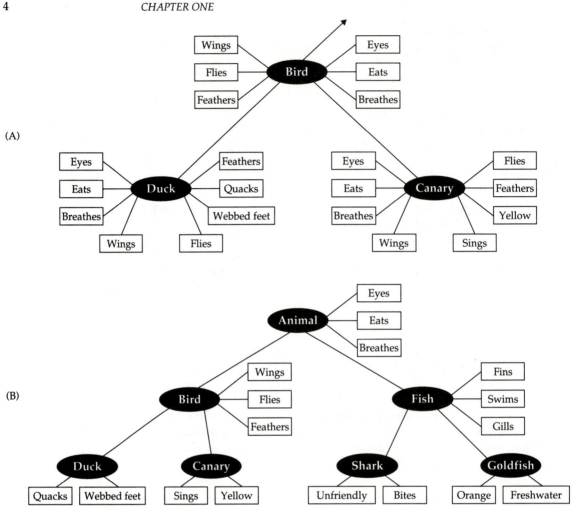

F I G U R E   1 – 1 Models of semantic memory. The model shown in (A) is redundant and inefficient, whereas the model shown in (B) is efficient and nonredundant. Reaction-time experiments suggest that semantic memory is organized as shown in (B).

people taking part in the experiment knew the answers to the questions; Collins and Quillian were interested in measuring reaction times—how long it took subjects to give their correct answers. The researchers' interest was not in reaction time itself, but in using reaction time to get an idea of how knowledge is stored. Consider the diagrams shown in Figures 1–1(a) and 1–1(b). Both diagrams show some nodes or cognitive units and some connections among these nodes. Assume that hearing or seeing a word leads to activating one of these nodes, and assume that activation spreads from a node to other nodes with which it is connected. Finally, suppose that a person says "yes" if the nodes activated by a question reach a certain level of activation after some interval of time. If the model shown in Figure 1–1(a) is correct, the two sample questions should be answered in the same amount of time. Activation should reverberate between *duck* and *quack* just as much as between *duck* and *eye*. On the other hand, the model shown in Figure 1–1(b) makes more efficient use of nodes. Because all animals have eyes, this fact is stored only once—with *animal*—rather than with each specific animal. According to this model, "Does a duck quack?" should be answered more quickly (because the *duck* and *quack* nodes are close together) than "Does a duck have eyes?" (because the *duck* and *eye* nodes are distant from one another). Collins and Quillian's results were consistent with the model shown in Figure 1–1(b). This example illustrates how one can use behavioral data such as reaction time to shed light on mental structures.

If activation spreads among nodes, then activating any one node will eventually activate a lot of other nodes, which will, in turn, activate yet other nodes. Let us say that one reads a sentence such as "I had to duck to avoid getting hit by the ball." Seeing these words corresponds to activating nodes such as those just described. Note that two of the words in this example are ambiguous: *duck* can mean a type of bird or to stoop down quickly; *ball* can mean either a dance or a round thing used in games. Why don't the incorrect nodes become activated? As it happens, they do seem to—at least partially.

Now, how could one know that? Let's say that we have people listen to the sentence above, then have them perform what is called a *lexical-decision task.* In this task, a person is shown a string of letters and must indicate, by pressing one of two keys, whether or not the letter string is an English word. We are again interested in reaction time, or how long it takes to make this decision. If the word shown were *quack*, people could more quickly decide that it is an English word if they had just heard the sample sentence than if they had heard one totally unrelated to ducks. In general, seeing or hearing an ambiguous word seems to activate the nodes coding *all* of its meanings for at least a fraction of a second (Simpson, 1984).

Usually, we are not consciously aware of the alternate meanings of potentially ambiguous words. Context activates the node that codes (stands for) the appropriate meaning much more intensely than it does the node that codes the wrong meaning. You have probably noticed, however, that some rather odd and seemingly irrelevant ideas occur to you while you read. It is likely that some of these ideas may have been cued off by spreading activation of the kind I have just described. On the other hand, there is evidence that stimuli one is not even consciously aware of having seen can activate nodes. If a word is presented for an extremely short time, people will not be able to tell if they have been shown a word or just a flash of light, especially if the word is followed by a *pattern mask* (a jumbled array of letter fragments). Marcel (1983) and others have produced evidence that such a brief exposure may initiate a cascade of activation that reaches all the way to nodes representing the meanings of words. Even though the person is not consciously aware of having perceived anything, these nodes are partially activated. In one experiment, Marcel briefly exposed words followed by pattern masks. Subjects were first asked whether a word had been presented or nothing at all. They could not tell, so they had to guess. Then, they were given a card on which two words were printed and had to indicate which of the words was a synonym of the word they had just *not* seen. Subjects in psychology experiments are usually rather accommodating, but this was asking a bit much. They explained that one can't possibly know the meaning of something he or she hasn't seen. They would just have to guess, and that would be silly. For that matter, the whole experiment was silly. But the subjects went ahead and guessed, and their "guesses" were correct at far above chance levels. Apparently the invisible word had partially activated nodes coding its definition.

Because this experiment caused so much argument from subjects, Marcel tried another approach. Correct responses in a lexical-decision task are speeded up if a word is preceded by a related word; for example, a person can verify that *butter* is an English word if it is preceded by the word *bread* more quickly than if it is preceded by an unrelated word (Meyer, Schvaneveldt, & Ruddy, 1974). Activation from the node coding *bread* spreads to the node coding *butter*. Because the *butter* node is already partially activated, it becomes fully activated more quickly when the word is actually presented. Marcel used this procedure, but in his experiment, the first word was presented so quickly that it was invisible. He found that related invisible primes speeded up reaction times. There is controversy over whether such subliminal or subconscious effects are real (Holender, 1986); these experiments exemplify, however, how we can test interesting and nonintuitive hypotheses about how the mind works by means of completely objective behavioral measures such as reaction times.

COGNITIVISM VERSUS BEHAVIORISM

Behaviorists were interested in what goes on within the organism only as a last resort; they postulated "intervening variables" such as motives or drives only when it became impossible to explain responses solely in terms of stimuli. Where a response was precisely predictable from a stimulus, the behaviorists felt no need to discuss intervening psychological processes. In the same situation, a cognitive psychologist would still be interested in the internal processes that link stimulus and response, whereas the real interest of behaviorism was in overt and observable behavior. Cognitive psychology, on the other hand, focuses primarily on what goes on in the mind, and behavior is of interest only to the extent that it sheds light on internal processes.

INFORMATION PROCESSING VERSUS BEHAVIORISM

At first, cognitive psychology involved an "information-processing" approach to questions concerning mental activity. This approach was based on a computer model of the mind; that is, cognitive psychologists tried to understand mental workings by analogy with the operations of computers. A computer takes input (for example, a sequence of keys pushed on a keyboard) and transforms the input into a qualitatively different internal representation (a pattern of electrical charges). It performs operations on this internal representation and transforms it into output (for example, a pattern on a monitor). The output is qualitatively different from either the input or the internal representation. One cause of the development of cognitive psychology was that it seemed rather silly to maintain that computers can perform operations on internal representations and produce obviously useful results but to deny—as behaviorists insisted upon doing—that human beings have this capacity.

The model of the mind at any given time often seems to reflect the technology of the age. Early views, such as vitalism, mirrored the agricultural economy of the times. The mind was seen as following predetermined patterns of growth, just as plants seem to do. With the advent of mechanical technology, mechanistic metaphors soon followed. In the steam age, hydraulic metaphors came into fashion. Freud's view of the mind as a thermodynamically regulated "machine" is the clearest example of such a model. Perhaps the behaviorists' telephone switchboard model was not so much a consequence of failures of earlier models as of a fascination with the analogies between the behavior of organisms and electrical switching circuits. The new computer models again illustrate the power of humanity's inventions in shaping our view of ourselves.

Although talking about inputs, central processing, and outputs may not at first seem any different than talking about stimuli, intervening variables, and responses, there are several differences. Behaviorist or stimulus-response psychology saw internal events in terms of associationistic connections. According to Bolles (1975), behaviorist psychology rested upon what he called a *correspondence assumption*, the assumption that there is a similarity between observable external events (stimuli and responses) and unobservable internal events. A change in the strength of a response to a given stimulus was attributed to the strengthening of a bond or link between the neural event representing the stimulus and the neural event representing the response. Thus, any internal processes were considered merely series of covert stimulus-response bonds. This left no place at all for theoretical constructs such as goals, purposes, or intentions, let alone ideas or images, because these constructs cannot easily be modeled as simple stimulus-response associations.

On the other hand, because of its implicit computer analogy, the information-processing approach is more prone to consider internal events in terms of "programs" and transformations that are not easily modeled by simple associations or connections between two points. As Paivio (1975) pointed out, cognitive psychologists see the basic elements of mental activity as differing qualitatively from covert stimuli, covert responses, or covert stimulus-response bonds—just as the elements of a computer's internal activity are qualitatively different from both its inputs and its outputs. A second difference is perhaps more important: a telephone switchboard is a linking device that does nothing but connect two callers. Behavioral psychologists tended to think as little as possible about what went on between the two callers (between stimulus and response). The cognitive approach inverts this emphasis, focusing more on central processes, such as thought and consciousness, and on looking at behavior to infer laws of mental activity rather than trying to formulate laws of behavior per se.

NEURAL NETWORKS AND INFORMATION PROCESSING

A metaphor may be helpful in explaining a concept, but if one carries it too far, it may do more harm than good. The mind works somewhat like a computer, but for that matter, it also works somewhat like a philodendron plant. Recently, many cognitive psychologists have started to think that the mind does not work exactly like a conventional computer (Rumelhart, Hinton, & McClelland, 1986). They suggest replacing the "computer metaphor" with a "brain metaphor." Because mental activity takes place in the brain, this model seems undeniably reasonable. This new neural network or connectionist version of cognitive psychology is the one we shall examine in this book. Figure 1–1 shows a small fragment of a neural network. The basic idea is simple: all cognitive operations are carried out by activation of nodes and the connections among these nodes.

How does this approach differ from the information-processing version of cognitive psychology? Consider the original cognitive explanation of language. The premise is that when we learn a language, we learn a set of rules, rather than a set of simple stimulus-response connections. These rules can be listed, and experiments have shown that people understand and produce speech in accordance with the rules. The theory is that the rules are contained in something like a computer program that is executed whenever speech is heard or produced. The information-processing approach gives descriptions on the symbolic level; that is, it deals with abstract rules. How is this "program" learned? How is it stored? How is it executed? The connectionist approach tries to answer such questions. It complements the information-processing approach.

In the case of language, it is clear that we know abstract rules of grammar, because we can produce an endless number of novel sentences that follow these rules. Most of us, though, can explicitly state very few of these rules. Symbolic-level explanations of language involve the assertion that we *do* in fact know a huge set of explicit grammatical rules. The problem is that we can't consciously access most of these rules (Pinker, 1984). Connectionist theorists say that we *don't* know the rules in this way, but that the rules are *implicit* in the connection strengths among the nodes involved in language production and comprehension. We could thus say that the connectionist approach gives descriptions on the "subsymbolic" level. Connectionist theorists ask how the rules could actually be implemented if one were wiring a computer—or a brain. By analogy, a computer program in a high-level language such as BASIC or LISP is symbolic. It uses statements that symbolize *what* is supposed to be done. When the program is compiled into machine language, it is subsymbolic, with the statements now more oriented to *how* things are going to be done.

Information-processing and connectionist predictions are often identical, differing merely in that the predictions derive from theories on different levels of analysis. There is a greater difference in the two types of explanations when the brain could not plausibly "run" a "program" proposed by information-processing theorists. More exciting is the possibility that the brain *could* run programs or execute operations not envisioned by information-processing theorists. In developing a neural network that could implement an information-processing "program," the hope is that the network may have some interesting emergent properties that allow us to go beyond information-processing theory. An emergent property is one possessed by a whole but not by its component parts; for example, water is composed of oxygen and hydrogen, but the properties of water are quite different from those of hydrogen or oxygen alone. Combining water with yet other chemicals yields still more emergent properties; the brain is 98% or so water, but certainly has some properties lacking in plain tap water. As we shall see, neural networks do have emergent properties that seem to tell us new things about the mind.

A computer has a central processing unit that operates serially—it does one thing at a time. It does things very quickly, of course, and in fact, operates about a million times faster than the average neuron (Feldman & Ballard, 1982). A computer can thus do long division problems a good deal faster than you can, but there are some tasks—for example, perceiving and understanding a visual scene—that the brain performs much faster than a computer. In such a case, the brain could not possibly work like a computer; it must be solving the problem of vision in a different way than a computer solves it. We know the brain is different from a computer in several ways; among other things, the brain does not have anything we could really call a

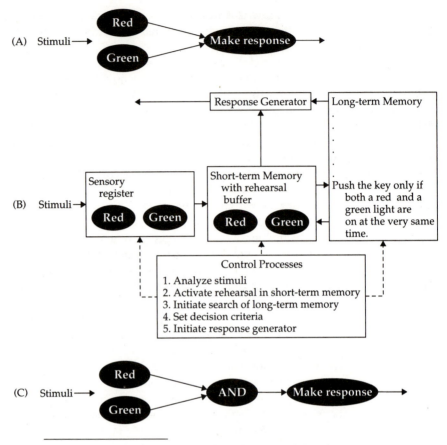

F I G U R E   1 – 2 Classical behaviorist (A), information proc-essing (B), and neural-network (C) explanations of configural conditioning. The model shown in (B) is based upon Shiffrin and Schneider (1977).

central processing unit, and it tends not to work in a serial fashion. The brain is more like a large number of very slow computers all operating in parallel (at the same time) and each dedicated to a fairly specific task.

An example will clarify the differences among behaviorism, the infor-mation-processing approach, and the connectionist approach to how the brain operates. In configural conditioning, an organism is supposed to make a response if and only if both of two stimuli—say a red and a green light—are present. Figure 1–2(a) diagrams a classic behaviorist explanation of con-figural conditioning. A node representing the red light is directly connected to a node controlling the response, as is a node representing the green light. Note that this arrangement will not work properly because *either* the red or the green light will elicit the response, although it would be adequate if we were dealing with a fish or an amphibian, because such creatures are com-pletely incapable of learning a configural conditioning task (Wickelgren, 1979a). Birds and mammals, however, quite easily learn such tasks, so their brains must be wired differently. Figure 1–2(b) is a diagram of a possible information-processing explanation based on Schiffrin and Schneider's (1977) information-processing model of cognition. The flow chart in the figure has extra gadgetry because this is a general-purpose model meant as a framework for explaining all types of mental activity. The point is that the explanation is a "program" that states the rule for correct performance. Figure 1–2(c) presents a connectionist explanation. If we assume that the "hidden" or "chunking" unit labeled AND is activated if and only if both of its inputs are on, the problem is solved. Wickelgren (1979a) reviews evidence that supports the idea that, at least in humans, nodes are always connected in this indirect way.

At first glance, the connectionist diagram looks more similar to the behaviorist diagram than to the information-processing diagram. This is true, but connectionist theorists (when necessary) postulate much more complicated "wiring diagrams" than behaviorists did. The connectionist and the information-processing explanations are not really contradictory; the connectionist model merely shows how the information-processing program might be implemented in a brain. For a simple process such as configural conditioning, the neural network approach tells us more; for a more complicated task, it might tell us too much. The explanation could be so complicated that we might be more satisfied with an information-processing explanation. By analogy, if you wanted to know how a telephone works, you would probably be quite sorry you had asked if the explanation consisted of a transitor-by-transitor description of the entire wiring diagram. As a rough generalization, the connectionist approach tends to offer more satisfying explanations for simpler, more perceptual mental operations. The information-processing approach tends to do better at explaining more complex cognitive tasks. This generalization may hold because the connectionist approach is fairly new, or because the approach breaks down or becomes too convoluted once we get beyond a certain level of complexity— it is still too early to tell. Ultimately, the relative merits of connectionist and information-processing theories will be decided in the same way we decide between any scientific theories: where theories make the same predictions, the simpler theory wins by default; where theories make different predictions, the theory from which the correct prediction is derived has a marked advantage.

NEURAL NETWORKS AND THE MIND
BASIC PRINCIPLES

A neural-network or parallel-distributed process model of cognition is aimed at explaining how and why we experience mental phenomena. In this purpose, such a model is not different from information-processing approaches to cognition. The difference lies in the type of explanation a neural-network model offers. As the name implies, the goal is to offer explanations consistent with what we know about the brain. Such models have been around for a long time. In the 1930s and 1940s, Rashevsky (1948) proposed a number of network models of psychological phenomena, but he was too far ahead of his time, because we didn't know enough about the brain then. Also, Rashevsky's theories were expressed in terms of difficult mathematical equations, and many people simply didn't understand what he was talking about. Later, Rosenblatt's (1962) perceptron model elicited a good deal of interest; however, the model was too simple to account for much (Minsky & Papert, 1969). As a consequence, network models fell out of fashion.

Konorski (1967) proposed a useful and general network model. Perhaps because he focused more on topics like Pavlovian conditioning than on cognition, Konorski's theory did not get the attention it deserved. Beginning in the 1960s and continuing until today, Grossberg (e.g., 1969, 1980, 1987, 1988a) has developed a powerful neural-network theory of the mind. Because Grossberg's theories are stated in complex mathematical terms, it has only gradually become apparent how truly revolutionary and important they are. More recently, a number of theorists, such as Rumelhart and McClelland (1982, 1986b), have proposed neural-network theories that are easier to understand than Grossberg's theory, yet they can elegantly explain a number of interesting phenomena. This book presents a neural-network model of cognition, based mainly on the work of theorists such as Konorski, Grossberg, and Rumelhart and McClelland, in a simple and understandable way.

A neural-network model is composed of several components (Rumelhart, Hinton, & McClelland, 1986).

1. A set of processing units, referred to as "nodes" or "cognitive units." They are similar to neurons, but not nearly as complicated. The only thing a node can do is to take on some level of activation.

2. A state of activation. Nodes can be activated to varying degrees. If some nodes are activated beyond some threshold, we are conscious of whatever they code. The set of these activated nodes corresponds to the contents of consciousness. The most activated nodes represent whatever is being attended to at the moment. Other nodes, such as those dealing with much of motor behavior, operate outside of conscious awareness.

3. A pattern of connections among nodes. Nodes are connected to one another by either excitatory or inhibitory connections that differ in strength. The strength of these connections constitutes long-term memory for associations between whatever the nodes represent. All long-term memories are coded in this way.

4. Activation rules for the nodes. These rules specify such things as exactly how a node "adds up" its inputs, how it combines inputs with its current state of activation, the rate at which its activation decays, and so on.

5. Output functions for the nodes. How does the output of a node relate

to its activation? If the output of a node were exactly the same as its input, the node wouldn't be good for much of anything. If we assign thresholds or make output a nonlinear function of the node's activation, we get useful results.

6. A learning rule. We need to explain how learning occurs; in a network model, learning means strengthening the connections between nodes. The simplest learning rule is Hebb's (1949) idea that the connection between two nodes is strengthened if they are simultaneously activated, especially if the activation is accompanied by attention (Crick & Asanuma, 1986). Of course, we also have to explain how forgetting or unlearning occurs.

7. An environment for the system. We shall follow Fodor (1983) and others in segregating nodes into modules devoted to specific processes (e.g., recognizing faces) because this is the way the brain seems to work. Of course, these modules are massively interconnected. We follow Grossberg (1980), Konorski (1967), and Martindale (1981) in arguing that the nodes in any analyzer are organized into several layers. Connections among nodes on different layers are generally excitatory, and connections among nodes on the same layer are usually inhibitory. Again, this seems to be the way the brain works.

According to network models, cognition is a massively parallel process, meaning simply that all the nodes are doing whatever they do simultaneously. That is why neural-network models are also called parallel-distributed processing models. The mind is *not* like a general purpose computer that runs all kinds of different software; it more closely resembles a huge number of dedicated computers that are wired up to perform specific tasks. There is thus no "software"; each computer is "hardwired" to do one specific thing. Learning corresponds to changing some of the wiring, not to running a revised version of a program. Within any analyzer or module, some computations may be done in a roughly serial fashion. Unlike a computer, however, a brain does not really work in a serial fashion. When a computer needs to find something in its memory, it engages in some kind of search. A brain or a neural network does not. It does not need to do so, because its memory is content addressable: an item automatically defines its place in memory—a stimulus or retrieval cue (via its connections to other nodes) automatically activates the nodes coding what was to be remembered. Remembering *is* activation of these nodes. When a computer finds something in memory, it moves the item to its CPU (central processing unit) to perform operations on it. A brain does not seem to do this; any computation has to be done "in place," for several reasons. If memories are defined as the strengths of connections among nodes, it is unclear what it would mean to move these connection strengths. Even if these weights could be moved, where would they be moved? The brain has no CPU. To say that the brain has a CPU would be equivalent to saying that the brain has a brain (compare Rychlak, 1987).

Information-processing models of cognition compare the way the mind works to the way a conventional computer works. If we have reason to believe this is not a good analogy, such theories are sometimes not very satisfying. Information-processing models generally include an executive processor or something similar (e.g., Dodd & White, 1980; Shiffrin & Schneider, 1977). This executive is often more like a computer *operator* than like anything one would find inside a computer. It does things such as voluntarily direct attention, perform searchs of memory, make decisions, move things back and forth between short-term memory and long-term memory, and the like. Network models do not include an executive processor. The brain does not have an executive, which would be a node or an analyzer that had all the abilities of all the other nodes or analyzers. Because there is no part of the brain that could serve that function, we don't want one in our model (Rumelhart & McClelland, 1986b). A mechanism that voluntarily directs attention is unnecessary, anyway, because redirection of attention can be explained mechanistically (Grossberg & Stone, 1986). A mechanism for search of memory is not needed for the simple reason that memory is not "searched" in the usual sense of this term (Wickelgren, 1979b). There is nothing wrong with talking about searching memory if one keeps in mind that this is a metaphor; however, it is all too easy to forget that it is a metaphor and start treating it as a reality. Although you can and do make decisions, to say that the executive processor in your head makes these decisions for you doesn't explain anything; it merely restates and complicates the problem. If short-term memory or consciousness *is* activation of a set of nodes and long-term memory *is* the connection strength among these nodes, it is unclear how or why something would be moved from one memory to the other. We don't need an executive processor to perform this seemingly unnecessary operation.

It may strike you that neural-network models are mechanistic, and they probably are. All scientific explantions are by their nature mechanistic. Information-processing theorists compare the mind to a computer, which is as mechanistic as one can get. Information-processing theorists sometimes forget that you have emotions and motives. Perhaps because they use the "brain metaphor," network theorists are less likely to overlook these aspects of mental life. Information-processing theories do a good job of explaining processes that are governed by rules that can be explicity stated. Network theories can handle this kind of behavior as well as cases where rules are vague and intuitive (Smolensky, 1988). Thus, network models offer at least the promise of a fuller and more complete account of what passes through your mind.

PROFESSORS AND STOCKBROKERS

At this point, it may be useful to examine a simple neural-network model to give you an idea of how such models work. The network shown in Figure 1–3 is an interactive activation and competition model based on the work of

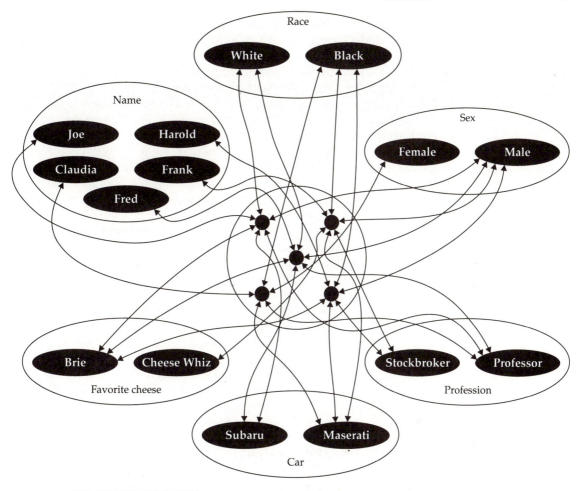

F I G U R E   1 – 3 A competitive-interaction network for storing knowledge about people. The nodes in each circle inhibit each other. Black lines indicate bidirectional excitation. Activating any node will inhibit nodes in the same circle and activate nodes with which it is directly or indirectly connected.

McClelland (1981). The network concerns knowledge about five people, represented by the five nodes in the center of the figure. There is nothing *in* these nodes. Knowledge about what they represent lies in their connections to other nodes. The five people's attributes, including their names, are represented by nodes in the circles surrounding the center circle. Here is how the network works: the lines indicate two-way excitatory connections. We assume that the nodes within each circle exert mutual lateral inhibition on one another. When any one node is activated, it inhibits nodes in its own circle and excites nodes with which it is connected in other circles. These nodes go on to do the same. After excitation and inhibition reverberate back and forth, some nodes will be maximally activated and others will be inhibited.

If you follow the lines back and forth between the circles, you will see that the network stores information; for example, it "knows" that Joe is a White male professor who drives a Subaru and likes Brie cheese. Fred has somewhat similar characteristics. Claudia sounds more interesting, although the network does not know her favorite cheese. It does know that she is a Black woman who is a professor and drives a Maserati. Harold and Frank are Black stockbrokers. They both drive fancy cars. Frank likes Cheese Whiz, but Harold is partial to Brie.

The network has several properties that mimic the way people really think. First is a *content addressable* memory. Asking the network about Claudia corresponds to activating the node coding her name. Very soon, the nodes coding her properties will be activated automatically. There is no need to search through memory to find out about her; simply asking automatically retrieves the information, or activates the nodes that contain information about her. The network also shows *default assignments*. Missing information is automatically "guessed." The node coding Brie cheese is likely to be partially activated after the network has been asked about Claudia. Why? Because it will have received activation from the node coding professors, as Claudia is a professor. This partial activation can be interpreted as a "hypothesis" that Claudia likes Brie cheese (Rumelhart, Hinton, & McClelland, 1986). The network also makes *spontaneous generalizations*, an extremely desirable property. If people did not have this ability, they would have to learn every fact explicitly. After seeing a thousand ducks, they would not know that the next duck would quack rather than warble. This ability can cause problems, however, if one has been exposed to a biased sample of instances. If our network were asked what Black men are like, it would reply that they are stockbrokers who drive fancy cars. By the same token, it would think that all White men are professors who drive Japanese cars. Our network is prejudiced! From the standpoint of mental modeling, that is good: A lot of people are prejudiced, too. The network can be fixed by exposing it to many more people about whom it would store information. The greater the number of different people to which our network is exposed, the less likely it will be to make incorrect generalizations.

PRACTICAL APPLICATIONS

In the last several years there has been an explosion of interest in neural networks. Some of this interest is on the part of cognitive psychologists who think the neural-network approach may be more useful than the information-processing approach in explaining some aspects of human mental behavior. Much interest comes from researchers in artificial intelligence and from computer scientists—who are not focally interested in how people think, but want to build better computers. Perhaps if they study how the mind works, they will be able to build computers that work as it does.

If you have a microcomputer, you realize one of the big problems with computers: the input bottleneck—everything must be entered by means of a keyboard. That process can be slow and boring even for a good typist, so it would be nice if one could just tell the computer what to do. There has been a great deal of progress in making computers that can recognize human speech, but a method has not yet been perfected. Words must be pronounced slowly and clearly, and machines can only recognize one voice.

It would be especially nice if your computer could not only recognize but also understand speech. Then, with the right programs, you could even ask it for advice. No matter how you get language into a computer, it turns out to be exceedingly difficult to write programs that can understand language. The problem is not in teaching the computer the meaning of words—one can put in the entire *Oxford English Dictionary* and all the rules of grammar that linguists have discovered. But you end up with an extremely complicated program that completely misunderstands most of what you say. If you listen closely to spoken speech, you will notice that it contains amazingly few complete and grammatically correct sentences. We say a bit and let the other person figure out what we mean from context. On the level of meaning, language is much more metaphorical than most people realize (Lakoff & Johnson, 1980); we constantly "bring up" "points," "put them on the table," "reverse" our opinions about them, and so on. A related problem is that meaning is extremely context-sensitive: words mean very different things in different contexts; for example, we use a great many *anaphors* (pronouns that refer back to some noun that was referred to implicitly or explicitly). People have no problem with any of this, but computers do, because understanding involves many loose constraints and much implicit knowledge. Conventional computers cannot handle loose constraints because they are binary, either/or machines. Neither can they handle intuition; they are hopelessly concrete. Almost every sentence contains an unclear referent and a metaphor or two, but people don't even notice. We need computers that will not be bothered by it either.

Let's say that we fixed these problems and developed computers that could actually understand what we say. What real use would they be? Take, for example, the sentence "Go out and pick up a loaf of bread." Imagine that the computer actually understands that we mean "go to the grocery store" and that it is not only supposed to "pick up" the bread, but also pay for it and bring it home. We still have a major output problem: the computer cannot walk or drive. One of the ultimate goals of artificial intelligence research is to produce computers that can do these things—robots. Robot computers could cook for us, do the laundry, paint the house, or whatever we told them to do. Will we ever have robots like this? Probably much sooner than you might imagine. Their wiring, however, will probably be nothing like that of present-day computers; instead, it will be more like the wiring of the brain. The brain is wired in a way that allows for very fast and efficient vision, understanding, motor movement, and so on, whereas, fast as they are, conventional computers are very slow and inefficient at such tasks. There is thus a practical reason to study neural networks: neural-network computers will be the brains of the robots that completely revolutionize our lives.

SUMMARY AND CONCLUSIONS

Cognitive psychology is the study of how knowledge is gathered, stored, and used. We may also consider cognitive psychology as the currently dominant paradigm in psychology. The first paradigm in psychology was structuralism, which encountered difficulties because of its reliance on introspection. The next paradigm was behaviorism, which successfully explained some of the behavior of lower organisms, but was unable to explain human behavior very well. Cognitive psychology asserts that knowledge exists in the form of mental representations. Information-processing theorists and neural-network theorists agree on this concept, but disagree as to what these mental representations are and how they work. The information-processing approach to cognition relies heavily upon the analogy between computers and the mind. Though there are similarities, conventional computers work very differently from the human mind. Neural-network theorists rely instead upon a "brain metaphor." They try to construct cognitive theories that are consistent with what we know about the brain and how it works. The practical side to studying neural networks is that researchers are already working on neural-network computers that mimic the way the brain functions. One of the goals of this research is to build robots that will understand what we say and actually do whatever we tell them to.

Pattern Recognition

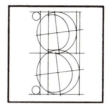

THE PROBLEM OF RECOGNITION

One of the most important tasks the brain performs is to recognize objects in the environment. The problem of recognition is a good topic with which to begin our discussion of neural networks, because neuroscientists have discovered a good bit of evidence about the workings of the neural circuits involved in perception. We can examine concrete evidence about systems that use excitation and inhibition among nodes to make useful computations. When we get to topics such as decision making or thinking, we can propose only rather tentative neural-network models. The argument will be, however, that the basic circuitry is similar to that described in this chapter. Here we shall focus on visual pattern recognition, simply because we know more about vision than about the other senses.

Perception is an active response. Rather than involving the movement of a copy or image into the brain, perception involves the activation of pre-existing neurons. Perception is the construction of a model of the world; it consists of turning on a set of neurons rather than passively receiving "pictures" of the world. To explain perceptual recognition, we have to explain how information from external stimuli makes contact with the correct neurons. How, for example, does one recognize and know the meaning of the letter "B," the word *dog*, or a friend's face? How does one pattern of light—or, more correctly, a whole family of patterns of light—on the retina yield the response "that's my dog," but another family of patterns yields the response "that's my grandmother." Once we have agreed that perception is the activation of nodes, it is a small step to saying that there are "grandmother" nodes or neuron assemblies in the brain. A "grandmother" node is the neuron or set of neurons that is activated when you recognize your grandmother. Before we can profitably consider the question of how you recognize your grandmother, we need some information about how you see in the first place.

ANATOMY AND PHYSIOLOGY OF THE VISUAL SYSTEM

Figure 2–1 shows the flow chart for human visual perception. The physical stimulus for vision is electromagnetic waves. These fall on the lens of the

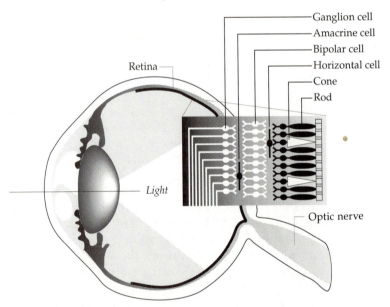

F I G U R E   2 – 1 The human eye, with an enlarged portion of the retina shown at right. Connections from rods and cones to bipolar cells to ganglion cells are excitatory. Horizontal and amacrine cells exert lateral inhibitory effects. Note that light actually passes through ganglion cells and bipolar cells before getting to the rods and cones. This arrangement is odd, but it works because the neurons are transparent. From *Eye, Brain, and Vision*. By David H. Hubel. Copyright © 1988 by Scientific American Library. Reprinted by permission by W. H. Freeman and Company.

eye, which focuses the stimulus and projects it in inverted form onto the retina. The retina is a cortical structure consisting of several discrete layers of neural tissue, as illustrated in Figure 2–1. The retinas of other vertebrates are quite similar. The receptor cells are called *rods* and *cones.* The rods are specialized for reception of brightness information, and the cones are specialized for detecting color. There are about 130 million rods and eight million cones in the human retina (Sekuler & Blake, 1985). The rods and cones contain light-sensitive chemicals—chemicals that react to light. In general, the more light they receive, the greater the chemical reaction. This chemical reaction causes a change in the electrical potential of the receptor. In other words, rods and cones are *transducers.* They translate light into a direct-current voltage by means of an intermediate chemical reaction.

The change in voltage is sensed by the bipolar cells, which in turn excite the ganglion cells. Both receptor cells and bipolar cells work in an analog fashion, by which I mean that their activation is continuously variable rather than an all-or-nothing phenomenon. It is not until we get to ganglion cells that discrete action *potentials* (electrical spikes) are produced. If its electrical potential crosses a certain threshold, a ganglion cell will fire (produce an action potential). Other things being equal, the more activity in the receptors with which it is connected, the more action potentials a ganglion cell

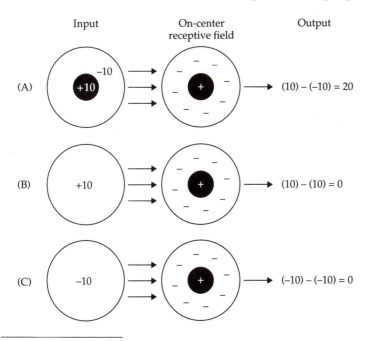

F I G U R E   2 – 2 On-center reception fields. In (A), there is light in the center of the field and darkness in the surround. This causes the ganglion cell monitoring the receptive field to fire. Light (B) or darkness (C) falling on the entire receptive field does not elicit a response by the ganglion cell.

will produce. Be warned that other things are *not* equal, however; if receptor cells were simply light-sensitive devices and if ganglion cells simply received excitatory input from a set of receptor cells, ganglion cells could detect nothing more than the mere presence or absence of light.

Each ganglion cell receives input from about 100 receptors. These receptors make up what is called the *receptive field* of the ganglion cell. There are two types of ganglion cells (Robson, 1975). On-center cells are maximally turned on if there is brightness in the center of their receptive field and darkness in the surround (periphery) of their receptive field, as shown in Figure 2–2(a). We might call these on-center cells "dot detectors." On-center ganglion cells receive excitatory input from the receptors in the center of the field and inhibitory input from the receptors on the periphery of the field. If an equal amount of brightness (Figure 2–2[b]) or darkness (Figure 2–2[c]) falls on the receptive field, the ganglion cell does not respond, because excitation from the center and inhibition from the surround cancel each other out. Note that in Figure 2–3(a) there seem to be gray spots where the white rows and columns intersect. These spots are not in the physical stimulus. The reason you see them is that dot detectors monitoring the intersections are not receiving quite enough inhibitory input (see Figure 2–3[b]). Therefore, you see gray spots rather than just white space. As also shown in Figure 2–3(b), dot detectors *do* get enough inhibitory input if they are not monitoring input at the intersections.

Off-center ganglion cells are the opposite of on-center cells. They are "spot" detectors looking for a spot of darkness surrounded by light. They do not respond if their entire receptive field is covered by brightness or darkness. Ganglion cells of both types are sensitive to contrast or difference between center and surround. They are not sensitive to absolute levels of brightness; in fact, they "discount" absolute levels of brightness and report to the brain about the relative difference between brightness levels in their center and their surround.

The retina has a lattice-like structure, as shown in Figure 2–1. We have mentioned the vertical connections from receptors to bipolar neurons to ganglion cells. Perpendicular to these pathways are cells—the amacrine and horizontal neurons (see Figure 2–1)—that have horizontal rather than vertical connections. The vertical connections are excitatory, and the horizontal connections are inhibitory (Hubel, 1988). Activating a receptor will activate a bipolar neuron that will, in turn, tend to activate a ganglion cell. The receptor will also activate a horizontal cell, however, which will inhibit neighboring receptors. The result of this structural arrangement is that activation of a receptor will activate both bipolar cells and horizontal cells. The bipolar cells will pass the activation on to ganglion cells; the horizontal cell will inhibit neighboring receptors. Bipolar cells also activate amacrine cells, which inhibit neighboring bipolar cells. The ultimate consequence of all this activation is that neighboring receptors and ganglion cells exercise a lateral

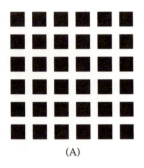

(A)

This dot detector receives enough inhibitory input

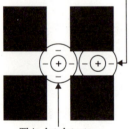

This dot detector does not receive enough inhibitory input

(B)

FIGURE 2–3
The Hermann grid is shown in (A). Note the patches of gray that seem to flicker on and off at the intersections of the white lines. Part (B) shows the reason for this effect.

inhibitory effect on each other because of the inhibitory amacrine and horizontal cells. The closer two receptors are, the greater the inhibition. This inhibition is the anatomical basis for the on-center and off-center ganglion cells described earlier. Inhibitory lateral connections and excitatory vertical connections are a general feature of nervous tissue that is organized into layers (von Békésy, 1967). We find this arrangement not only in the retina, but also in the skin, the cochlea, the cerebellum, and the neocortical and paleocortical areas of the brain. Later, we shall use this wiring arrangement to describe what happens in modules or analyzers in the cortex.

Action potentials travel along the axons of the ganglion cells. These axons are bundled together to form the optic nerve, which goes to the lateral geniculate nucleus, a part of the midbrain. Here, the axons connect with other neurons whose axons run to the occipital cortex of the brain, the primary receiving area of the visual system. Surrounding the primary visual receiving area are association areas where perception of visual inputs finally occurs. Damage to the primary visual receiving area leads to blindness; damage to the visual association areas leads to *agnosia*. A victim of agnosia can still see but is unable to recognize what is seen. Depending upon what area is damaged, one may lose the ability to recognize faces, written words, or other specific types of objects (as described in Chapter 3).

VISION AS TRANSDUCTION

It is apparent that the mental event of seeing is the end result of a number of translations. We go from electromagnetic waves to a chemical reaction to a change in direct-current voltage to an alternating-current signal (the action potential). After all these translations, we have gotten only to an impulse traveling along the axon of a ganglion cell. When this electrical impulse gets to the end of the ganglion cell's axon in the midbrain, it must produce another action potential in the next neuron in the series. Neurons excite one another not by a direct electrical contact, but via an intermediate chemical reaction involving release of neurotransmitters. To get from receptors in the retina to the primary receiving area of the cortex requires traversal of three neurons. To get to the association areas—where we recognize or understand what is seen—requires traversal of several more neurons. Interposed between each of these neurons is a chemical reaction. Thus, there is a long series of translations and retranslations from chemical to electrical codes between the initial reception of the stimulus and its final recognition. It seems highly likely that all this translation and retranslation serves some useful purpose. If it did not, nature would have made the axons of the ganglion cells longer, so that they could be attached directly to the neurons in the association areas where recognition ultimately takes place.

TEMPLATE MATCHING

A possible solution to the question of recognition involves template matching, an idea first proposed by Gestalt psychologists in the 1930s. Recognition requires that a stimulus make contact with a memory trace. One way of doing this would involve the connection of a set of ganglion cells to form a template or pattern, as shown in Figure 2–4. Output from the ganglion cells

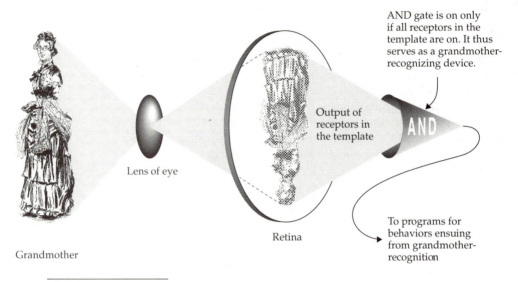

AND gate is on only if all receptors in the template are on. It thus serves as a grandmother-recognizing device.

Output of receptors in the template

Lens of eye

Retina

Grandmother

To programs for behaviors ensuing from grandmother-recognition

F I G U R E   2 – 4   A retinal template for recognizing one's grandmother.

making up the template would be connected to a neuron in the brain. Whenever a pattern of excitation on the retina fit the template, the recognizing neuron in the brain would be activated.

This approach immediately presents problems. Whereas you can recognize your grandmother from a variety of perspectives and distances, a template would work only if she were standing, say, exactly four feet away. If she were any closer, her size would appear too large on your retina. If she were lying down, you would be at a total loss. This difficulty could be solved by having a whole family of grandmother templates—one for grandmother standing four feet away, another for grandmother standing three feet away, and so on. All of these templates would be connected to the same "grandmother" neuron in your brain. The problem with this solution is that literally an infinite number of templates would be necessary just to enable you to recognize your grandmother from all possible distances and in all possible orientations. The same would be true of every other object you are capable of recognizing. You would run out of neurons before enough templates had been constructed to account for all the things you can recognize.

FEATURE ANALYSIS

Since template matching does not provide a very good explanation of how we recognize things, let's consider a different possibility. This approach involves the idea that recognition is based on the detection of distinctive features. A distinctive feature is an attribute that characterizes an object and can be detected throughout a wide range of circumstances; for example, it remains the same at various distances. Any object is defined by a unique set of distinctive features. When they are present, the object is recognized as being present. After we discuss the general theory of feature analysis, we shall examine some evidence based on research with frogs, cats, and crabs suggesting that organisms are sensitive to distinctive features and that the detectors for these features are wired together so as to permit recognition of complex patterns. We shall also investigate how distinctive features are detected in the first place.

WHAT IS A DISTINCTIVE FEATURE?

A distinctive feature is an invariant cue or signal. Is it possible that detection of distinctive features could be used as a basis for recognition? Some lower animals use exactly such an approach. The male stickleback fish stakes out a bit of territory that he considers uniquely his own. If another male stickleback fish enters this territory, he does so at considerable risk, for the original owner will attack him. On the other hand, the owner doesn't care if other species of fish pass through his territory. Evidently, then, one male stickleback is able to recognize another one. How does he do so? Recognition is based upon a single distinctive feature: the presence of a red underbelly. Tinbergen (1951) prepared a number of fake fish, of which one looked exactly like a male stickleback fish except that it was not red on its underside. Others were red underneath but did not look much like fish, let alone those of the stickleback variety. Tinbergen floated these models through stickleback territory and found that anything with a red underside elicited attack. Anything lacking it, including the otherwise realistic model, was ignored. It would seem that male sticklebacks recognize one another by the presence or absence of a single distinctive feature—a red underside. Tinbergen (1951) describes a number of other species that respond to the presence of a single distinctive feature in this manner.

Is it possible that recognition in higher organisms could work in a similar way? Perhaps recognition is based not on a complete analysis of a pattern of sensations but on the detection of a feature that uniquely defines an object. Suppose that your grandmother were Hester Prynne, the heroine of Hawthorne's *The Scarlet Letter*. Hester Prynne was compelled to wear a scarlet letter "A" on the bodice of her dress. Although she did not wear the scarlet letter to help people recognize her (it was a punishment for adultery), the presence of such a scarlet letter would be a tremendous aid in recognition. To recognize Hester Prynne, one would need only to detect the presence of this single attribute.

A problem with this idea is how one would recognize the scarlet letter in the first place. How could one differentiate among the true Hester (*A*), a red cross nurse (+), and a lazy wolf in Hester's clothing who thought that people would fall for any scarlet letter at all (say, *R*)? For that matter, how would one tell the difference between any of these and one of Tinbergen's fake stickleback fish? Even a letter of the alphabet is a complex pattern defined by the simultaneous presence of several distinctive features. Perhaps lower organisms recognize things on the basis of single features such as redness, but higher organisms recognize them on the basis of combinations of distinctive features.

PANDEMONIUM AND HIERARCHICAL FEATURE ANALYSIS

Pandemonium is the name the poet John Milton gave to the capitol of Hell. This was certainly Hester Prynne's ultimate destination in the eyes of her Puritan judges. The devil who came to escort her there, however, would be up against the same problem we are facing: how to recognize her. Selfridge (1959) proposed a general feature-detection model for pattern recognition and called the model *Pandemonium* in reference to the "demons" that make the model go. Let us consider a Pandemonium system for recognition of letters of the alphabet. A Pandemonium system is organized into several hierarchical layers. Figure 2–5(a) shows part of a Pandemonium system for recognizing letters of the alphabet. Note that Hester is not providing the stimulation; the demon has gotten the wolf instead. At the lowest level of the system is the "image demon," whose task is to hold an image of the incoming stimulus so that it can be examined by demons on the level above— the "feature demons." All of them simultaneously examine the image for their own particular feature. One of them might be interested in right angles, another in acute angles, another in continuous curves, and so on. Whenever one of these demons sees its feature, it begins yelling. On the next tier are the "cognitive demons"—one cognitive demon for each of the things to be recognized. We would want twenty-six of them, one for each letter of the alphabet. These demons listen for cries from the feature demons. The "A" demon, for example, would be listening for very loud and excited yells from the obtuse-angle demon, since an "A" contains two obtuse angles. It would also be listening for some vociferous yelling on the part of the acute-angle demon, because an "A" has three acute angles. The more the "A" demon hears what it is listening for, the more it, too, begins to yell; that is, the more yelling it hears from the relevant feature demons, the louder it yells. In Figure 2–5(a), the "A" demon does not have much to shout about; however,

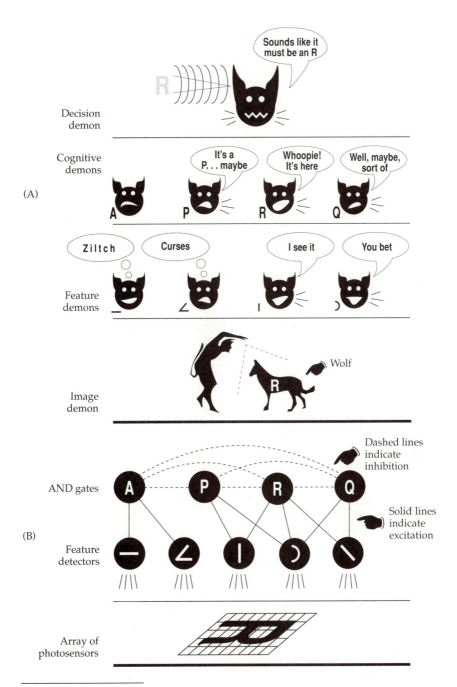

F I G U R E   2 – 5   A Pandemonium letter-recognizing system composed of demons (A) and of electronic devices (B).

several of the other demons—most notably the "R" demon—are yelling. On the top level lives the "decision demon." Selfridge put it there because a lot of voices are rising from the Pandemonium below. Whenever an "R" is put in, the "R" demon should be yelling the loudest, but anything that excites it will also set the "P," "B," and "F" demons to yelling as well. They would not be yelling quite as loudly, however, because they would have detected fewer of the features they were looking for. The decision demon decides which letter demon is yelling loudest.

IMPLICATIONS OF THE PANDEMONIUM MODEL

The important thing to note about the Pandemonium system is its efficiency. First, it is what is called a parallel processing system: all the demons work simultaneously. Second, it is economical—there need be only a few feature demons; certainly, there can be fewer feature demons than letter demons. Third, it ignores the types of minor differences that should be ignored, such as the size, orientation, and details of the input letters. Also note that when the system recognizes a letter, one of the cognitive demons yells loudly. The image has been transduced, or changed into something qualitatively different. The internal representation (the yelling of a cognitive demon) has no qualitative similarity at all to the physical characteristics of the input stimulus.

SUBSTITUTING LOGIC GATES OR NEURONS FOR DEMONS

In building a Pandemonium, we could economize by employing electrical circuits rather than demons; that is, we could construct an electronic neural network. Figure 2–5(b) substitutes an array of light-sensitive detectors for the image demon. At higher levels, AND gates rather than demons are used. Rather than listening for yelling, these logic gates simply detect inputs from lower levels. An AND gate is an electronic device that will go on if and only if all of its inputs are simultaneously on. The detector for "A" would be connected to detectors for obtuse and acute angles on the lower level. All of the other letter detectors would also be connected to feature detectors. Of course, we would have to be careful that each different letter of the alphabet was defined by a unique combination of distinctive features. (We shall consider later how these features would be detected in the first place.) Note that we have also economized by eliminating the decision demon. We no longer need it because all of the letter-detecting units are connected to one another by inhibitory connections, and the most activated unit inhibits the less activated ones. Thus, no decision unit is needed. (This is good, since otherwise we should have to explain how the decision unit makes its decision.)

It is possible that a set of neurons could operate as a Pandemonium system, which would look as it does in Figure 2–5(b). The only difference would be that it would be constructed of neurons (rather than electronic devices) and their axons (rather than wires). Neurons communicate in terms of rate of firing rather than by yelling or by simply producing a steady voltage level. In Figure 2–5(b), the neural pandemonium would "know" that an "R" was present because the R-detecting neuron would be firing most rapidly, thus laterally inhibiting the other letter-detecting neurons. We shall see later in this chapter that there is a good deal of evidence for the existence of neural feature-detection networks that work exactly this way.

WHAT THE FROG'S EYE TELLS THE FROG'S BRAIN

Lettvin, Maturana, McCulloch, and Pitts (1959) conducted an interesting experiment with a living frog's eye. Lettvin et al. were investigating what turned out to be a very simple neural network: the frog's retina. To their question, "What does the frog's eye tell the frog's brain," we might give the brief answer, "not much." The details of this brief answer, however, have revolutionized our view of perception. A schematic diagram of the frog's

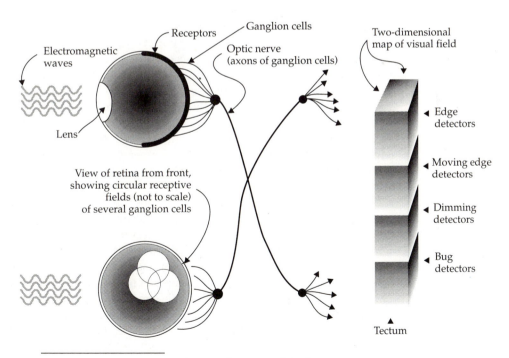

F I G U R E   2 - 6   The visual system of the frog.

visual system is shown in Figure 2–6. The frog's retina is composed of light-sensitive receptors. Ganglion cells receive inputs from a number of receptor cells in roughly circular areas. These are the receptive fields of the ganglion cells. The axons of the ganglion cells are collected into optic nerves that run to an area of the frog's brain called the *tectum*.

FEATURE DETECTION IN THE FROG'S RETINA

In the Lettvin et al. experiment, the frog's eye was fixed at one point inside a metal hemisphere. By means of magnets, a variety of objects could be presented and moved around in the frog's visual field. Meanwhile, the experimenters were recording impulses from single ganglion cells. This was done by inserting a recording electrode into the axon of the ganglion cell. The logic of the experiment was to find out what would make a ganglion cell fire at its maximal rate—theoretically, whatever the ganglion cell was constructed to detect. Of course, if a stimulus were not falling upon a ganglion cell's receptive field, there would be nothing for it to detect, so it would remain silent.

The results that Lettvin and his co-workers obtained were little short of astounding. There are only four types of ganglion cells sending information: (1) *edge detectors* respond to any border between light and dark regions; (2) *moving contrast detectors* respond to moving edges; (3) *dimming detectors* respond to an overall decrease in illumination; and (4) *convex edge detectors* respond only to small, dark, moving objects. It takes little imagination to dub the last as "bug" detectors. These four types of ganglion cells have overlapping receptive fields. In a given region of the frog's retina, one ganglion cell responds to edges, another to bugs, and so on.

It is important to note three things about the results of this experiment. First, the ganglion cells are responsive to abstract features rather than to specific attributes or nuances; for example, edge detectors respond to any edge at all to about the same degree, whether the edge of a leaf, the edge caused by the shadow of Hester Prynne, or an artificial edge created by an abrupt change in light intensity. The same is true of bug-detecting ganglion cells, which exhibit exactly the same response to moving dark spots as to real bugs. The ganglion cells, then, are very abstract or general in respect to what they detect. Second, although the detectors do not "know" or "care" what caused the thing they detect, they are attuned to respond only if it is unambiguously present; for example, an edge detector will not respond if an edge is too fuzzy—that is, if the transition from light to dark is too gradual. A bug detector will not respond if the small, dark spot is not moving. A frog will starve to death in the presence of a generous supply of freshly killed bugs; because they are not moving, it cannot see them. Third, each of the four types of ganglion cells are specialized—each completely ignores the features that the others detect. An edge detector, for example, is unresponsive to a general dimming of its receptive field.

ORGANIZATION OF THE TECTUM

The axons of each of the four types of ganglion cells end up in a separate layer of the tectum (Arbib, 1972). All of the axons from edge detectors go to one layer, those from bug detectors to another layer, and so on. Interestingly, though, they remain in registration; that is, information about any receptive field on the retina ends up in the same "column" of the tectum. As shown in Figure 2–6, the tectum is not so much a map of the visual field as a three-dimensional data matrix. For any region in the visual field, the frog "knows" four things: Is an edge there? Is it moving? Is the area dim? Is a bug there? The answers to each of these questions is coded in a binary or yes/no fashion. The frog thus has four "bits" of information about each region of its visual field.

A frog is a biological machine for killing bugs and avoiding moving shadows. Outputs from the tectum to the frog's motor regions code two basic programs: (1) escape from moving shadows (possible predators) toward dim regions, while taking care not to run into things like rocks and trees (indicated by edges), and (2) place your (sticky) tongue in the spatial coordinates occupied by a bug. Arbib (1972) gives a fascinating and plausible description of how this circuitry must operate.

SOMATOTOPIC MAPPING

The frog has information about spatial location. In fact, space is the organizing principle of the tectum. Spatial location is not coded explicitly, however; wherever it is relevant, the brain tends to operate in this sort of "somatotopic" fashion. It stores information about location not explicitly, but by preserving the relative relationships of data cells to one another. The frog's tectum is built so as to organize its information about the world in spatial terms. It is prewired so that it *has* to perceive in this way. A given column of the tectum contains all the information about a given region of space, and the columns are rationally arranged so as to constitute a spatial map. If the axons of ganglion cells all went to random places in the tectum, the frog could not perceive the world in spatial terms. Information about the same point in space would not be in registration. There would be no way to tell what was where. Information about neighboring points in space would be scattered randomly. No matter how much or how little learning influences the development of the frog's visual abilities, if these abilities develop at all, they will develop such that objects are seen in a spatial framework. To say that the frog learned to see in spatial terms is as implausible as saying that it learned its brain. Though they spoke of human rather than frog knowledge, philosophers from Plato through Kant have argued that we could not *learn* to arrange our experiences in spatial terms. Quite the contrary: the mind must arrange information about the world in spatial terms before we can learn anything about the world in the first place.

IMPLICATIONS

The frog's visual world consists of bugs and shadows, but it is at least a little better off than the creatures in Plato's cave, who could see only shadows. Let us consider the broader implications of Lettvin's study. First, the frog—if it could conceive at all—could not conceive of our world. Color, for example, is excluded by the nature of its feature-detection system, because it has no detectors for color. This raises the possibility that we, too, are limited by our feature detection systems. It could not be otherwise if perception is the activation of preexisting feature detectors. Second, the brain gets only a few bits of information and constructs a model of the world on the basis of this information. The brain has to construct a model, because it is information about abstract features that are transmitted to the brain, not information about whole images. Third, even the idea that the brain constructs an image is misleading. In vision, patterns of electromagnetic waves falling on the retina are transduced not into patterns of neural firing that correspond to the intensities of the impinging light but into patterns of firing that represent the presence or absence of specific features, such as edges. The transformation is not merely quantitative but qualitative. The world you see is a pattern of neural activity inside your brain. You seem to see objects "out there" in the world. You really *construct* an idea of the world based on hints given by patterns of light on the retina. If you are not willing to agree with Schopenhauer that "the world is my idea," perhaps you will agree that "the world is my hypothesis."

LATERAL INHIBITION AND FEATURE DETECTION

How do ganglion cells extract features such as edges from the activity of retinal receptors? We know that there are four types of feature detectors in the frog's eye, but how does each one find the feature that it detects?

EDGE DETECTION

Edge Detection in a Lateral Inhibitory Network

The latticework arrangement (vertical excitation and lateral inhibition) of the frog's retina must somehow function to extract features. Let us consider the problem of detecting edges. First, imagine a case in which lateral inhibitory connections are not present. One receptor is connected to one ganglion cell. This sort of 1:1 arrangement is of no real value. As shown in Figure 2–7(a), the output of such a system is the same as the input. Here, an edge, represented by the numbers at the top of the figure, is being shined onto the receptor cells. Let us assume that the vertical connections are excitatory and that for every unit of stimulus brightness we get a proportional number of

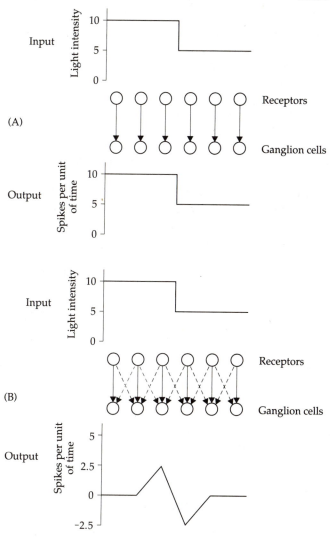

F I G U R E 2 – 7 In (A), input (top) and output (bottom) are the same in a retina with no lateral inhibition. Such a retina is useless. Part (B) shows that a retina with lateral inhibition can detect edges.

action potentials out of the ganglion cells. When ten units of brightness arrive at a receptor, the ganglion cell to which it is connected produces ten spikes per unit of time. This system cannot detect edges; the ganglion cells can only code whether or not light is present in the region of the retina they monitor.

Lindsay and Norman (1977) and others have discussed how we might modify such a system by adding lateral inhibition to construct feature detectors. Figure 2–7(b) shows Lindsay and Norman's design for an edge detector. They assume that a receptor excites its own ganglion cell but inhibits neighboring ganglion cells—via lateral inhibitory connections—to a degree proportional to one-half its input. If each of the receptors were receiving ten units of input, the output of each ganglion cell would be zero: it would get ten units of input from its receptor, but from this we must subtract five units because of the inhibitory input coming from the receptor on one side and another five units from the receptor on the other side. Clearly, 10 - 5 - 5 = 0. Figure 2–7(b) shows what happens when a whole array of ganglion cells are connected to one another in this fashion. Note that the input is the same as it was in Figure 2–7(a); however, the output is quite different.

When we compute the output from the ganglion cells, we find that it is zero, except for the cells at the edges of the light. This network will detect edges. The output of a ganglion cell is zero if no edge is present over the receptor that it monitors. Note that the output will be zero regardless of whether its region is bright or dim. On the other hand, the output of a ganglion cell will *not* be zero if there is in fact an edge near its receptor. If it is on the bright side of the edge, its output will be +2½ spikes per unit of time. If it is on the dim side of an edge, its output will be –2½ spikes per unit of time. Thus, we have an array of detectors that ignores brightness and responds only to edges. One minor problem is that one of our outputs is –2½. It doesn't make sense for a ganglion cell to be emitting a negative number of spikes, so something is amiss—this could not be the way the real circuit in a frog's eye works. The problem is easy enough to fix. Assume that the ganglion cells fire continually at a spontaneous rate of, say, five spikes per unit of time. An edge would now be indicated by 5 ± 2½ = 7½, or 2½ spikes per unit of time. This eliminates the problem of negative rates of firing. Nature solved the problem in exactly the same way—neurons do in fact exhibit just such spontaneous firing.

Edge Detectors in the Eye of the Horseshoe Crab

We have seen how we could construct an edge detector. If we were engineers building a machine, we could stop here; however, our question must now be whether this is in fact the way that edge detectors are constructed in real organisms. Ratliff's (1965) work with the visual system of *limulus*, the horseshoe crab, sheds light on this question. Limulus is an ideal creature for the study of vision because of the anatomy of its eye. It has a compound eye constructed of individual receptors or *omatidia*. The omatidia are interconnected in a lateral inhibitory network. Stimulating only one omatidium inhibits neighboring ones. If one removes the lens and other biological matter covering the eye, exactly one receptor can be stimulated. By recording the action potentials coming from the ganglion cell collecting information from the omatidium in question, one can observe the effect of stimuli on the receptor. Ratliff tested the effect of an edge of light on the output of ganglion

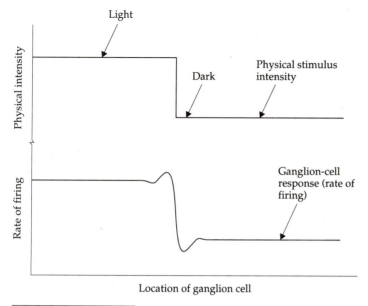

F I G U R E   2 – 8   Results of Ratliff's experiment on the eye of the horseshoe crab: the ganglion cells detect both brightness and edges.

cells. The results of his experiment are shown in Figure 2–8. Although this is not exactly what Ratliff did, the logic of the experiment was to record the output of a number of ganglion cells while some were exposed to light and others were exposed to dark. As shown in Figure 2–8, the physical stimulus had an abrupt transition from light to dark—that is, it was an edge. As may be seen in Figure 2–8, the ganglion cells were responsive to the edge: those on the bright side of the edge exhibited the highest rate of firing, and those on the dark side of the edge exhibited the lowest rate of firing. The ganglion cells, however, were also responsive to brightness per se. Those exposed to light fired at a higher rate than those exposed to darkness. Thus, the ganglion cells detect both edges and brightness. If the inhibitory coefficients in Figure 2–7(b) are reduced from one-half to one-fifth, the system will mimic the response of the eye of the horsehoe crab very nicely (Lindsay & Norman, 1977), as you can verify by working out the arithmetic.

Mach Bands and Edge Enhancement

The human retina works similarly to that of the horseshoe crab. It, too, is sensitive to *both* brightness and edges. In the 19th-century, Ernst Mach (1865) first described what have come to be called Mach bands. In Figure 2–9(a), observe that the bands of gray seem to be separated by slightly darker strips. The actual physical changes in brightness are as illustrated in Figure 2–9(b). Your subjective impression is diagrammed in Figure 2–9(c). The reason for

(A)

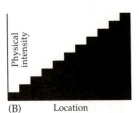

(B)   Location

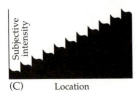

(C)   Location

F I G U R E   2 – 9
Illustration of Mach
bands. The bands of
gray shown in (A) are
of uniform brightness,
as shown in (B),
although they seem to
be separated by dark
bands, as shown in (C).

the difference between the physical input and the resultant sensation is that the human eye detects both brightness and edges, of which one effect is that our eyes tend to enhance or intensify the edges of things. Most of the stimuli we see really have much fuzzier edges than we perceive them as having. Consider how realistic a line drawing seems to be. In fact, line drawings of objects can be identified as quickly and accurately as can photographs (Biederman, 1985). If you are asked to draw a human face, it is likely that your drawing would consist wholly of lines or edges rather than of shadings. The Italian painter Botticelli actually painted thin black lines around his figures to accentuate their edges. Presumably, he outlined in this way because he wanted to be realistic. He "knew" and "saw" that objects have edges, so he put them there in his paintings. The reason for our sensitivity to edges is the edge enhancement brought about by the lateral inhibitory networks in our retinas.

MOTION DETECTION

We perceive not only the form of objects but also their motion. Perception of form and of motion seems to be accomplished by neural networks that are partially independent (Zeki, 1974). You can demonstrate this by showing a friend a harmless object. A crumpled piece of paper will do. With your friend attending to the paper, throw it violently at him or her. Of course, you want to aim a bit low so you don't hit the person in the eye. As likely as not, your friend will duck or wince. Why? The paper could not possibly do any harm. Motion-detecting neurons have been activated and have produced a reflex reaction. There is a natural tendency to get out of the way of speeding objects before we know what they are. This is an adaptive response. The brain is not fast enough to analyze the form and meaning of such objects before analyzing their speed. Some speeding objects can do considerable damage, so speed is actually analyzed before form and meaning. If analyzing took place the other way around, the speeding object might become embedded in the brain before its speed had been computed. There is physiological evidence that information about motion is collected by different ganglion cells from those that collect information about stationary forms (Tolhurst, 1973). There is also evidence that these neurons project to a different area of the cortex than do neurons that gather information about form (Zeki, 1978). Damage to this area can impair ability to perceive motion without harming ability to perceive stationary objects.

Lateral Inhibition and Motion Detection

How is motion analyzed? Lindsay and Norman (1977) have suggested a neural network similar to that shown in Figure 2–10 for a detector that would be sensitive to motion from left to right. Here, the inhibitory connections are

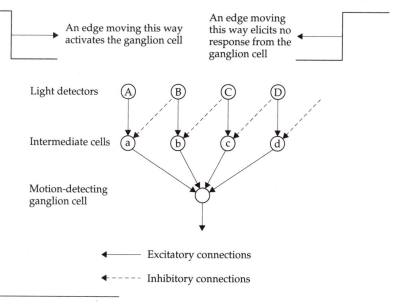

F I G U R E   2 – 1 0 Design for a motion detector sensitive to an edge of light moving at a certain speed from left to right.

all biased in one direction. Inputs to the motion detector come from light-sensitive receptors. Assume that whenever a given receptor is stimulated, it immediately activates the intermediate cell with which it is connected. Furthermore, after a delay comparable to the speed of the motion the system is supposed to detect, the receptor laterally inhibits the intermediate cell to the left of it. Finally, assume that the ganglion cell shown at the bottom of Figure 2–10 functions as what is called an OR gate: it fires whenever it gets input from *any* of the intermediate cells.

A light moving from left to right would elicit continuous firing of the ganglion cell. When the light was over *A*, *A* would activate intermediate cell *a*, and the latter would in turn activate the ganglion cell. By the time the light was over *B*, it would begin activating the ganglion cell via intermediate cell *b*, and so on. On the other hand, a light moving from right to left would elicit no activity in the ganglion cell. When the moving light was over *C*, *C* would activate intermediate cell *c*, but at the same time the delayed inhibitory signal from *D* would deactivate *c*. Thus, the activation and inhibition would cancel each other. By the time the light was over *B*, the delayed inhibition from *C* would be arriving at intermediate cell *b* just in time to cancel the excitatory input from *B*.

Illusions of Motion

It may strike you that this is a rather faulty network, which could malfunction under certain circumstances. Consider what would happen if a small spot of light were shined steadily only onto receptor *B*. The spot of light would elicit activity in the motion-detecting ganglion cell because no inhibitory input would be arriving from receptor *C*. In fact, if you fixate on a small spot of light in a completely dark room, it *will* appear to move about erratically. This is called the *autokinetic effect*. If two stationary lights are quickly flashed in an alternating fashion, one will perceive a single light moving back and forth between the two points. This is called the *phi phenomenon* (Wertheimer, 1912). Our hypothetical motion detector would be susceptible to this illusion as well if the spots of light were small enough to stimulate only one receptor.

A light moving very quickly from right to left would be able to outrace the inhibition in the system and activate the ganglion cell. Such a light would, however, lead the ganglion cell falsely to detect a slower left-to-right motion, because the meaning of the ganglion cell's firing is that a left-to-right motion of a certain speed is present. Such an illusion is exactly what you see in a motion picture when the spokes of stagecoach wheels seem to be slowly rotating in the wrong direction. Thus, Lindsay and Norman's motion detector would be susceptible to illusions of motion that are actually found in human beings. This is a point in its favor, because the goal was to devise a model of how people perceive motion rather than to build a foolproof motion detector.

Motion-Detecting Neurons in Humans

The neural network described above was only good for detecting left-to-right motion. We would need another network for detecting right-to-left motion. Experimental evidence supports the idea that there are in fact neurons that are tuned to detect motion in specific directions (Nakayama, 1985). All neurons show adaptation effects: prolonged stimulation causes a decrease in the response of the neuron. Adaptation effects can be taken as evidence for the existence of a feature detector. The logic is that for adaptation to occur, something must have been adapted, and this something is a feature detector. Sekuler and Ganz (1963) exposed subjects to black and white gratings moving either from right to left or from left to right. Then, they tested their subjects' luminance thresholds for moving gratings (that is, how much black-white contrast was needed before the gratings could be seen). If the test gratings were moving in the same direction as the adapting gratings, large increases in threshold were observed; that is, they were harder to see than they had been before adaptation. This finding suggests that direction-specific motion detectors had been fatigued in the first part of the experiment.

We not only perceive direction of movement, but also its speed. An obvious way to perceive speed would be to code speed by rate of firing of ganglion cells. The faster something was moving, the faster would be the firing rate of the neuron detecting it. Although this seems a quite reasonable supposition, it is wrong. Sekuler (1975) adapted peoples' motion detectors with gratings moving at different speeds, then tested their ability to detect gratings moving at various speeds. Adaptation with a slowly moving grating impaired ability to detect slow motion but had no effect on ability to detect faster motion. Conversely, adaptation with fast-moving gratings hurt ability to detect fast motion but did not affect ability to detect slower motion. Thus, we must have neurons that are specialized as to both the direction and the speed of the motion they can detect.

HIERARCHICAL FEATURE DETECTION IN THE CAT'S BRAIN

STRUCTURE OF THE CAT'S VISUAL SYSTEM

In the frog, a lot of feature analysis goes on right in the eye itself. Lower animals often possess more complex retinas than do higher ones. The higher up the phylogenetic scale we go, the more feature analysis seems to be deferred to the brain. Hubel and Wiesel (1965) investigated visual processing in cats. The cat's visual system is similar to that of humans. Ganglion cells collect information from roughly circular fields of receptors. There are two basic types of ganglion cells (Robson, 1975); one type has an on-center receptive field. This type of ganglion cell is maximally activated if there is a spot of light in the center of its receptive field surrounded by darkness on the fringes of the field. The other type of ganglion cell has an off-center receptive field. It is maximally activated by a spot of darkness surrounded by light in its receptive field. Thus, one type of ganglion cell (on-center) detects dots, and the other type (off-center) detects spots, just as is the case in the human retina.

Signals from retinal ganglion cells are relayed to the lateral geniculate nucleus of the cat's thalamus. There, they connect with neurons that send their axons to the occipital cortex. The cat's visual cortex is composed of five layers. Axons from the lateral geniculate nucleus neurons end up in level four of the cortex. (For no particular reason, cortical layers are numbered from the outside inwards.) The cat's visual cortex is somatotopically arranged; that is, it is a map of the visual field. Input from the two eyes is collated at the cortical level so that a point in the cortex contains information about a point in space.

PANDEMONIUM IN THE CAT'S BRAIN

Hubel and Wiesel's Experiment

Hubel and Wiesel (1965) presented visual stimuli to cats and recorded the activity of individual neurons on different layers of the cats' cortexes. The goal was to find out what each neuron was specialized to detect. Hubel and Wiesel found evidence that supports the hypothesis that the cat's visual cortex operates as a hierarchical feature-detection network. Neurons on lower levels detect simple features, while neurons in successively higher layers of the cortex detect more and more complex features. The more complex feature detectors receive input from the lower-level detectors, just as in Selfridge's Pandemonium model.

The feature-detecting neurons on all cortical levels share a number of properties. Each exhibits a maximal response to a specific visual feature, but it will respond somewhat to similar features. The closer the fit of a stimulus with the feature that the neuron detects, the faster its rate of firing. Each of the neurons can be fatigued by prolonged exposure to the thing it detects; that is, prolonged stimulation lessens the detector's sensitivity. The neurons on each layer of the cortex are arranged in a lateral inhibitory network (Nelson & Frost, 1978; Sillitoe, 1979). When a neuron is activated by the feature it detects, it laterally inhibits surrounding neurons, which code similar features in nearby areas of visual space. Presumably, the lateral inhibitory arrangement is useful in feature extraction in the ways explained earlier.

Simple Cells

In Layer 4 of the occipital cortex, Hubel and Wiesel discovered circularly symmetric cells (see Figure 2–11). These neurons get input from on-center and off-center ganglion cells in the retina. Output from these neurons goes to what Hubel and Wiesel called simple cells. These neurons are detectors for visual features such as edges, slits, and lines. Circularly symmetric cells in the brain and retinal ganglion cells have small circular receptive fields. Simple cortical cells have larger, more oblong receptive fields. As also shown in Figure 2–11, firing in an edge-detecting neuron can be elicited by shining a light anywhere along a specific area on the retina. Right next to this line is a line that, if light is shined on it, will depress the cell's spontaneous rate of firing. Light shined anywhere else on the retina would have no effect. The maximum rate of firing of this type of cell is elicited by positioning an edge of light over the receptive field such that the + line is in light and the – line is in darkness. On the other hand, overall illumination of both the + and – fields elicits no change in the neuron's spontaneous firing rate. In this case, the inhibition from the – field and the excitation from the + field cancel each other out.

Closely related to edge detectors are the slit detectors. These cells have a central excitatory field surrounded by an inhibitory field on both sides (see Figure 2–11). They respond maximally only if a bright line surrounded by darkness on both sides is positioned over their receptive field. They respond minimally—that is, their spontaneous firing rate is depressed—if a dark line surrounded on both sides by a bright field is presented to the receptive field. Line-detecting neurons are just the opposite, responding maximally to a line of darkness surrounded by brightness (see Figure 2–11). Slit and line detectors are constructed similarly to edge detectors, but the wir-

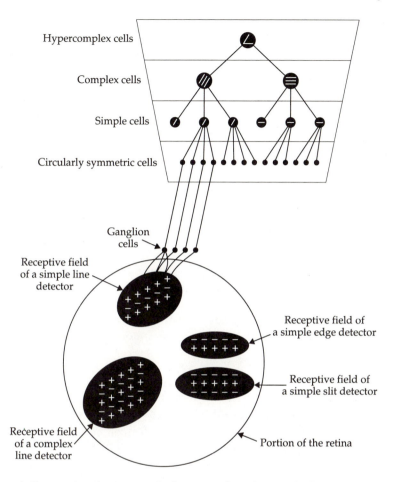

+ indicates points that increase the firing rate of simple cortical cells
− indicates points that decrease the firing rate

F I G U R E   2 – 1 1   Connections of circularly symmetric cells, simple cells, complex cells, and hypercomplex cells in the cortex. Also shown (not to scale) are the retinal receptive fields of simple cells and complex cells.

ing is a bit more complex. The cat's visual cortex is somatotopically arranged; that is, a given region corresponds to a small patch of visual space. Within this region, organization is based on similarity. If a neuron codes a horizontal line, its neighbor will code a line oriented about ten degrees from horizontal, the next neuron will code a line oriented twenty degrees from horizontal, and so on (Hubel, 1988).

Hubel and Wiesel reasoned that simple cells must receive input from a number of retinal ganglion cells via the circularly symmetric neurons. If we wanted to build a line detector in the cat's cortex, it would make sense to connect together the output of a string of off-center ganglion cells to one simple cortical cell, as shown in Figure 2–11. The simple cell could be thought of as an AND gate. An AND gate goes on only if *all* of its inputs are on. Each ganglion cell would be on only if there were darkness in the center of its own field and brightness on the periphery. All of them would be on only if a line of darkness were correctly positioned over the whole series. The simple cell would be on only if all of the ganglion cells were on. Thus, it would be on only if a line were present.

Complex Cells

In Level 3 of cat cortex, Hubel and Wiesel found neurons, which they called complex cells, that extract more general information. Here again were edge, slit, and line detectors, but they could be turned on by a wider variety of stimuli. The specific location of a slit, line, or edge was not particularly crucial, but orientation was still important. A complex line detector might be specialized for the detection of 45-degree lines of a certain width at any place over a fairly wide area of the visual field. An obvious way to build this kind of cell is merely to connect the outputs of a number of simple line-detecting cells to the complex cell. In this case, we might think of the complex cell as an OR gate. An OR gate goes on whenever *any* of its inputs are on (also shown in Figure 2–11).

Hypercomplex Cells

Moving higher in the cortex, Hubel and Wiesel found what they labeled hypercomplex cells. One type of hypercomplex cell actually shows more specificity than simple and complex cells. It is sensitive to lines and edges of a specific length. A simple or complex cell that detects lines exhibits the same response if a line continues beyond its receptive field as it does if the line exactly fills its receptive field. A line must be of a specific length to excite a hypercomplex line detector, although its exact position on the retina is not crucial. Hubel and Wiesel speculated that this type of cell must receive inputs from complex cells. Hypercomplex line-segment detectors must receive excitatory input from some complex line detectors (indicating the presence of the line) and inhibitory input from others (indicating the end of the line).

Another type of hypercomplex cell, the angle detectors, are more general than the complex cells. As the name implies, these cells are sensitive to angles. They have rather wide receptive fields, but are very picky about the type of angle to which they will respond—some respond only to right angles, others only to acute angles, and so on. Hubel and Wiesel argue that the logical principle of construction would be to connect outputs from lower-level orientation-specific line- or segment-detecting cells to the angle-detecting cells, as illustrated in Figure 2–11.

CONCLUSIONS ABOUT CATS

The process involved in the feature-detection system in the cat's brain is quite similar to what happens in Selfridge's Pandemonium model. Animal perception does appear to be a hierarchical feature-analysis neural network involving parallel processing. Clearly, too, the system is content address-able. The act of perceiving *is* a lookup in memory: the cat's seeing an angle in some part of its visual field means that the angle-detecting neuron for that region has been activated. Perceiving and activating the neuron are the same thing. We should mention that the feature-analysis system in the cat's brain is now known to be a lot more complicated and less rigidly hierarchical than Hubel and Wiesel originally thought; for example, some complex cells begin to respond to a stimulus before the simple cells that hypotheti-cally send them input (Hubel, 1988; Marrocco, 1986). Thus, at the very least, complex cells get some early "hints" from a source other than the simple cells. There is also evidence of even more complicated feature detectors that are sensitive to gratings or spatial frequencies—alternating patterns of light and dark (Ginsburg, 1986).

ARE THERE COMPLEX OBJECT DETECTORS?

It does not take much imagination to speculate that the output of hyper-complex cells could be used as input to other neurons that would detect more complex patterns. Output from angle detectors, for example, could be used to construct detectors for squares, triangles, and so on. Eventually, mouse detectors and grandmother detectors could be constructed. This would solve the problem of recognition; that is, it would explain how a mouse or a grandmother is recognized regardless of where it is in the visual field. Monkeys have a hierarchy of feature detectors in their visual cortex that is almost identical to the hierarchy found in the cat (Hubel & Wiesel, 1965). In other areas of monkey cortex, Gross (1973) found neurons that seem to be detectors for much more complex patterns. One type of neuron seems to be a monkey-paw detector. It exhibits a maximal response only to a monkey paw in a certain orientation! It responds somewhat to a human hand and other things resembling monkey paws, but not at all to other stimuli. Other neurons have been discovered that seem to be detectors for triangles, squares, and even faces (Bruce, Desimone, & Gross, 1981).

Is it possible that output from detectors for monkey paws, monkey faces, and so on converge on neurons that serve as general monkey detec-tors? It is certainly possible, but most investigators think it is rather unlikely (Erickson, 1984). It seems much more likely that a whole distributed array of neurons serve as the ultimate monkey, mouse, or grandmother detector; that is, seeing a monkey, mouse, or grandmother corresponds to activation of a whole set of neurons coding the features of these stimuli rather than to activiation of a single neuron. If this is the case, finding the exact set of neurons would be extremely difficult, given that there are billions and billions of neurons in the brain. As psychologists, though, our real concern is whether there are nodes or cognitive units coding percepts such as monkeys, mice, and grandmothers. We can leave to neuroscientists the task of figuring out exactly how these cognitive units are constructed from neurons.

SUMMARY AND CONCLUSIONS

Some lower organisms solve the task of recognition by detecting simple invariant features, whereas higher organisms need to recognize objects defined by many features. The basic idea behind Selfridge's Pandemonium model of recognition is that complex stimuli can be defined in terms of the simultaneous presence of unique sets of distinctive features. Recognition, in this view, consists of hierarchical extraction and combination of these features. The classic experiment of Lettvin et al. on the eye of the frog showed that frogs are indeed sensitive to distinctive features. The latticelike structures of the retina and of the brain can serve to extract distinctive visual features such as edges. A variety of evidence ranging from Ratliff's studies of the eye of the horseshoe crab to Mach's demonstration of edge enhancement in human perception suggests that the retina and brain not only could, but in fact do, extract such features. The experiments of Hubel and Wiesel on cats and monkeys show that these animals process visual stimuli with a hierarchical feature analytic neural network similar to that proposed by Selfridge. Presumably, human pattern recognition works about the same way as pattern recognition in cats and monkeys.

Mental Modules and Mental Contents

INTRODUCTION

This chapter describes the systems involved in perception of the various classes of objects that people can recognize, then previews the modules that come into play after recognition has occurred. These modules are sensory systems, perceptual systems, the semantic system, the syntactic system, the episodic system, and the action system. After you learn what happens in each system, we shall discuss evidence that suggests information is processed in the theoretically specified order. We shall then discuss some experimental and subjective phenomena—sensations, percepts, ideas, mental images, and hallucinations—in terms of different types of activity in the cognitive systems.

An example will help to illustrate the stages of cognition. Suppose that an attractive and mysterious stranger hands you a note that reads, "Meet me at midnight on the library steps." This note will elicit analyses at the sensory level (you sense bright and dark patches on the sheet of paper), the perceptual level (you recognize the words), the semantic level (you understand what the words mean), and the syntactic level (you understand how the words combine to yield a meaningful message). You would already have analyzed the stranger on sensory, perceptual, and semantic levels—otherwise, you could hardly know that the person was attractive, mysterious, and a stranger. Unless your brain is wired up differently than mine, other mental activities would ensue. Emotions and motives would be aroused. Mental images concerning the meeting might occur, and images foretelling what would happen after the meeting could arise. If you were actually going to meet the mysterious stranger, more mental work would be needed. The message would have to be stored in what is called *episodic memory;* otherwise, you would forget it. At the appointed hour, you would need to get from wherever you were to the library steps. This involves two more modules. The action system contains general programs or "scripts," such as those for walking, opening car doors, driving, and so on. It controls the motor system, which contains the programs for the specific muscle movements necessary to execute the behaviors called for by the action system.

MENTAL DIVISION OF LABOR

Theorists of various persuasions agree that there is more division of labor in the brain than our conscious experience would suggest (Fodor, 1983; Minsky, 1986; Treisman & Gormican, 1988). The brain operates very slowly, yet it can carry out many tasks quite rapidly. One way to accomplish this rapid functioning would be to divide the tasks into subtasks, with a different module or analyzer performing each of the subtasks in parallel. A module or analyzer refers to a neural network devoted to a specific subtask. Evidence for the existence of such modules comes from three sources. First, localized brain damage may impair a specific ability. Second, anatomical and physiological investigation may show that neurons in a given area of the brain are responsive only to a specific type of stimulus. Third, psychological experiments may indicate that some tasks are independent of one another. Anatomically, there are about 100 cortical regions in each hemisphere of the brain (Crick & Asanuma, 1986). The tasks carried out by many of these regions are known to be duplicated in both hemispheres, so we can speculate that there may be around 150 separate cortical modules. This is just a guess; the point is that it would be implausible to postulate the existence of many fewer or many more modules.

THE ARCHITECTURE OF MENTAL MODULES
BASIC DESIGN

Konorski (1967) and Martindale (1981) have argued that the mind is composed of a large number of analyzers or modules, all constructed in exactly the same way. Each has several layers; most have four. Each layer has a large number of nodes. We can think of each layer as a two-dimensional sheet that works similarly to a slab of cortex. The vertical connections among nodes on different layers are almost always excitatory, whereas the lateral connections among nodes on the same level are almost always inhibitory. Both vertical and lateral connections are usually bidirectional: if node A is connected to node B, then B is also probably connected to A. The strength of these connections is not necessarily the same; in fact, it usually is not. One reason to postulate this vertical excitation and lateral inhibition arrangement is its similarity to the wiring diagram of the cortex. As we saw in Chapter 2, it is also the same as the wiring diagram of the retina. An important difference is that the strength of connections among neurons in the retina do not change, but the strength of connections among nodes in cortical modules can change because of learning. If the structure of all the analyzers is almost the same, we should expect to find that they work in similar ways. To take an extreme example, if the structure of the retina produces Mach bands, we should find something similar in all of the analyzers. In fact, as you will see in Chapters 4 and 8, this is exactly what we do find. A side benefit of this hypothesized wiring diagram is that it severely constrains the neural network so that it yields explicit testable predictions. In some neural-network models, any node can be connected to any other node by either an excitatory or an inhibitory connection. Massaro (1988) and others have pointed out that such models are so unconstrained that they don't really predict anything; that is, by tinkering with the connection strengths among nodes, such models can—at least after the fact—be adjusted to fit any possible set of data. One cannot do this with the model we shall be using.

In all of the analyzers, vertical excitatory connections code part-whole relationships; for example, the node coding the letter "A" is connected with nodes on another level that code its component features. Thus, the vertical connections tell us what a node *is,* or what it represents. On any one level, connections tend to be inhibitory. These connections can be seen as coding what a node does *not* code. The principle of arrangement on any layer of an analyzer is one of similarity: the more similar the things two nodes code, the closer together they are; hence, the more they can laterally inhibit one another. Of course, what is similar varies from analyzer to analyzer and from layer to layer. In the analyzer for speech, similarity has to do with sound, whereas in the semantic analyzer, similarity has to do with meaning. We shall not go into how nodes coding similar things automatically get close to one another, but Martindale (1981) and Kohonen (1989) have dealt with this issue.

LATERAL INHIBITION

Psychologists do not generally agree that there is lateral inhibition among cognitive units; however, there is increasing use of this concept on the part of cognitive theorists (e.g., Grossberg, 1988b; Hoffman & Ison, 1980). Why is lateral inhibition important? Consider early mathematical models of networks with only excitatory connections such as those developed by Beurle (1956) or Ashby, von Foerster, and Walker (1962). These models deal with nodes and connections among these nodes. In such networks, input to the network can eventuate in only two possible outcomes: either activation decays gradually until all of the nodes in the network are off, or it increases explosively until all of the nodes are on and continue to be on. Neither of these outcomes even remotely corresponds to the reaction of the brain to stimuli or to the spontaneous and sustained activity of the brain in the absence of stimuli. When you meet a mysterious stranger, you do not go into a coma (all the nodes are off); on the other hand, you do not have a fatal seizure either (all the nodes are on). Purely excitatory networks have been rejected in favor of models incorporating both excitatory and inhibitory connections (Wilson & Cowan, 1972). Activation in such networks exhibits a closer fit with actual cognition and brain activity—it oscillates back and forth, just as our thoughts wax and wane.

WHAT HAPPENS ON EACH LAYER OF A MODULE

At least for the higher senses, such as vision and hearing, input from receptors goes first to sensory analyzers located in the primary receiving areas of the cortex. Output from these sensory analyzers serves as the input to the bottom layer of perceptual analyzers. At the top level of each perceptual analyzer are cognitive units that code what Konorski (1967) called unitary percepts. A unitary percept would be the sound pattern of a particular word for the speech analyzer or the face of a friend for the analyzer that deals with recognition of faces. All the things we can recognize are hypothetically coded by such units that are located on the top layer of a perceptual analyzer. Feldman and Ballard (1982) take a similar viewpoint, but Grossberg (1988a), McClelland and Rumelhart (1986), and many other connectionist theorists argue that unitary percepts are *not* coded by individual nodes; rather, they are coded by the large number of nodes representing their features. There are good reasons for this view: the nodes coding whole things or unitary percepts may not really be necessary and can actually cause problems if one gets into the details of how a neural network functions (Fodor & Pylyshyn, 1988). An analogy may clarify this issue. A microcomputer may have a register composed of eight "nodes" that contains numbers in binary format; for example, 16 is coded as 00010000 and 17 is coded as 00010001. Each number corresponds to a specific pattern of zeros and ones. This binary distributed representation has a lot of advantages. There would be no advantage, and a lot of disadvantages, to taking the output of each "node" to "unitary percept" nodes that represented each specific number in decimal form. We would need 129 nodes—one for every number from zero through 128—and they would serve no earthly purpose. It would be far better to dispense with them and just stick to the eight nodes that code these numbers in binary form; however, when we talk about what the computer is doing, it is easier to speak in terms of numbers that we readily understand rather than binary numbers. The same is true of neural networks. A whole set of nodes can *function* as if they were a single node coding a unitary percept (Stone & Van Orden, 1989). Thus, although we may not really need the unitary percept nodes, we shall quickly become confused if we don't include them in the network. In an introductory book such as this one, it won't hurt to think of one node, rather than a whole pattern of nodes, as coding one thing.

Between the highest and lowest levels of an analyzer are several intermediate levels. As we move upward, units on each level code more specific aspects of the class of stimuli dealt with by that analyzer. The higher the level, the more specific the features detected by the units at that level. Higher-

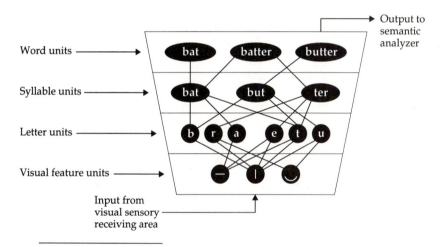

F I G U R E   3 – 1   The perceptual analyzer for printed words. Only a few sample nodes are shown at each level.

level units receive excitatory inputs from lower-level units. The analyzer for printed words is shown in Figure 3-1. Hypothetically, there is a cognitive unit for each printed word one can recognize at the highest level of this analyzer. At the bottom level, there is a small number of nodes. Each node codes a distinctive feature of printed letters—examples would be vertical lines, diagonal lines, angles, and so on. Levels in between contain nodes for individual letters of the alphabet and for letter groups. (Note that this is just an expanded version of Selfridge's [1959] Pandemonium network described in Chapter 2.) The higher we go in a perceptual analyzer, the larger the number of units. A huge number of different units at the highest level of a perceptual analyzer can be activated by a small number of units at lower levels. On each layer of the module, nodes exert mutual lateral inhibition upon each other. For all modules or analyzers, the basic "wiring diagram" is the same: vertical connections are excitatory and horizontal connections are inhibitory. As we shall see in later chapters, this circuitry allows modules to make useful computations—as it certainly should, since vertical excitation and lateral inhibition is a basic wiring principle of the cerebral cortex.

SENSORY ANALYSIS
GENERAL PRINCIPLES

Sensory analyzers lie in the primary sensory receiving areas of the cortex. There is at least one of them for each of the senses. Activation of nodes in these analyzers causes raw sensations rather than perception of meaningful objects. In the case of vision, sensory analysis deals with such things as brightness, color, and spatial location; in the case of audition, sensory analysis deals with loudness and pitch. Nodes in sensory analyzers code what Wundt (1896) called *psychical elements,* the basic building blocks of subjective experience. Brain lesions in the primary receiving areas cause specific sensory deficits—for example, damage to the primary auditory receiving area will result in deafness or inability to hear sounds in a specific frequency range.

SEGREGATION OF VISUAL SENSATIONS

Evidence is accumulating from several sources that analysis of visual sensations does not take place in only one sensory module, but occurs in a surprising number of distinct analyzers. There is physiological evidence that different areas of the cortex must be involved in

1. Distinctive feature analysis—detection of basic features such as lines, edges, angles, and so on (Hubel, 1988). (This is the process described in Chapter 2.)
2. Spatial frequency analysis—detection of repetitive light-dark patterns (Tootell, Silverman & DeValois, 1981).
3. Binocular disparity or depth analysis (Blakemore, 1970).
4. Color (Livingstone & Hubel, 1984).
5. Motion (Zeki, 1974).
6. Location (Ungerleider & Mishkin, 1982).

Of course, all this information is normally kept in synchrony. The analyzers are structurally separate but massively interconnected, so they all function together. Otherwise, you would not know what was where. If stimuli were presented very quickly, though, you might get confused. Suppose that you were very briefly presented with arrays of the letters "A" and "O" that were either scarlet or blue. You would make a lot of mistakes, such as seeing a scarlet "A" when you were shown a blue "O" (Treisman & Schmidt, 1982).

Visual displays divided so that each half is composed of stimuli coded in different ways by different sensory analyzers automatically segment themselves (Beck, 1982; Triesman & Gormican, 1988). Look at Figure 3-2(a). It is

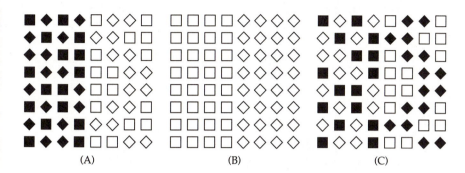

(A)   (B)   (C)

F I G U R E   3 – 2   Illustration of texture segregation effects predicted by Treisman's feature integration theory. In (A) the right and left halves differ in brightness, and in (B) they differ in line slope. Thus, the two halves are automatically and rapidly segregated. In (C) the right and left halves differ because of a combination of features: the squares are black and the diamonds are white on the left, whereas the squares are white and the diamonds are black on the right. In this case, segregation is not automatic. (From J. E. Hoffman [1986]. The psychology of perception. In J. E. Le Doux and W. Hirst [Eds.], *Mind and brain: Dialogues in cognitive neuroscience*, p. 12. Copyright © Cambridge University Press. Reprinted by permission.)

easy to see at a glance that it is composed of two parts. The same is true of Figure 3-2(b). Figure 3-2(c) is also composed of two halves, but they don't jump out at you. Theoretically, the reason is that no single visual sensory analyzer automatically performs the segmentation. If you inspect the figure closely, the principle of division will be clear. The problem is that neither the analyzer for color nor the one for form allows you to see it automatically.

PERCEPTUAL ANALYSIS

Perceptual analyzers are located in the association areas of the cortex. These areas surround the sensory analyzers. Nodes in perceptual analyzers code what Wundt (1896) called *psychical compounds*. As the name implies, psychical compounds are composed of psychical elements. This makes sense, because input to perceptual analyzers comes from sensory analyzers. Brain lesions in the association areas (perceptual analyzers) lead to specific, and often bizarre, difficulties in *recognition* of various objects. With this type of brain damage, one can still see or hear perfectly well; however, one is unable to recognize a specific category of stimuli, such as spoken words or other people's faces. Data from the effects of brain lesions give us an idea about the variety and location of perceptual analyzers. These data suggest the independent existence of a number of different types of analyzers that we would probably never guess at on the basis of purely psychological experimentation.

VISUAL ANALYZERS

Konorski (1967) postulated separate visual analyzers for the following types of things:

1. Small manipulable objects
2. Large nonmanipulable objects
3. Human faces
4. Expressions of human faces
5. Animate objects (human figures and animals)
6. Signs (e.g., printed words)
7. Handwriting
8. The postures of one's own limbs

The independent existence of each of these analyzers is suggested by brain lesions that destroy only the ability to recognize the class of objects in question and leave all other visual perception and recognition undisturbed. The strangeness of problems arising from localized damage is suggested by the title of the book in which Sacks (1985) describes some of these disorders: *The Man Who Mistook His Wife for a Hat.*

Printed-Word Analyzer

As an example of what kinds of nodes occur on each level of an analyzer, let us consider the perception of printed words. There is supposedly a perceptual analyzer devoted to just this task. This analyzer is hypothetically a layered structure, as shown in Figure 3-1. Input to units at the lowest level is from the sensory visual analyzers. The lowest level of the analyzer for printed words is composed of units coding distinctive visual features of letters, such as curves, vertical lines, right angles, and so on. At the next higher level are nodes coding the letters of the alphabet. The next higher level contains units coding printed syllables or letter groups. Hypothetically, output from syllable units goes to units at the highest level that code individual printed words. There is general agreement that perception of printed words must work in this sort of hierarchical fashion (e.g., Rumelhart & McClelland, 1982).

Alexic agnosia is a disorder involving the inability to recognize printed letters and words. Konorski (1967) described the problems of patients suffering from this syndrome. There is nothing wrong with their vision; with one exception, they have no difficulties in perceiving visual stimuli. The exception is that they cannot recognize printed words. Such patients cannot read, though they had previously been able to do so. Either they cannot read printed words at all, or they respond with completely incorrect words. On the other hand, the patients can copy down a dictated text. Even stranger, they have no trouble at all in reading familiar handwriting! They can also understand spoken language. These extremely selective losses suggest that separate perceptual analyzers must be involved in the three different tasks of reading printed text, understanding spoken language, and reading hand-written text. Patients with alexic agnosia apparently have brain damage restricted to the area containing the analyzer for printed words.

Visual-Object Analyzer

Another analyzer deals with small, manipulable objects such as eyeglasses, knives, forks, keys, clocks, and so on. Such stimuli share several attributes: they have sharply defined edges, they can be moved, and they are routinely seen from various angles, so they must be represented by a number of different mental images. In some cases of brain damage, visual recognition of exactly such objects is impaired in the absence of any other visual deficits—a disorder called *visual-object agnosia*. Hécaen and Ajuriaguerra (1956) had a patient who could not recognize such objects when shown them. He could not recognize an ashtray visually, but could immediately recognize it if he took it in his hand. He had no problem recognizing larger objects, human faces, and so on.

Facial Analyzer

Another type of agnosia is called *prosopagnosia*, or facial agnosia. Patients with this disorder have lost the ability to recognize even familiar human faces, but have no other visual deficits! Cole and Perez-Cruet (1964) describe one such patient who could recognize individual parts of faces, such as the nose or the mouth; however, as the patient stated, he "could not put it all together." He could not recognize his wife—in fact, he could not really recognize himself when he looked in a mirror. The patient could, however, easily recognize other objects; his problem was quite specific to faces.

AUDITORY ANALYZERS

Konorski (1967) postulated the existence of at least four separate perceptual analyzers for auditory inputs, concerned with:

1. Known sounds such as those of bells, whistles, and different musical instruments

2. Voice quality
3. Speech
4. Musical melodies

The reason for saying that these categories of stimuli are processed by different analyzers is that there are people with localized brain damage in whom perception of just one of the categories is defective.

The most important of the auditory analyzers is the one that deals with speech sounds. The unitary percepts of speech are the sound patterns of individual words; that is, the cognitive units at the highest level of the speech analyzer code the sound patterns of individual words. In *audioverbal agnosia*, patients lose the ability to recognize speech sounds, but have no hearing loss and no problem in recognizing other kinds of sounds. These patients say that they hear an indistinct murmuring rather than speech. In less severe cases, the patient may be able to recognize some words, but has trouble discriminating similar words from each other. The patient may, for example, hear *bat* when *pat* should be heard. Remarkably, such patients can copy a written or printed text with no problems.

The task in speech recognition is to make a connection between a complex pattern of sound waves impinging upon the ear and cognitive units that code whole words. Almost everyone agrees that this process involves a hierarchical series of analyses (e.g., Lamb, 1966; McClelland & Elman, 1986). The speech analyzer is structurally identical to the analyzer for printed words. The difference, of course, is that it is devoted to processing auditory rather than visual inputs. At the top level of the speech analyzer are cognitive units representing the sound patterns of individual spoken words. There would need to be at least 50,000 of these units, because this is the number of words the average person knows. Words are composed of syllables, which are encoded at the next lower level. There are about 10,000 syllables in the English language, so there would have to be at least this many syllable units. At the next lower level are phoneme units. A phoneme is the smallest unit of sound that makes a difference in the meaning of a word. For example, if we change the phoneme /a/ in *tap* to /i/, we have a completely different word, *tip*. There are about 30 to 50 phonemes in any language, which do not correspond exactly to the letters of the alphabet. As you have no doubt noticed, English words are often not pronounced the way they are spelled. A phoneme is defined by the simultaneous presence of a set of distinctive features, each of which is signalled by acoustic cues. An example of a distinctive feature is the property of voicing. All phonemes are voiced in the sense that they are made up of vocal noise. The term *voicing* refers to something else: in a voiced phoneme, the vocal chords begin to vibrate as soon as production begins; in an unvoiced phoneme, they do not. This difference in production causes a detectable difference in the resultant sound wave. Only about ten distinctive features are needed to specify the properties of all of the phonemes in any language.

CONCEPTUAL ANALYSIS

LEVELS OF PROCESSING

Craik and Lockhart (1972) introduced the concept of "level of processing." That is, stimuli can be analyzed to varying depths. Shallow processing corresponds to activation of nodes in sensory analyzers, whereas a medium level of processing corresponds to activation of nodes in perceptual analyzers. At the medium level, we not only sense the stimulus but also perceive it as a recognized object. Several degrees of depth are possible according to how many levels of a perceptual analyzer are activated. When you listen to a foreign language that you do not know, no word nodes will be activated, although units on the featural, phonemic, and syllabic levels will be activated. On the other hand, when you listen to your native language, units of all these levels, as well as units on the word level, will be activated. Thus, processing will be deeper. Even deeper processing involves understanding or interpreting the stimulus. Another type of analyzer must be postulated to account for the deeper levels of processing, which we shall call a *conceptual analyzer*— one that deals with mental processes more abstract than sensation and perception.

CHARACTERISTICS OF CONCEPTUAL ANALYZERS

Conceptual analyzers receive input from the highest levels of perceptual analyzers. This input goes to nodes on the highest level of the conceptual analyzer rather than to nodes on the bottom level, as was the case with the perceptual analyzers. Perception consists of recognizing a huge number of different objects on the basis of a few distinctive features. Understanding, which is carried out by the conceptual analyzers, consists of abstracting a few basic conceptual features from a large number of concepts or ideas. Consider what happens when you read a novel. A small number of units coding distinctive perceptual features for printed words activate a very large number of printed-word units. These in turn activate a very large number of conceptual units, but these conceptual units ultimately activate only a few conceptual features, such as the typical-love-story node or the hero-is-deceived-by-villain node.

SEMANTIC ANALYZER

The *semantic analyzer* stores our knowledge of the meanings of concepts and percepts. The semantic analyzer is a multilayered system like the perceptual analyzers. The units at the highest level—semantic nodes—receive hypothetically code abstract concepts rather than unitary percepts. There is one unit for each concept a person knows, which means there would have to be many thousands of them. Semantic units serve to collate units in many different perceptual analyzers; for example, the semantic unit coding the concept *mallard duck* receives inputs from units in the speech analyzer (the units coding the sound of the words), the visual analyzer for small objects (the unit coding the visual image of a mallard duck), and so on. Everything a person knows about a mallard duck is coded by connections between the mallard duck unit and semantic units coding the relevant concepts. A crucial difference between perceptual analyzers and the semantic analyzer is that the semantic analyzer has no direct input from sensory systems to the units at its lowest level. What is the multilevel structure good for then? Presumably, the units at each lower level code successively more and more abstract concepts. Thus, units at the highest level code elementary concepts or "ideas," such as the concept of a mallard duck or a merganser duck. Units at the next deeper level might code what Rosch, Simpson, and Miller (1976) call basic-level categories, such as *duck*. At the next lower level would be units coding more abstract superordinates, such as the general concept of *bird*. Units at the next lower level might code even more general concepts, such as *animal*. As with the other analyzers, the lower the level, the smaller the number of units. Figure 3-3 presents a diagram of a portion of the semantic analyzer.

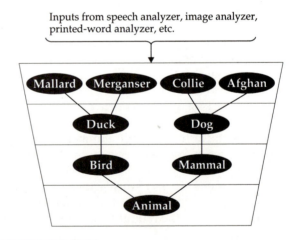

FIGURE 3 – 3 The semantic analyzer, with examples of nodes on each level. Note that input is to nodes on the top layer of the analyzer. (Only a few sample nodes are shown.)

SYNTACTIC ANALYZER

Recall the example at the beginning of this chapter—the note about meeting on the library steps. After it has activated units in the relevant sensory and perceptual analyzers, the meaning of each word is automatically "looked up" in semantic memory. To understand the message, you need to know more than the meaning of each individual word. You must also know where and when who is supposed to do what. Theoretically, understanding arrives through combining the meanings into an abstract proposition (Anderson, 1985). A proposition describes an event in terms of "cases," such as action, agent, object, time, location, and so on. The note in question might be represented in propositional form as *meet (self, stranger, midnight, library steps, imperative)*. The cognitive units in the syntactic analyzer code and decode such propositions. Any one syntactic unit would receive inputs from units in the printed word analyzer and from semantic memory units. The syntactic analyzer performs a grammatical analysis of a message, which we shall examine in Chapter 9.

EPISODIC ANALYZER

To remember a proposition, connections from the semantic and syntactic analyzers to the episodic analyzer must be established. According to Tulving (1985), we have several distinct types of long-term memory: semantic memory contains our general store of knowledge, whereas episodic memory is "time-tagged." Episodic memory contains memories of events that have occurred to us or that we have heard about. As shown in Figure 3-4, the episodic analyzer is also a multilayered structure. The idea is that nodes in each lower level are more general or abstract. Suppose you meet the stranger on the library steps, and the two of you take a walk in a moonlit forest. Each specific action in the forest will be coded by an *event unit*. The entire promenade will be an *episode* in your life, and an episodic unit will be

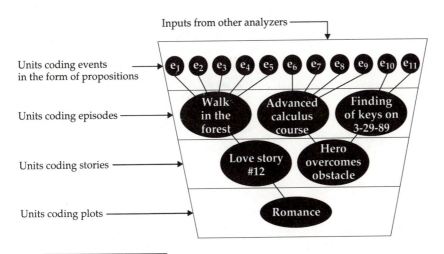

F I G U R E   3 – 4   The episodic analyzer, with examples of nodes on each level.

established to code it. The episodic unit will be connected to the event units that code its component parts. At the next lower level are units coding stories. We tend to classify our memories not only according to when they happened, but also according to what happened. Story units give us a way of representing this classification system. The walk in the forest might be the first episode in Love Story #12 or something of the sort. At the lowest level of the episodic analyzer are hypothetically plot units. We might envision ten or so of them—one for each of the small number of very basic components from which a story (including the story of one's life) can be composed.

THE ACTION SYSTEM

We have gotten ahead of ourselves. You cannot get to the forest before first getting to the library steps. Shallice (1978) has postulated the existence of what he calls the *action system*. In the adaptation (Martindale, 1980) of Shallice's action system, as illustrated in Figure 3-5, we have placed what he calls *action units* on the top layer. There is an action unit for every basic act a person performs. At a minimum, Shallice argues that there would be one unit for every action that can be described by a transitive verb. These units

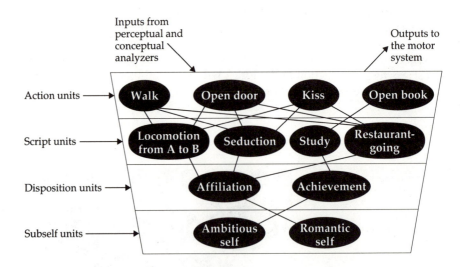

F I G U R E   3 – 5 The action system, with examples of nodes on each level.

code actions such as *walking, sitting down, kissing,* and so on. Output from action units goes to the motor system. The main reason for postulating action units is that after we decide upon a given act, it is executed by the motor system in an automatic fashion. You can decide to kiss, but you cannot control or even be conscious of all the specific muscle movements involved in kissing. The motor system takes care of these details—not merely because your mind is otherwise occupied while kissing; the same is true of all actions.

At lower levels of the action system are nodes controlling more and more general types of action. At the second level are nodes coding what Schank and Abelson (1977) call *scripts*. A script codes a sequence of actions such as "going to a restaurant" or "seducing a stranger." Lower yet, I have placed units coding dispositions. These are connected to a large number of script units. An achievement disposition, for example, would be connected to scripts having to do with achievement, such as studying, sewing a dress, repairing a motor, and so on. At the bottom level of the action system, I have placed units coding "subselves." These nodes hypothetically allow us to exert some self-control over our behavior. Whichever node is currently activated laterally inhibits competing subselves and activates the disposition, script, and action units with which it is vertically connected. Among other things, subselves are useful in explaining how we remember to act in quite different ways in different situations: the situation activates a subself node. The latter primes (partially activates) the disposition nodes with which it is connected. In turn, the disposition nodes prime the script nodes with which they are connected, and the latter prime the action nodes with which they are connected. All this activation also leads to lateral inhibition on each level, lessening the probability of inappropriate actions, such as laughing at a funeral or trying to seduce the bride at a wedding. Subself nodes also give us a good excuse for occasionally acting out of character: an alien or unusual subself may become activated, so we behave in a different way than we usually do.

The example of getting to the library steps would involve all levels of the action system. If the currently active subself and disposition units all had to do with achievement, you might not go at all. If you did go, a script node coding the script for something such as "locomotion from one point to another" would take over. This node would serially activate action units coding such things as opening doors, starting cars, driving, parking, walking, and so on. Eventually, you would arrive at the steps of the library. At that point, you would be confronted once more with the problem of recognition. The facial analyzer would be of help; then, the whole process will begin again—the stranger will say something, you will have to understand the message, and so on.

OVERVIEW OF HUMAN COGNITION

It may help to step back and get an overview of the modules described so far. Figure 3-6 presents a schematic diagram of some of the more important

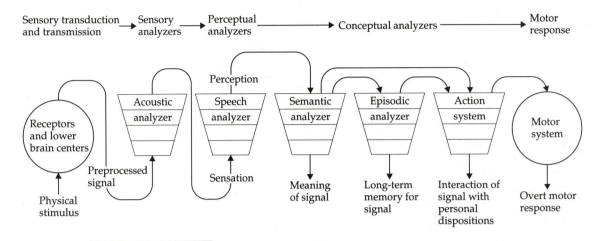

F I G U R E   3 – 6   Flowchart of cognitive processing, illustrated by the analyzers involved in responding to a spoken message.

analyzers. There is fairly general agreement that discrete systems, such as those shown in Figure 3-6, must be postulated to account for human perception, thought, and action. There is also agreement that the flow of information must be as shown in the diagram; for example, one cannot very well understand a stimulus prior to activation of nodes in sensory and perceptual analyzers. It is likely, however, that perceptual analysis begins before sensory analysis is completely finished. Likewise, conceptual analysis begins before perceptual analysis is completed. Furthermore, conceptual analysis feeds back and influences perception and even sensation. The further to the right we go in the diagram, the less consensus there is as to the structure of the systems. Most cognitive psychologists would probably agree that the perceptual analyzers must have a hierarchical structure something like that shown, but the structures of the conceptual systems are much more in doubt. Semantic memories and episodic memories, for example, may actually be stored in the same analyzer. We have put them in different analyzers partly because this will simplify our discussion later. There must be something like the action system, but we do not know much about its structure.

MENTAL CHRONOMETRY

DEPTH OF PROCESSING

Posner (1986) defines *mental chronometry* as the study of the time course of information processing. Mental chronometry can be used to gather evidence about whether the different levels of processing just described actually occur in the hypothesized order. Is there any evidence that, when we understand a spoken word, the stimulus goes through successive stages of acoustic, phonemic, word-level, and semantic processing? Is there any evidence that, when we understand a printed word, the stimulus goes through successive levels of visual, featural, word-level, and semantic processing? On any layer of an analyzer, everything is done in parallel. There must, however, be some serial order as we go from one layer to another or one module to another; if not, it would make no sense to talk about layers and modules in the first place. If these successive stages of processing occur, then each must take some amount of time. A decision that calls only for a shallow level of processing should be faster than one that requires deeper processing. If understanding does not involve the sequential series of stages postulated, no such time differences should be found.

Posner (1969) introduced a letter-matching technique to get at this question. Subjects are simply shown two letters of the alphabet and asked whether or not they are the same. The letters can be physically identical (e.g., *AA* or *bb*), phonetically identical (e.g., *Aa* or *bB*), or semantically identical (e.g., both vowels or both consonants). Posner found that people can make correct "same" judgments in an average of 549 milliseconds when they have to judge exact physical identity. (There are 1000 milliseconds in one second, so 549 milliseconds is a tiny bit more than half a second.) It takes 623 milliseconds to judge phonetic identity (e.g., *A* and *a* are phonetically identical). Semantic judgments (e.g., *A* and *e* are both vowels) take even longer. We can interpret results such as these as evidence that sensory analysis occurs before perceptual analysis, and perceptual analysis occurs before semantic analysis.

SPEED/ACCURACY TRADE-OFF STUDIES

Reaction time studies are prone to speed/accuracy trade-offs. A person can try to maximize accuracy by sacrificing speed or vice versa; for example, most methods of speed-reading maximize speed by sacrificing accuracy or comprehension. Whether in reading or in an experiment, different people may decide to make different trade-offs. A way to avoid this problem is to force, or at least plead with, people to respond at specific times after a stimulus is presented. If they are forced to respond too early (before the relevant nodes are activated), they will just have to guess, so their performance should be at chance levels. Somewhat later, responses may be based upon only partial activation of the relevant nodes. At some point, accuracy should reach an asymptote—the time necessary for the relevant nodes to become fully activated. Allowing even more time should lead to no further increases in accuracy. Thus, if I show you the word *duck* and ask you what the word

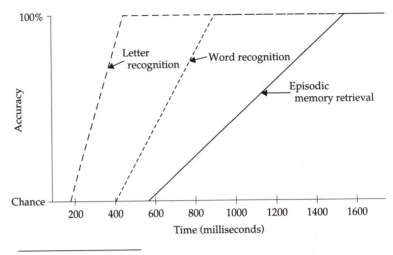

100% ┐

Accuracy

Letter
recognition ← ← Word recognition

Episodic
memory retrieval

Chance ┴┼┼────┼────┼────┼────┼────┼────┼────┼────
        200   400   600   800 1000 1200 1400 1600
                      Time (milliseconds)

F I G U R E   3 – 7   Results of speed/accuracy trade-off studies.

spells, your performance will be no better after an hour than after a second or so.

Figure 3-7 presents in idealized form the results of several speed/accuracy trade-off studies. As you can see, the deeper the level of processing involved, the longer it takes to reach asymptotic performance. Wickelgren and Corbett (1977) tested recognition memory for a paired-associate list of words. First, they taught their subjects lists of word pairs. Then they showed them a variety of pairs of words and asked if these pairs were on the list they had just learned—a task that requires activating units in episodic memory. When subjects were forced to respond within the first 550 milliseconds after presentation of a word-pair, performance was at chance levels. After 550 milliseconds, accuracy began to climb rapidly. An asymptote of correct responding was reached around 1500 milliseconds, or 1.5 seconds. What does this mean? Wickelgren and Corbett (1977) argue that it takes about 1.5 seconds completely to activate an episodic memory unit. Responses before this time are based upon only partial activation; responses at any point after this time are based upon full activation of the unit. After full activation has been achieved, there can be no further increase in accuracy.

Polf (1976) used a similar method to study visual letter recognition and word recognition. She found that asymptotic performance for letter recognition was reached around 400 milliseconds and around 800 milliseconds for word recognition. Letter recognition involves activation of nodes at a low level of the printed-word analyzer, whereas word recognition involves activation of nodes at the highest level. It thus makes sense that letter recognition occurs more quickly than word identification. Furthermore, because perceptual analysis hypothetically occurs before episodic analysis, it makes sense that both letter units and word units can be activated more quickly than episodic units.

PERCEPTS, IMAGES, IDEAS, AND HALLUCINATIONS

BOTTOM-UP VERSUS TOP-DOWN ACTIVATION

A node in a perceptual analyzer can be activated in at least two different ways. First, it can be activated by sensory input, called *bottom-up activation,* corresponding to perception of the stimulus object coded by the node. Second, the node can be activated via connections with units in conceptual analyzers, called *top-down activation,* corresponding to having a mental image of the stimulus.

Perceiving involves activation of units in a perceptual analyzer along with activation of units in the corresponding sensory analyzer. Such activation is most likely to occur in the presence of an external stimulus. We *hear* speech when nodes in both the auditory sensory analyzer and the speech analyzer are active. We *see* objects when nodes in both the visual sensory analyzers and at least one of the visual perceptual analyzers are active. On the other hand, a mental image corresponds to activation of nodes in a perceptual analyzer in the absence of full activity of nodes in sensory analyzers. This state of affairs is most likely when the activation has originated from inputs from a conceptual analyzer or from another perceptual analyzer. You have an image of "inner speech" when the speech analyzer is active in the absence of much activity in the auditory sensory analyzer. A more general way of putting the distinction between a mental image and a perception would be that a perception is mainly the result of bottom-up activation. It consists of the activation of a perceptual unit by, and along with, all of its lower-level component sensory units. On the other hand, a mental image is the result of top-down activation. It consists of the activation of a perceptual unit along with some—but not all—of its lower-level component sensory units by an internal rather than an external source of stimulation.

Another common distinction is that between a mental image and an abstract idea or an imageless thought. We can define an abstract idea as corresponding to activation of units in a conceptual analyzer in the absence of activity in perceptual or sensory analyzers. Such pure thought is rare; when we think, there are usually bits and pieces of inner speech, visual images, and so on present in the stream of consciousness. These bits and pieces may not be the basic components of thought at all. Perhaps thought consists of a sequence of activity in conceptual analyzers corresponding to ideas, insights, deductions, and so on. Because the nodes in conceptual analyzers are strongly connected with perceptual units, activation tends to overflow into perceptual modules so that our thoughts are accompanied by mental images that may often be superfluous.

THE CONTENTS OF CONSCIOUSNESS

Consciousness corresponds to the set of cognitive units in sensory, perceptual, and conceptual analyzers that are activated above some threshold at any given moment. Right now, you are looking at this book. Perception of it consists of the set of nodes in visual sensory and perceptual analyzers that it has activated. Simultaneously, there is more to your perceptual world than just this book. You are also aware of other stimuli in the periphery of your visual field and of tactual, somesthetic, and other sensations. There are less palpable mental contents as well; for example, I hope that you have a sense of understanding what you are reading. That understanding corresponds to activation of nodes in your semantic and syntactic analyzers. Some other nodes in these analyzers may also be activated that may correspond to the question of *why* activation of a set of nodes or neurons brings about conscious awareness. I don't have the slightest idea, but I am in very good company. No one else knows either.

The contents of consciousness receive quite unequal treatment. Until you read this sentence, you were not attending to the fact that your shoes are filled with your feet. Now that I mention it, this fact occupies the focus of your attention. Before, the feeling of your feet was in the far fringes of awareness because the nodes coding the feeling were very weakly activated. There is a difference between something's being in the fringe of awareness and your being completely unconscious of it. Being unconscious of something corresponds to the units' coding it being more or less completely inactive . . . as were the nodes coding your middle name until I brought up the issue. Not very many nodes can be simultaneously activated in perceptual and conceptual analyzers at any one time. We refer to the one or two most activated nodes as "occupying" the focus of attention. Perhaps four or five other nodes on any level of an analyzer may be activated to some degree. These nodes correspond to what psychologists refer to as *short-term memory*.

MENTAL IMAGERY

Perceiving something and forming a mental image of it must involve activation of the same perceptual units. What differs is only the manner in which these units have been activated. The distinction between percepts and images is especially poor for the more primitive analyzers—examples are those for touch, taste, and smell. These analyzers have rather few different unitary percepts to detect. The average person may know 50,000 or so different words that must each be coded by a cognitive unit. In contrast, we can discriminate rather few tastes, smells, or types of touch. We certainly cannot recognize anywhere near 50,000 distinct tastes. With the primitive analyzers, Konorski argues that all of the feature analysis goes on right in the primary sensory receiving area. The sensory units and the perceptual units are either the same or very closely connected; therefore, the very same units may be activated by sensory input and by associative input from other analyzers. Thus, there is little subjective difference between images and perceptions for these analyzers. Consider seeing someone else's finger being cut. Most of us have an empathic and queasy sense of real pain. Seeing someone else being cut leads to a mental image of pain that is much like the perceived pain we would actually experience. Ribot (1911) cites an interesting example: "A butcher remained hanging by one arm from a hook, he uttered frightful cries, and complained that he was suffering cruelly, while all the time the hook had only penetrated his clothes, and the arm was uninjured." It is difficult to form mental images of touch, taste, or smell, but when they are formed, they seem to be percepts rather than images (Titchener, 1910).

It is clear that many operations on visual mental images resemble perceptual rather than conceptual processes. Shepard and Metzler (1971) showed people pairs of pictures, two-dimensional drawings of three-dimen-

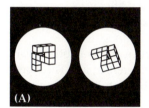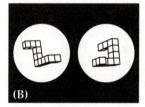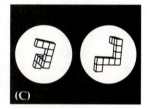

F I G U R E   3 – 8   Examples of the stimuli used by Shepard and Metzler (1971). Subjects had to say whether the two members of a pair were identical except for spatial orientation. The stimuli in (A) and (B) are identical but rotated, whereas the stimuli in (C) are different. (From R. N. Shepard and J. Metzler [1971]. Mental rotation of three-dimensional objects. *Science,* 1971, *171,* p. 702. Copyright 1971 by the American Association for the Advancement of Science. Reprinted by permission.)

sional objects, such as those illustrated in Figure 3-8. The task in this experiment was to say whether or not the two drawings were of the same object in different spatial orientations. When they were the same, the difference in orientation varied from zero degrees to 180 degrees. Reaction time to determine that the two members of a pair were the same was a linear function of the degree of difference in orientation. To answer the question, subjects seemed to be mentally rotating mental images at a constant speed. It must be that they formed images of the members of the pair and then mentally rotated one of these to see if it could be made to correspond with the other member of the pair. The more rotation necessary, the longer the mental process took, hence, the longer it took to answer the question. Subjects' behavior in looking at mental images was similar to what their behavior would have been if they had been looking at actual objects rotating in space.

Several other lines of evidence suggest that people form mental images that resemble percepts and then look at them so as to make decisions. Podgorny and Shepard (1978) used a five-by-five square grid such as that shown in Figure 3-9. On each trial, subjects had to say whether a probe dot in one of the squares fell on a stimulus figure (a letter of the alphabet, such as the "F" in Figure 3-9) or outside it. There were three conditions: in the *perceptual* condition, the stimulus figure was actually shown; in the *memory* condition, it was shown before the trial, so subjects had to remember where it was; and in the *mental imagery* conditions, subjects were given a verbal description of what and where the stimulus figure was supposed to be and then had to project a mental image of it onto the grid. Reaction times to say whether the dot was on or off the stimulus figure were practically identical in all three conditions. Furthermore, other details of responding were the same in all three conditions. Reaction times for on-figure dots, for example, were always faster, and reaction time for off-figure dots was faster the further the dot was from the figure. There were no real differences in the pattern of responses to percepts and to mental images, suggesting that the same cognitive units were involved in both cases.

Finke and Kosslyn (1980) investigated an even more subtle effect. People were shown pairs of dots six, 12, or 18 millimeters apart. Their task was to indicate the point in the visual periphery at which it was no longer possible to tell whether there were two separate dots. In the perceptual condition, this was easy enough, because the experimenter actually moved the dots. In the imagination condition, subjects had to *imagine* that the dots were moving toward the periphery of the visual field. Subjects with good imagery ability showed practically identical results for the perceptual and imaginative condition, which could not have been because of their implicit knowledge about peripheral vision. When Finke (1980) asked subjects to guess the answer rather than to look at mental images, they were systematic in their guesses, but their guesses were quite wrong.

Questions about salient attributes (for example, "Do cats have claws?") can usually be answered more rapidly than questions about less salient attributes (for example, "Do cats have heads?"). The difference in response time should not be the case, however, if one were answering questions by looking at mental images. If you were to form an image of a cat, the claws would be small in comparison to the large and prominent head, if claws were even represented at all. If you were answering questions by looking at mental images, you should be faster if the questions concern larger parts of the image (for example, "Do cats have heads?") than if they concern smaller parts (for example, "Do cats have claws?"). This response is exactly what

Stimulus figure

Probe dot

F I G U R E 3 – 9
Example of a pattern used in Podgorny and Shepard's (1978) experiment on probe dots. (Adapted from P. Podgorny and R. N. Shepard [1978]. Functional representations common to visual perception and imagination. *Journal of Experimental Psychology: Human Perception and Performance*, 4, p. 25. Copyright © 1981 American Psychological Association. Reprinted by permission.

Kosslyn (1976) found. In his experiment, half the subjects were told to answer questions by reference to mental images, and half were given no such instructions. The questions concerned attributes of objects that are salient but small and attributes that are nonsalient but large. Reaction times for the imagery group were a function of attribute size, whereas reaction times for the nonimagery group were a function of attribute salience. Moyer (1973) presented subjects with pairs of animal names. Their task was to say which member of the pair was larger. The greater the difference in size, the quicker the reaction time; for example, the decision could be made more quickly for *fly* versus *elephant* than for *fly* versus *duck*. This finding makes sense if subjects formed images to answer the questions; on the other hand, such differences in reaction time would not be expected if more abstract semantic units were used to answer the questions.

HALLUCINATIONS AND DREAMS

Hallucinations involve nonsensory activation of perceptual units that *are* sensed as perceptions rather than as mental images. To explain hallucinations, we have to assume that vertical connections in an analyzer go from higher to lower nodes as well as vice versa and *from* perceptual analyzers *to* sensory analyzers as well as vice versa. If such connections are there, why don't we hallucinate all the time? One reason we do not probably has to do with the strength of downward vertical connections, which are relatively weak compared to the upward vertical connections.

Another reason we don't have more hallucinations is probably a result of lateral inhibition. While we are awake, sensory input continually activates perceptual nodes corresponding to external stimuli. These nodes laterally inhibit other nodes that might happen to be activated by top-down connections. If such is the case, then shutting off external sensory inputs should lead to hallucinations—and it does. The most common example occurs with dreaming. During sleep, sensory inputs are systematically reduced. Dreaming meets the basic criterion for being a hallucination rather than a series of mental images; hallucinations are confused with perceptions, whereas mental images are not. While you are dreaming, the dream images have perceptual reality. You are not usually aware that you are just dreaming while the dream is occurring.

SUMMARY AND CONCLUSIONS

Response to a stimulus involves sequential activity in a number of different analyzers: the sensory, perceptual, semantic, syntactic, episodic, action, and motor analyzers. Reaction-time studies and speed/accuracy trade-off studies support the contention that processing does occur in this order. We may further assume that each of these analyzers is a hierarchical latticelike neural network consisting of nodes and connections among these nodes. The nodes in an analyzer are organized into several layers. Higher levels of an analyzer have more nodes, which code more specific things. Conversely, lower levels have fewer nodes, which code more abstract features. The wiring diagram of all of the analyzers is hypothetically the same: vertical connections among units on different levels tend to be excitatory, and lateral connections among units on the same level tend to be inhibitory. These structural similarities lead us to expect that all analyzers work similarly.

To perceive something is to activate a set of cognitive units by means of hierarchical feature analysis. Cognitive units in one analyzer are connected to units in other analyzers; for example, the perceptual unit coding the unitary perception of the printed word *duck* is connected to a cognitive unit in the semantic analyzer coding the meaning of this word. This concept raises the possibility that the perceptual unit could also be activated by top-down connections—that is, it could be activated via its connection with units in the semantic analyzer as well as by bottom-up connections with sensory nodes. A brief review of mental imagery showed that mental images do in fact behave much like percepts, giving support to the notion that at least some of the same cognitive units must be involved in imagination and in perception.

The Structure and Dynamics of Neural Networks

COGNITIVE UNITS AS LOGIC GATES AND AS HYPOTHESES

No matter what they code, all cognitive units have many properties in common. Most neural-network theorists would say that cognitive units are composed of neurons and behave like neurons (McClelland & Rumelhart, 1986). They would not want to say that one node equals one neuron. Conceptually, nodes are like AND gates and OR gates: an AND gate is an electronic gadget that is turned on only if *all* of its inputs are on; an OR gate is a device that is turned on if *any* of its inputs are on. AND gates and OR gates are called *logic gates* because they can be hooked together to make logical "deductions" electronically. The node coding the letter "A," for example, is an AND-gate that will be fully activated only if *all* the units coding its component features are on: feature #1 *and* feature #2 *and* feature #3 and so forth.

69

The cognitive unit coding the concept *human being* works like an OR gate. It will become activated if any one of its component units—*woman, man, boy,* or *girl*—is on. The figures in this chapter show a picture of the word or the thing each cognitive unit codes; cognitive units do not, however, actually contain a little picture of the thing they code. They do not contain anything at all. Perception of the letter "A" is simply a state where a specific set of cognitive units are simultaneously activated. The more activated the units are, the greater the confirmation for the *hypothesis* that an "A" is present.

INTERACTIONS OF NODES AND LAYERS

ACTIVATION FUNCTIONS

We have already implied how a cognitive unit computes its activation: it adds up excitatory input and subtracts inhibitory input. We must also add a spontaneous decay factor: activation decays as a function of time. If nothing else, the decay factor saves us from embarrassment. Consider seeing your grandmother, for example. When you see her, she turns on the nodes that code her. When she goes away, she stops activating the nodes. She doesn't take the activation the nodes already have along with her, though. We could hope that subsequent activation of neighboring nodes would laterally inhibit grandmother's unit, but the best laid plans of theorists sometimes go wrong. Let us put in the decay factor just to make sure you are not haunted by the ghost of granny long after she is gone—leaving us with an "equation" that shouldn't scare anybody:

$$\text{Activation} = \text{Excitation} - \text{Inhibition} - \text{Decay}$$

But this equation is so general, it does not tell us much. Let's consider excitation first. Activation must be a monotonic function of excitation—activation increases as excitation increases. We do not want the two to be related in a completely linear fashion, however, because there is a ceiling on how activated a node or a neuron can become. Activation cannot increase with excitation without any limit. If there were no limit, we could show you a lot of stimuli so that your neurons generated a lot of electrical potential, then we could use your brain for a battery. Your brain is good for a lot of things, but it makes a worthless battery. Grossberg (1980) suggests that excitation contributes to activation as follows:

$$\text{Increase in Activation} = (\text{Maximum Activation} - \text{Current Activation}) = \text{Excitation}$$

This equation simply means that the closer to its maximum activation a node is, the less excitatory input counts for. To understand this notion better, think in terms of money rather than of activation and excitation. A hundred dollars means a lot to a poor person, because it increases his wealth considerably. The same amount means almost nothing to a millionaire, because it adds a negligible amount to what that person already has. As we shall see, this is not a bad analogy: activation is the currency of a neural network.

Similar considerations apply to inhibition, as we want nodes to have a minimum below which they cannot be inhibited. That minimum might be less than zero. In terms of money, we could think of a node as being able to go into debt. There is a limit as to how far a person can go into debt, though. Grossberg (1980) suggests that

Decrease in Activation = (Current Activation – Minimum Activation) = Inhibition

Finally, don't forget that activation also decays, so let's let

Decrease in Activation = (Current Activation – Resting Level Activation) = Decay Rate

This formula makes activation decline as a function of not only the absolute decay rate, but also of how activated a unit is. Think in terms of money again—the more you have, the more you spend.

Masking Fields

On any level of an analyzer, nodes are arranged in a lateral inhibitory way. When a node is activated, it inhibits surrounding nodes; the closer they are, the more the first node inhibits the others. Assume that every node on a layer inhibits every other node. Nodes that are very remote, of course, exert very little inhibition on each other. What good does this arrangement do? Any network faces what Grossberg (1980) has called the noise-saturation dilemma. Small signals coding a stimulus need to be amplified so that they do not get lost in random noise. Too much amplification, however, would backfire: all activation would get amplified so that all the nodes in the field were activated. Lateral inhibition takes care of this situation, however, by amplifying the activation of more activated nodes and suppressing the activation of less activated ones. Thus, lateral inhibition causes *contrast enhancement*, as shown in Figure 4-1(c) and 4-1(d). The edge enhancement shown in Figure 4-1(d) is also a consequence of lateral inhibition, as described in Chapter 2.

It may not be obvious that there is any "noise" to be eliminated, because perceptual noise has already been filtered out before you become conscious of anything. As noted in Chapter 1, introspection is not a good basis upon which to build scientific psychology. Here is a simple demonstration of noise suppression (von Békésy, 1967): a small vibrating tip is placed on someone's upper arm and sets up a traveling wave all over the arm and

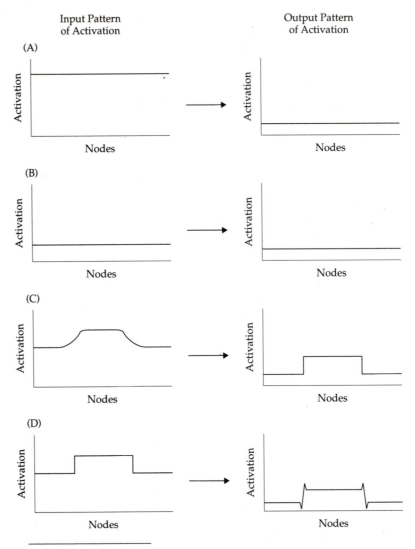

F I G U R E   4 – 1 Consequences of lateral inhibition. In *normalization,* absolute level of illumination is discounted, so that a bright field (A) or a dim field (B) yield about the same response. For *contrast enhancement,* a fuzzy edge is sharpened (C) and a sharp edge is sharpened even more (D). Compare the edge enhancement shown in (D) with that shown in Figures 2–8 and 2–9. Note that (C) and (D) illustrate both contrast enhancement and normalization.

chest. This wave is clearly visible, but the person does not feel it. The person feels vibration only within about one centimeter of the tip—the vibrating tip is the signal, and the wave is the noise. The noise is filtered out, so only the signal reaches consciousness. The vibrating tip has strongly activated nodes that have laterally inhibited nodes coding the smaller vibrations across the rest of the skin.

A layer of nodes exerting lateral inhibition upon one another has some other nice properties. For one, it automatically *normalizes* its own activity. Normalization means that the total amount of activation across the layer tends to be conserved or kept constant. Each node adjusts its activation so that it will be proportional to the total amount of activation available to the layer. How could a node do this without knowing how activated every other node is? It couldn't, but every node *does* "know" the total amount of activation across the field. Its inhibitory connections with all the other nodes keep it constantly informed about total activation. Figure 4-1(a) shows a situation where all the nodes are activated to about the same degree; the result is that there is *no* activity in the nodes. Each node automatically subtracts activity in its surround (all other nodes on the layer) from its own activity. Because activation in the surround is the same as activation of the node, the result is zero. If this field of nodes dealt with detecting visual objects, the result would be to discount the overall level of illumination. An object would elicit about the same pattern of activity in bright light (Figure 4-1[a]) as in dim light (Figure 4-1[b]). In fact, overall illumination *is* discounted in perception (Rock, 1983).

OUTPUT FUNCTIONS

We shall only get the nice results described above if nodes have a certain output function, which refers to how the output of a node is related to its input. If the output were linear, as shown in Figure 4-2(a), the result would be worthless. Noise would be amplified as much as signals. Making output less than linear (Figure 4-2[b]) would make things worse. Noise would be amplified more than signals, and the nodes would saturate; that is, they would all become maximally activated. Making output increase at a faster than linear rate (Figure 4-2[c]) does not work either: weaker parts of the signal would get suppressed along with random noise. A compromise works best. If the output function has the S-shaped or sigmoid shape shown in Figure 4-2(d), the system will work the way we want it to. Nodes with sigmoid output functions have a *quenching threshold,* meaning that activation *above* a certain level gets amplified and activation below this level is quenched or suppressed. Fortunately, real neurons do seem to have sigmoid output functions (Grossberg, 1980).

AMPLIFICATION OF ACTIVATION

A neural network may seem abstract and dry; however, it is like a society in which life is "nasty, brutish, and short." The brain has been compared to a

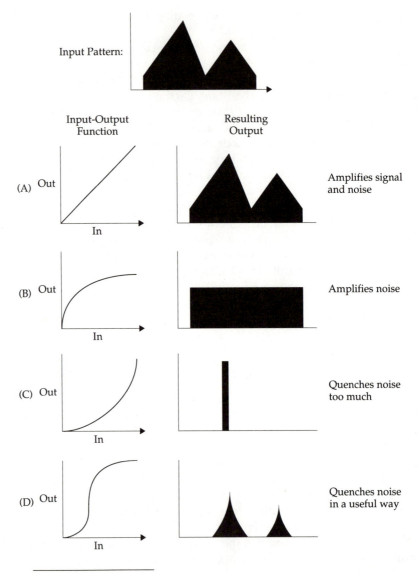

F I G U R E   4 – 2 Consequences of different input-output functions of nodes. The input pattern is shown at the top and output patterns are shown in the middle column. (Adapted with permission from *Neural Networks, 1,* S. Grossberg, "Nonlinear neural networks: Principles, mechanisms, and architectures," Copyright 1988, Pergamon Press plc.

Republican system in which the rich get richer and the poor get poorer. We might instead compare it to a feudal system in which the rich get everything and the serfs get nothing. I hope your grandmother is a nice person; if so, she wouldn't like the nodes that code her in your brain. As soon as they start to accumulate activation (wealth), they try to get more and more of it, through alliances with nodes on other layers. At the same time, they try to destroy the wealth of their neighbors on the same level: the more activated they get, the more they inhibit neighboring units. In a real society, no class stays in power forever. Eventually, some of the rich become poor, and some of the poor become rich. The same thing happens in the brain. If you stop seeing her or thinking about her, Granny's nodes lose their wealth and get inhibited by neighbors that were once poor.

RESONANCE AND UNCONSCIOUS INFERENCE

Let us consider the interaction of nodes on two layers of an analyzer. Assume that the top layer contains units that code faces, and the units on the bottom layer code the features that compose faces. Units on the bottom layer are connected to and therefore activate units on the top layer. The units on the top layer are also connected to the lower-level nodes and can thus feed activation back to the bottom layer. A closed or resonant loop is set up *if* the activated units on the bottom level are connected with the most activated unit on the top level. Say that the most activated unit on the top layer codes the face of your friend, Julia. Julia is actually the stimulus, so she is turning on the feature nodes corresponding to her face. In such a case of correct identification, units on both levels become maximally active and laterally inhibit any "accidentally" activated units on their own level.

Why do we need the feedback and resonance? Why not just let the nodes at the bottom level activate the nodes with which they are connected at the top level and leave it at that? The evolutionary purpose of "adaptive resonance" is noise suppression (Grossberg, 1980), allowing us to recognize stimuli in noisy situations—for example, in poor lighting, at a distance, when only part of the stimulus is in view. Without resonance, you would not recognize Julia very well at a distance or unless you saw her whole face. Unless you saw her whole face, all of the feature detectors would not be activated, so there might not be enough activation of the correct face unit on the top level. As we shall see later, adaptive resonance does lots of other things—some rather unexpected—besides suppress noise. Resonance would occur if you saw Julia after only a few hours' absence. Imagine that you see Julia after a few years. Her facial features will have changed a bit, but they are still likely to activate the correct unit on the top level, so resonance will still occur. The unit on the top level will now activate some feature units on the bottom level that were *not* activated by the stimulus, and these units may inhibit some units actually turned on by Julia's face. The result will be that resonance causes you to "regularize" Julia; that is, you see a compromise between what you expect to see and what you "should" be seeing, as illustrated in Figure 4-3(a).

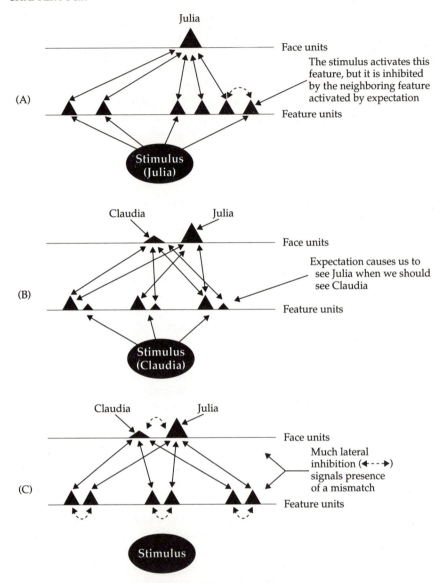

F I G U R E   4 – 3 Adaptive resonance can cause regularization (A), mistaken perception (B), or detection of mismatches in cases where we expect one stimulus and are confronted with another (C).

Consider now a case of mistaken identity. You think that you see Julia, but it is really Claudia. This mistake could happen because of top-down effects. The node coding Julia's face is primed, or partially activated, because you are expecting to see her. The expectation would cause special problems if Julia's and Claudia's faces were similar. How do the units know that a mistake has been made? There is no executive monitor overseeing this process. All we have is a bunch of "mindless" nodes—no one of them could detect a mistake. There are two answers to the question. If the two faces were sufficiently similar, you would "regularize" Claudia into Julia and actually make a mistake (see Figure 4-3[b]). Claudia might be insulted; whether or not she was, she would probably let you know that you had made a mistake. If Claudia and Julia are sufficiently different, feedback from the second level will *mismatch* the already activated units to a degree that will produce a good deal of inhibition on the first level, because the feedback is activating one set of nodes, whereas the stimulus is activating another set. Recalling that activated nodes on the same level inhibit one another, look at Figure 4-3(c). A sense of confusion will be the subjective aspect of inhibition, which is detected by the arousal system. The arousal system can send diffuse, or nonspecific, activation to all nodes in all analyzers. The reason to put it in our neural network is that it is a key system in the brain. The arousal system has a difficult job: it must inhibit the *most* activated node on the second level—the one coding Julia's face—and leave the other nodes alone. If it did *not* do so, you would keep making the same mistake over and over again. It is difficult to see how the arousal system could accomplish this task. It *can* accomplish it because cognitive units are organized into what Grossberg (1980) calls *dipoles*. Leaving you stuck for the moment trying to figure out whether you are seeing Julia or Claudia, we shall look for more information to explain how you extricate yourself from this situation. (The details of how you do so will be covered in Chapter 5.)

I have implied that perception is a compromise between expectation and sensation, involving a great deal of what Helmholtz (1866) called *unconscious inference*. Although it may seem completely contrary to your intuitions, this "inference" is built into the wiring diagrams of the analyzers. Listening to speech is probably the best example of the degree to which perception really is a compromise. Did you ever overhear people speaking a language you don't understand? You cannot tell where one word ends and the next begins. On the other hand, American English seems to consist of a sequence of clearly spoken words—but this is not true at all. English sounds the way it does because your brain is segmenting it into words. Many of the pauses you hear between words are simply not there in the speech signal. To someone who does not speak it, English sounds almost exactly the way French may sound to you if you don't know how to speak French.

In some cases, expectation can lead us to see the wrong thing altogether. Edgar Allan Poe's short story, "The Sphinx," is about a man who looks out a window and sees a horrible creature of monstrous size crawling along the distant horizon. Suddenly, he realizes that he is in fact observing a tiny insect crawling along the window pane a few inches in front of his eyes. The apocalypse is transformed into a perceptual mistake. Castaneda (1971) reports a similar encounter with the "guardian of the other world." The guardian was a huge and grotesque animal approaching from a distance that turned out to be a gnat a few inches in front of Castaneda's eyes.

Everyone has had the experience of seeing something that, upon closer inspection, turned out to be totally different than what it initially seemed to be. Bruner and Potter (1964) brought this phenomenon into the laboratory. People were tachistoscopically shown unfocused pictures. (A *tachistoscope* is a device that exposes a visual stimulus for a brief period.) On each successive presentation, the picture was brought into clearer focus. After each presentation, the subject was asked to guess what the picture was. Subjects who had made early incorrect guesses were unable to correctly recognize the picture even when it was focused enough so that nonguessing subjects had no difficulty at all in recognizing it. The early hypothesis imposed on the picture prevented or delayed correct recognition. This situation illustrates another case of adaptive resonance not working the way it is supposed to.

Dipoles and Opponent-Process Nodes

Konorski (1967) says there are two types of nodes: *on-units* and *off-units*. On-units code *something*—the presence of a certain line in a certain place in the visual field, for example. Off-units code the *absence* of whatever the units on the level of an analyzer are specialized to detect. The brain has a large number of neurons corresponding to off-units that fire only in the absence of whatever their region of the brain is specialized to detect. Grossberg (1980) points out the need for off-units. Consider a task that you quite obviously could do: Pressing a switch when a light goes off. You could not perform this task unless you had cognitive units that detected the fact that the light had gone off, which is precisely what off-units do. Grossberg's theory is that an off-unit is briefly turned on when its companion on-unit is turned off, not that the off-unit is permanently on if the on-unit is off. The second possibility wouldn't work, because almost all off-units would be constantly turned on. Say that you know 50,000 words. At any one moment, you can only hear one of them. We wouldn't want the off-units for the other 49,999 words to be turned on just to allow that.

Grossberg (1980) suggests that on-units and off-units are systematically paired into what he calls *dipoles*. Suppose that an on-unit codes presence of a black line of a certain orientation at a certain place in the visual field, and its companion off-unit codes *absence* of a black line of that orientation at the same place in the visual field. The pair of nodes composing a dipole inhibit one another, as logically they would have to. They cannot both be on at the same time, because that would correspond to the line's being simultaneously present and absent. (On-units also laterally inhibit neighboring on-units, and off-units laterally inhibit neighboring off-units.) When they first hear about it, most people think this notion of dipoles is downright silly. And admittedly, it does not sound very plausible. Why not code the presence of something by the neuron's firing above its spontane-

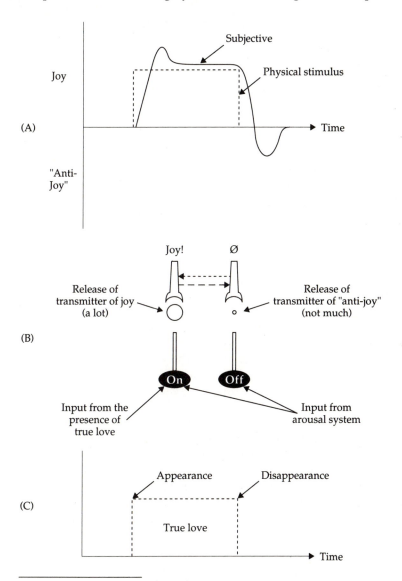

F I G U R E   4 – 4   How dipole circuits work. Subjective feelings are shown in (A). How they were "computed" is shown in (B), and the physical stimulus is shown in (C). As explained in the text, we could use exactly the same circuit to explain feelings of joy—as shown in the figure—or perception of brightness (the Broca-Sulzer effect).

ous rate, and its absence by a neuron's firing below its spontaneous rate? The reason is that the spontaneous firing rate of most neurons is far too low (Crick & Asanuma, 1986). We would be very good at detecting the presence of something and very bad at detecting when it went away. Why didn't nature make the spontaneous firing rate higher? It takes energy to fire a neuron. Giving all of them high spontaneous firing rates would consume too much energy.

The time has come to explore the details of how dipoles work. To make our task more pleasant, let us consider what happens when you are madly in love. What happens when your true love appears on the scene? Among other things, you feel an upsurge of joy. After a few moments, the surge of joy may subside a bit, but it is still quite strong. All lovers must part. What happens then? The positive glow lasts for a few seconds, then you are plunged into a forlorn feeling of sadness. This feeling of "anti-joy" may not last very long, but you probably agree that it occurs.

Figure 4-4 presents a circuit for the computation of joy. On the bottom, your true love is represented by a square wave. He or she shows up, stays awhile, and goes away. The top of the figure illustrates your subjective feelings. As described, the feelings overshoot a bit, settle down to a stable level, and then fade wistfully away as your true love disappears. Also diagrammed is the surge of "anti-joy" that follows your lover's departure. How is all this computed? The center of the figure shows the two channels of the dipole. We assume that each regularly obtains equal amounts of nonspecific input from the arousal system. Actual neurons do, so our nodes should too. So long as he or she is present, the on-channel also receives input caused by the presence of your true love. Clearly, the on-channel gets more input than the off-channel and thus is more activated. This activation gets to the end of the axon of the neuron coding joy. Now, each neuron has to tell the next one in the chain about its activation. To do so, each has to release a transmitter substance. The on-channel releases more of this transmitter substance than the off-channel because it is more activated. The on- and off-channels later- ally inhibit each other. Unsurprisingly, the on-channel wins this competi- tion. The initial overshooting in the joy channel happens because the lateral inhibition from the "anti-joy" channel takes a while to come into play.

Now for the dark side of love. The longer your true love stays around, the more he or she will deplete the transmitter used by the on-channel. The on-channel must use its transmitter to communicate, and the off-channel stores up its transmitter as it bides its time. The off-channel has *more* trans- mitter substance than the on-channel but cannot release it, because it can only be activated by the departure of your true love. What happens when your true love leaves? Both on- and off-channels are now receiving equal inputs from the arousal system; however, the off-channel has more trans- mitter substance. Its signal will thus be *stronger* than that of the on-channel. It will win the competition, and you will feel the aftereffect of joy. Rather quickly, the off-channel will deplete its neurotransmitter. Now, the two channels will emit equal amounts of transmitter. Their signals will then cancel each other because of lateral inhibition, and neither channel of the dipole will emit anything.

A dipole circuit can compute joy as well as many other things. This type of circuit seems to be used to compute emotions and motives of all types (Bower, 1981; Solomon & Corbit, 1974). Consider being frightened. The aftereffect is not just a return to baseline, but a feeling of relief, or even elation. The circuit is also used by many, if not all, perceptual and cognitive nodes. Opponent-process color cells in the retina are a good example. Stare for a long time at your lover's eyes. If they are blue, you should experience a yellow aftereffect. If they are green, you should experience a red aftereffect. The dipole for color cells consists of one neuron rather than a pair of neurons, but the principle is exactly the same.

ACTIVATION EFFECTS

OPERATING CHARACTERISTICS OF COGNITIVE UNITS

If cognitive units are like electronic logic devices (AND gates and OR gates), it makes sense to ask about their operating characteristics. What is their rise time—how long does it take fully to activate one of them? Do they have a minimum dwell time? (By this we mean that once a cognitive unit has been activated, does it stay in the on-state for some minimum length of time?) What is their fall time? When a unit goes off, at what rate does it do so? These questions will be dealt with in more detail in Chapter 6 regarding primary memory, but we can give some preliminary answers now. The top and bottom graphs in Figure 4-4 also diagram what is called the *Broca-Sulzer effect* (Broca & Sulzer, 1902). The bottom of the figure shows a stimulus of constant brightness appearing and disappearing abruptly; the top of the figure shows subjectively perceived brightness. Subjective brightness corresponds exactly to what Grossberg (1980) says should be the reaction of a node in a dipole pair. Feeling joy and perceiving brightness work in the same way. Not surprisingly, there is a brief "dead time" between onset of the physical stimulus and onset of the sensation, because neurons take a few milliseconds to respond. Note that perceived brightness shows some initial "overshooting." Inhibition from the other member of the dipole then sets in and pulls activation to a lower level. After stimulus offset, the stimulus is still being seen. Again, this is to be expected: the physical stimulus can go off in a millionth of a second, but cognitive units respond on a millisecond time-scale. The undershooting or aftereffect is hypothetically the result of disinhibition of the other member of the dipole.

The speed/accuracy trade-off studies described in Chapter 3 give us some information about rise times. Nodes in episodic memory seem to take a second or so to become fully activated, whereas units in analyzers devoted to shallower levels of processing have faster rise times. As we shall see in Chapter 6, there is some evidence that cognitive units in sensory analyzers may have a dwell time of 100 milliseconds or so. Even if the stimulus does not last this long, the unit stays on at least this long. There is no real evidence about the dwell times of cognitive units in analyzers devoted to deeper levels of processing, but it would make sense that they probably have longer dwell times. The activation of cognitive units seems to decay at a rather leisurely pace, accounting for some of the short-term memory effects discussed in Chapter 6. There is reason to suspect that the fall time of units in analyzers devoted to deeper processing is on the order of at least several seconds; the fall time of units at shallower levels is a lot faster than this.

ALL-OR-NOTHING VERSUS GRADED ACTIVATION

Each node has a quenching threshold. When its inputs cause its activation to exceed this threshold, it becomes fully activated. Nodes are more complex than logic gates in that they can exhibit states intermediate between completely on or completely off—they can be partially activated. Nonetheless, cognitive units are enough like logic gates to lead us to expect that there should be something of a discrete all-or-nothing quality to perception. If perceiving something corresponds to activation of units that are usually either completely on or off, then this conclusion makes sense.

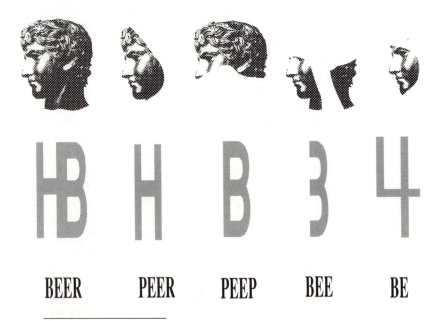

F I G U R E   4 – 5 Stopped visual images disappear in meaningful chunks. (From "Stabilized images on the retina," by R. M. Pritchard. Copyright © 1961 by *Scientific American*, Inc. All rights reserved. Reprinted by permission.)

Stopped Images

One line of evidence for the on/off activity of cognitive units comes from research on what are called *stopped visual images*. The human eye exhibits physiological *nystagmus*, which refers to rapid (30 to 70 per second) eye movements. These movements are so slight that we are unaware of them. Pritchard, Heron, and Hebb (1960) designed a special apparatus to compensate for these movements. By means of tiny mirrors, an absolutely stable retinal image could be presented. Every eye movement moved the image exactly the same distance and direction, so that the stimulus always remained over the same receptors—with a surprising result. The visual image disappeared! Even more amazingly, it did so in meaningful chunks (examples are shown in Figure 4-5). When subjects were shown a face, it didn't just gradually fade away; first the eyebrows might disappear, then the nose, and so on. Shown the word *beer,* the diagonal of the "R" might disappear so that the subject now saw *beep.* Finally, the stimulus would end up as "B," then "P," and so on. An explanation for these findings is that perception depends upon a feature-detection process. The slight oscillations of the eye serve to avoid fatiguing the receptors at any given point. Canceling this movement leads to fatiguing of the receptors, which then stop activating the feature detectors. If the process involved only fatiguing of the receptor cells, the image would fade away gradually rather than disappear in chunks.

Categorical Perception

People can often discriminate many more stimuli than they can identify (Miller, 1956). If you were presented with two tones that differed in loudness, you would be able to tell them apart readily; however, if you were later presented with a tone and asked if it were one of the earlier two, you might have great difficulty answering. In the case of stimulus intensity, we are much better at discriminating differences than at making absolute identifications. On the other hand, the reverse seems to be true of stimuli coded by unitary percepts, where we tend to be better at absolute identification than at discrimination.

Liberman, Harris, Hoffman, and Griffith (1957) constructed artificial speech stimuli that varied in small steps. Subjects had two different tasks: first, they were asked to categorize the stimuli. They showed good agreement on this task, dividing the continuum into three phonemes—/b/, /d/, and /g/. Second, subjects were given discrimination tests in which they were presented with pairs of sounds and asked whether they were the same or different. Here is where the interesting results were found. People were quite good at discriminating between stimuli classified as belonging to different phonemes, but very poor at discriminating between stimuli classified as belonging to the same phoneme. In fact, subjects performed at almost the level of chance, a phenomenon known as *categorical perception;* that is, if a speech sound is classified as representing a given phoneme, people cannot discriminate it from other sounds also classified as that phoneme. The finding is consistent with the notion that detectors for phonemes operate in an all-or-nothing fashion. If one of these detectors is activated, we hear the phoneme in question and are unaware of the subtleties of the sound pattern that activated the detector.

Other stimuli besides speech are perceived in a categorical way—for example, colors. Bornstein, Kessen, and Weiskopf (1976) showed infants a variety of colors. When an infant tires of something, he or she stops looking at it. If you show the child something different, it will look at it. One can use this fact to find out what the infant perceives as being different. After seeing one shade of red, Bornstein et al. found that infants do not find other shades of red of any interest; however, they do find a shade of orange or yellow interesting. This finding suggests that color is perceived in a categorical fashion.

EASE OF ACTIVATION

Each node has a *quenching threshold*. As long as activation of the node falls below this threshold, the node will be inhibited. As soon as the amount of input to the node rises above this threshold, the unit is likely to attain its maximal activation. It is logical to ask whether nodes differ in their thresholds. As mentioned earlier, things coded by nodes with lower thresholds should be recognized more quickly and more accurately—a *threshold effect*. There is reason to think that activation of a node leads to a temporary lowering of its threshold. If so, it should be possible to activate the node more easily at a later time, leading to *sensitization effects:* it should be easier to recognize a stimulus if the stimulus has been presented recently. On the other hand, repeated or continuous activation of a node should fatigue it, which is what happens to neurons and leads to *adaptation effects.*

Threshold Effects

Numerous studies support the contention that words that occur more frequently are recognized more easily and more quickly than less frequent words. Howes and Solomon (1951) found evidence for such an effect with brief visual presentations of words. Brown and Rubinstein (1961) got similar results when people were asked to recognize spoken words presented in noise. The same result has been found with lexical decision tasks (Monsell, Doyle & Haggard, 1989). Recall that a lexical decision task is one in which a string of letters is presented, and the subject's task is simply to say whether the letters make up a real word. The critical variable is reaction time, and the finding is that the decision is made more quickly for high-frequency words than for words of lower frequency. Hypothetically, this result occurs because the cognitive units coding more frequent words have lower thresholds (Clarke & Morton, 1983).

Sensitization Effects

There is also a substantial amount of evidence that a word is recognized more quickly on later presentations than on its first presentation. On a lexical decision task, reaction times are faster on a word's second presentation than on the first presentation (Roediger & Blaxton, 1987). We also find the same type of repetition effect for faces (Bentin & Moscovitch, 1988; Bruce & Valentine, 1985) and for drawings of common objects (Mitchell & Brown, 1988).

Adaptation Effects

If there are detectors for distinctive features, then it should be possible to fatigue or adapt them by repeatedly presenting the feature they detect. If a word is repeated over and over, for example, it seems to transmute itself into a series of different words, called the *verbal transformation effect* (Warren & Warren, 1970). If one hears the word *dress* over and over, what will happen? Of course, it will first be heard as *dress*. Fairly soon, though, it may be heard as *tress*, then *stress*, and so on. Warren and Warren (1970) found that when a word is repeated for three minutes at a rate of two times per second, the average person hears it as changing form about 30 times. The changes involve hearing about six different words, although all the while, exactly the same stimulus is being presented.

When people are asked to discriminate speech sounds, they are good at the boundaries between two phonemes, but not perfect. Detectors for distinctive features and for phonemes respond to a range of stimuli, and two neighboring detectors have a bit of overlap. Assume that there is a detector for early voice onset time (V+) and another detector for late voice onset time (V-). The difference between these two features has to do with how quickly the vocal cords begin to vibrate. One range of voice onset times activates the V+ detector, and another range of times activates the V- detector. But what of the gray area in between? There is some overlap where these ranges meet.

Eimas and Corbit (1973) followed this line of reasoning. Fatiguing one feature detector by repeated presentation of the feature it detected should lead to a shift in the category border between neighboring detectors. Stimuli formerly categorized as belonging to the fatigued detector should now be categorized as belonging to the unfatigued one. If the V+ detector were fatigued by repeated presentations of early voice-onset-time phonemes, for example, this detector would now be harder to activate. On the other hand, the detector for the late voice-onset-time property should be unaffected or even disinhibited. As a consequence, stimuli in the region of overlap that were formerly heard as a V+ phoneme should now be heard as a V- phoneme.

Eimas and Corbit (1973) studied a range of synthetic speech stimuli categorized as either /da/ or /ta/. The stimuli differed as to V+ (/d/)

versus V- (/t/). First, Eimas and Corbit repeatedly presented /da/. Then they asked their subjects to categorize stimuli from along the whole range of stimuli. As compared with judgments in a control condition, the category border shifted toward /ta/; that is, stimuli formerly heard as /da/ were now heard as /ta/. Just the reverse happened when the V- detector was fatigued with repeated presentations of /ta/.

CONNECTIONS AMONG COGNITIVE UNITS

Cognitive units in any analyzer—whether sensory, perceptual, or conceptual—are hypothetically arranged in a latticelike structure. As we have said, the general principle is that vertical connections joining units on different levels of the same analyzer are excitatory, and lateral connections joining units on the same level of the analyzer are inhibitory. In either case, the effect of one unit on another declines with the number of intervening units. At least some units also are connected with lower brain centers—the arousal system and the emotional system. Units at the highest level of an analyzer (and, probably, units on lower levels as well) are connected with units in

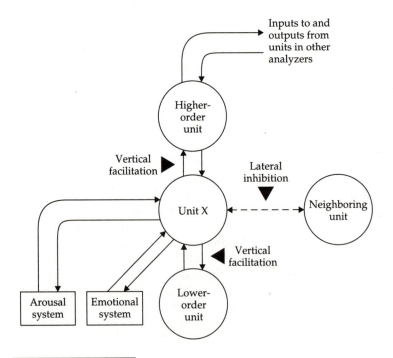

F I G U R E   4 – 6 Connections of a cognitive unit. Solid lines indicate excitatory connections and the dashed line indicates an inhibitory connection.

some other analyzers. Figure 4-6 illustrates the types of inputs and outputs a cognitive unit can have. All the connections tend to be two-way, but often a connection in one direction is stronger than a connection in the opposite direction.

VERTICAL EXCITATION

Vertical connections—those between nodes on different levels of the same analyzer—are excitatory. If we stimulate nodes on the lowest level of the analyzer, they activate nodes with which they are connected on the next higher level, which activate nodes on the next level, and so on. This process—when an external stimulus causes activation of the cognitive units that code it—is called *data driven* or *bottom-up* activation (Norman & Bobrow, 1976). There are also *descending* vertical connections between the nodes in an analyzer, although the ascending connections are usually stronger. The ascending connections account for perception and recognition—how we connect sensations with unitary perceptions. The descending connections account for the influence of deeper-level understanding on shallower levels of perception; for example, they allow us to explain why expectation and context can cause us to see or hear what we *know* the stimulus should be rather than what is actually is. As explained in Chapter 3, the descending connections also allow us to explain self-generated phenomena such as mental images and hallucinations. Cases in which more abstract cognitive units activate lower-level units are called *conceptually driven* or *top-down* activation (Norman & Bobrow, 1976).

Misreading

You may find one or two typographical errors in this book, despite the assiduous efforts of various proofreaders and the author. Why may we not have found all the mistakes? Proofreading is extremely difficult. Especially if the material is familiar, one tends to see what one knows should appear rather than what is actually printed. Long ago, Pillsbury (1897) found this expectation effect with brief visual presentations. If the fake word, *foyever,* is shown briefly, subjects are likely to report that they have seen the word *forever.*

One way to explain this effect is to argue that the cognitive unit coding the word *forever* receives input from the letter detectors coding "F," "O," "R," "E," and "V." Presentation of *foyever* activates most of the relevant letter detectors, which in turn activate the cognitive unit coding the word, *forever.* This word unit does not get quite enough input: the "R" detector should be more activated than it is. Cognitive units are not terribly picky, because they are used to operating under less than perfect conditions. Especially if no other units at the same level are activated, a cognitive unit may become activated even when all lower-level units feeding into it are not fully

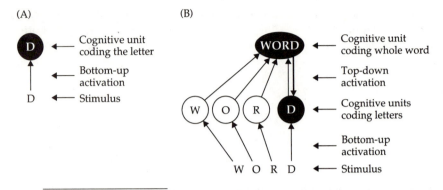

(A)   (B)

F I G U R E   4 – 7   Recognition of a letter of the alphabet corresponds to activation of the relevant cognitive unit. When a letter is presented in isolation (A), the unit can only be activated by a bottom-up process. When the letter is embedded in a word (B), top-down activation of the relevant unit is also present.

activated. The higher-level unit, in turn, *reactivates* its component lower-level units. Thus, in this case, people see the third letter in the stimulus as "R" rather than "Y," another example of what Grossberg (1980) calls *adaptive resonance.*

The Word-Superiority Effect

If the preceding reasoning is correct, we should recognize individual letters more readily when they are presented in a word than when they are presented alone. When a letter is presented alone, the relevant letter unit has only the bottom-up input to activate it (see Figure 4-7[a]). When a letter is presented in a word, the letter detector should be activated not only by the stimulus but also by the top-down reactivation from higher-level syllable and word detectors (see Figure 4-7[b]). In fact, individual letters *are* recognized better when they are embedded in words than when they are not, a phenomenon called the *word-superiority effect*. Reicher (1969) demonstrated this effect by briefly presenting either a four-letter word (for example, *word*), an anagram of this word that did not spell a word (for example, *owrd*), or a single letter. Subjects had to say which of two letters (for example, "D" or "K") had just been shown. Performance was better when the letter was embedded in the real word than when it was embedded in either the nonword or presented alone. The letter could occur in any of the four positions of the word, so it was not the case that subjects could always concentrate on one letter position. In fact, concentrating on just one letter position *destroys* the word-superiority effect. Johnston and McClelland (1974) instructed their subjects to attend either to the whole word being presented or to the specific location of the letter to be recognized. The word-superiority effect almost totally disappeared in the latter condition. Telling people exactly where to look for the particular letter led them to do worse than if they focused on the whole word! Looking at just one letter removed the top-down reactivation, because the word unit was never activated. Recall that Grossberg's (1988a) model of cognition does not have nodes that code whole words. He can explain the word-superiority effect, but the explanation is complicated, leaving us with one of the cases where postulating units coding unitary percepts is quite useful in that it provides a simple and straightforward explanation.

The Sentence-Superiority Effect

Pollack and Pickett (1964) surreptitiously tape-recorded conversations, then randomly presented isolated single words from these conversations to their subjects. Subjects correctly recognized only 47 percent of these isolated words! If we assume that we correctly hear almost 100 percent of words spoken in normal conversation, these findings imply that about half of this correct hearing is *not* because of the stimulus, but to our understanding of what is being said—that is, to top-down facilitation from deeper-level syntactic and semantic analyses.

The Object-Superiority Effect

Anything embedded in something meaningful seems to be easier to detect; the effect is not specific to speech. Williams and Weisstein (1978) gave their

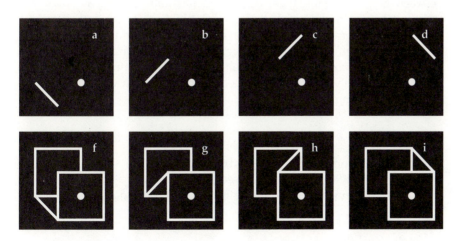

F I G U R E   4 – 8   The object-superiority effect. Subjects have to report which of the diagonal lines (a–d) is shown on each trial. This task is easier when the lines are embedded in figures that look like three-dimensional objects (f–i). (From N. Weisstein and C. S. Harris [1974]. Visual detection of line segments: An object superiority effect. *Science, 186*, p. 753. Copyright 1974 American Association for the Advancement of Science. Reprinted by permission.)

subjects the task of detecting whether lines of the type shown in the top row of Figure 4-8 were present in a visual display. Subjects performed better when the line was embedded in a meaningful figure (bottom row of Figure 4-8) than when the line was shown by itself (top row of Figure 4-8). Pomerantz (1981) asked his subjects to indicate which of four lines in a display was different in orientation from the others. Performance was much better if the lines were embedded in meaningful figures, and poorer if the lines were embedded in meaningless or disorganized figures.

LATERAL INHIBITION

On any level of an analyzer, adjacent nodes laterally inhibit each other and, the higher the level, the stronger lateral inhibition seems to be (Konorski, 1967). At the highest level of an analyzer, the units coding unitary percepts are extremely antagonistic to each other. Thus, it is difficult simultaneously to activate two units coding similar unitary percepts. It is hard to hear two words at the same time; it is certainly much more difficult than hearing a word and recognizing a face at the same time. Walley and Weiden (1973), Martindale (1981), and others argue that—on any level—the principle of arrangement is one of similarity. The more similar two percepts or features, the closer together are the units coding them. As a consequence, we should expect greater similarity between two percepts to lead to greater inhibition between the nodes coding them, because lateral inhibition is greater the closer together the two nodes are. If such lateral inhibition exists, activation of a node should interfere with activation of neighboring units. On the level of perception, this effect is called *masking*; on the level of long-term memory, it is called *interference*, and accounts for why we forget things. We shall also see that lateral inhibition seems to be important in both voluntary and involuntary focusing of attention.

Metacontrast

Averbach and Coriell (1961) showed subjects an array such as that illustrated in Figure 4-9(a) for a few milliseconds. Then, after a pause of about 50 milliseconds, they showed a circle aligned to fit around one of the letters

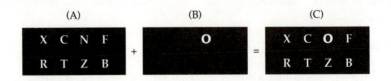

| (A) | (B) | (C) |

F I G U R E   4 – 9   What subjects were shown (A and B) and what they saw (C) in Averbach and Coriell's (1961) experiment.

(see Figure 4-9[b]). Subjects were supposed to report the circled letter. When stimuli follow each other this quickly, the letter array and the circle are experienced as being simultaneous. The subjects didn't do very well at this task. What they saw is diagrammed in Figure 4-9(c). The circle had erased the letter! This phenomenon is called *backward masking*. When stimuli that are similar in shape and close to one another produce masking, we call it *metacontrast*.

For metacontrast to occur, the second stimulus must appear within 100 milliseconds of the first. We know that metacontrast happens in the brain rather than in the retina: the two stimuli can be presented to different eyes and masking still occurs. The more similar the stimuli, the more masking there is. We also find that the second stimulus almost always masks the first one. Stimulus intensity is not important—even if the first stimulus is intense and the second is weak, one finds backward masking. Turvey (1973) established these principles in an impressive series of studies. The mechanism causing metacontrast is probably lateral inhibition. The more similar two stimuli, the more lateral inhibition there should be. Because the brain normalizes stimulus intensity, intensity is not important. Why does the effect work backward in time? Why don't we get forward masking? Because nodes in sensory analyzers have very rapid decay rates; the first stimulus is coded by nodes whose activation is fading, and the second stimulus is coded by nodes whose activation is reaching its peak.

Tilt Illusions

Look at Figure 4-10(a). Is line *a* vertical? It is in fact quite vertical, but it probably seems to tilt slightly in a counterclockwise direction because of the presence of line *b*. This effect is called a *tilt illusion* or *orientation contrast*. A similar effect is obtained if one is first exposed to line *b* and is then presented with line *a* alone—a *tilt aftereffect*. Both effects were first described several decades ago by Gibson and Radner (1937). An explanation of the tilt illusion is as follows: people have cortical orientation-specific line detectors that exist in a lateral inhibitory network. (As we learned in Chapter 2, this is certainly the case with cats and monkeys.) The detector activated by line *b* laterally inhibits the detector for line *a*, causing the latter to respond at less than its maximal rate. There are other plausible explanations as well. Fortunately, the case can be made much stronger. In Figure 4-10(b), the vertical line appears less tilted than the vertical line in Figure 4-10(a). Why? Hypothetically, the detector that responds to line *c* is now inhibiting the detector that responds to line *b*. As a result, the detector that responds to line *a* is *disinhibited*, because the *b*-detector cannot inhibit it as much. Carpenter and Blakemore (1973) first demonstrated this disinhibition effect for the tilt illusion. Magnussen and Kurtenbach (1980) showed that it also occurs with the tilt aftereffect. The disinhibition effect can be explained readily by the lateral inhibition theory, and it is difficult to imagine any other reasonable explanation.

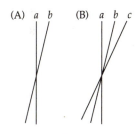

F I G U R E   4 - 1 0
The tilt illusion. In (A), the presence of line *b* makes line *a* seem to tilt away from verticality. In (B), the node coding line *c* inhibits the node coding line *b*, thus disinhibiting the node coding line *a*. Consequently, line *a* appears to be vertical.

ADAPTIVE RESONANCE VERSUS SERIAL SEARCHES

If people are given the task of saying whether a target letter appears in a briefly presented display, it is well established that performance worsens as the number of distractor items in the display increases (Estes & Taylor, 1964). Gardner (1973) argued that this results not from the number of items that have to be scanned before finding the target letter, but because as the number of items increases, more of the distractor items will be confusable with the target item. If letter detection involves a parallel-processing set of feature detectors, then the number of stimuli should be irrelevant because no scanning is involved. Only if letter detection involved serial processing should the number of items slow down detection. Gardner designed a simple experiment to test this idea. The subjects' task was to say whether an "F" or "T" was presented in a visual display. Distractor items were either dissimilar to both targets (an "O") or highly similar to both targets (the artificial letter, ⊤). The items were distant enough from one another so that sensory-level masking would not be a factor. The results were clear: performance was not at all affected by display size when the distracting items were not confusable with the targets. It took no longer to recognize an "F" in the presence of several "O"s than in the presence of only one "O." On the other hand, when the distracting items were similar to the target items, performance declined as display size increased. One explanation would be to postulate that cognitive units coding the features of the distractor items laterally inhibited the cognitive units coding features of the target item; the more distractors, the more inhibition there would be.

The results can be explained in this way, but Shiffrin and Schneider (1977) suggest a different interpretation. They attribute the interference caused by the presence of similar distractors to a decision-making stage. Their argument is that, at the end of each trial, several cognitive units are activated—those coding the target and those coding the distractors. They don't disagree that these units get activated in an automatic or parallel processing way; they disagree about what happens next. They argue that there is then a search through these units to decide whether an "F" or a "T" has been presented. The search takes longer if the activated units are confusable with each other. Similar arguments have been made in the case of recognition of whole words, and several "verification" models of word recognition have been proposed (Forster, 1987; Paap, Newsome, McDonald, & Schvaneveldt, 1982; Posner & Snyder, 1975). The basic idea of all these models is that preliminary feature analysis activates a number of nodes coding different words, especially if the stimuli are degraded or presented very briefly. Then, the set of activated units is searched in some way by an attentional mechanism to discover which activated node best matches the stimulus.

It takes longer to recognize a letter when other similar distractors are present, and it takes longer to recognize a word under some circumstances than under others. The problem with search models is that they don't explain how the search is carried out. How does attention get directed from one node to another? Grossberg and Stone (1986) provide a mechanism to account for this event. Lateral inhibition supplies part of the answer (more activated nodes inhibit less activated ones), and adaptive resonance provides the rest of the answer. Nodes on a level coding words resonate with nodes on a level coding features. The end result is that the two levels "compromise" on what the real stimulus probably is. The more degraded or conflicting the stimulus, the longer it will take to settle on a compromise. No search in the usual sense of this word is involved. The "redirection" of attention is the *outcome* rather than the *cause* of settling upon a response and is an example of how neural-network theory can explain how something— a search, in this case—postulated by a symbolic-level theory could be implemented. In so doing, new possibilities may be suggested; here, the possibility is that redirection of attention may be an effect of the search rather than the cause of it.

A word's "neighborhood size" refers to how many other words could be constructed by changing one letter of the word. *Dame*, for example, has a large neighborhood size; we could change one letter to get *fame, dome,* and so on. *Mesh* has a much smaller neighborhood size. Andrews (1989) points out that verification theories predict that it should take longer to recognize words with large neighborhood sizes, because there would be more alternatives to search through. On the other hand, connectionist theories lead to the prediction that neighborhood size could speed up the time it takes to recognize a word, because of reverberation between the word level and the letter level—all the incorrect word nodes that have been activated will feed activation back to nodes on the letter level. The latter will feed activation back to the word level, and so on. All activated word nodes will become more activated, but the correct word will benefit most, because it is the only one getting input from all four of the activated letter nodes. Andrews did several experiments using lexical-decision tasks and time taken to correctly name words to find out which prediction is correct. Neighborhood size does not have much effect for high-frequency words, but results for low-frequency words were clear: nodes coding words with large neighborhoods become activated more quickly. This result is consistent with the connectionist prediction and inconsistent with the verification-model prediction.

SUMMARY AND CONCLUSIONS

Nodes on each level of an analyzer laterally inhibit one another, thus normalizing the total amount of activation on the level. Lateral inhibition also produces contrast enhancement: nodes coding signals become more activated, and nodes coding noise are inhibited. The nodes on each level resonate with nodes on other levels. If the nodes on two levels "agree" with each other, resonance amplifies their activation and further suppresses noise. If there is a mismatch, the arousal system sends a "reset" signal.

Characteristics of the operation of nodes lead to several predictions. There should be an all-or-nothing quality to perception. Experiments with stabilized images on the retina support this idea, as does evidence on the categorical perception of stimuli as diverse as phonemes and colors. The connections among nodes lead to other predictions. Vertical connections are excitatory, causing several top-down effects: components of a percept are easier to perceive if they are embedded in an object than if they are presented in isolation. This effect is true of letters in words, words in sentences, and lines in forms. Vertical excitatory connections facilitate perception, whereas lateral inhibitory connections may interfere with it. Evidence for such interference can be found in phenomena such as backward masking. Everyone agrees that perception occurs in some way at least vaguely similar to the process we have described. Some theorists argue that after perception has occurred, there is a search through alternatives so that one can decide what he or she has perceived. The gist of our argument here is that it may not be necessary to postulate such a decision stage; the decision may be an automatic effect of the way neural modules are wired up.

Attention

THE STREAM OF CONSCIOUSNESS AND THE WAVE OF ATTENTION

According to Titchener (1910), consciousness can be "arranged into focus and margin, foreground and background, centre and periphery" (p. 266). Attention is the focus, the foreground, and the center; the other contents of consciousness are the background. The mental representation upon which attention is fixed is somehow *more* conscious. Titchener compared attention to a wave, as shown in Figure 5-1(a). Consciousness is shown as a stream moving toward you. The focus of attention is the raised wave in the middle, and the fringe of consciousness is the lower part. Titchener believed the drawing in Figure 5-1(a) best represented attention, in that something is either attended to or it is not. He called this division the "law of two levels." Like many laws in psychology, there is not much evidence for it. Other introspectionists said there are several degrees of focus, as shown

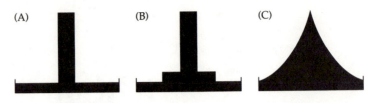

F I G U R E   5 – 1   The attention wave. Titchener argued that there is only one degree of attentional focus (A). Other introspectionists said there are two degrees of attentional focus (B), and still others said that degree of focus is continuously variable (C).

in Figure 5-1(b), and still others thought that there is a continuous gradient, as shown in Figure 5-1(c).

Introspection cannot give a final answer as to how to depict attention. The diagrams are helpful (if we aren't too fussy about their details) because they give us a way to ask some questions about attention that psychologists are still trying to answer. One question concerns the "width" of the attention wave—how many things can be attended to at once? William James (1892) gave the answer that is still generally held today: "not easily more than one, unless the processes are very habitual; but then two, or even three" (p. 220). Another question is about the "height" of the attention wave. "Height" deals with the intensity of attention—a higher wave represents more intense attention, and a lower one represents less intense attention. How many heights can the wave have? Can "height" actually be measured? We could multiply height and width to obtain the "volume" or capacity of attention. Is this capacity at all constant—for example, can we reduce height to increase width?

ATTENTION, ANALYZERS, AND COGNITIVE UNITS

Awareness consists of the set of cognitive units activated above some threshold in some of the analyzers. As mentioned before, some analyzers do their work outside conscious awareness. Attention is the subset of the most strongly activated units. Titchener's attention "wave" can better be depicted as shown in Figure 5-2. Here, the focus and fringe of consciousness are distributed across the surface of an analyzer. If we think about attention in this way, the introspectionists' questions can be rephrased into questions about activation of cognitive units. How many degrees or gradations of activation can a cognitive unit have—that is, can cognitive units take on only several levels of activation, or does their activation vary in a continuous manner? How many cognitive units can be maximally activated (attended to) at one time? We can also rephrase the question of capacity—is there a constant amount of activation available to the nodes in an analyzer? Is there a constant amount of total activation that must be divided up among the analyzers?

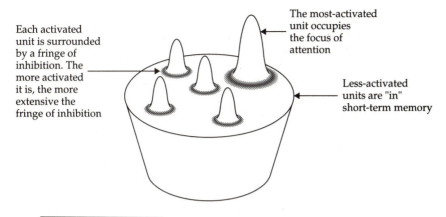

Each activated unit is surrounded by a fringe of inhibition. The more activated it is, the more extensive the fringe of inhibition

The most-activated unit occupies the focus of attention

Less-activated units are "in" short-term memory

F I G U R E   5 – 2   Attention depicted as a pattern of activation and lateral inhibition of cognitive units.

You cannot attend to all the things of which you are aware at any one moment in time. That is why we have defined attention as a subset of currently activated nodes. Most theorists argue that we can attend to only one or two things at one time. If so, attention imposes a severe *bottleneck* on cognition. There are two types of selectivity of attention. Selectivity may be automatic and involuntary, as when a sudden and unexpected noise seizes our attention, or effortful and voluntary, as when we force ourselves to attend to an uninteresting task. In both cases, the first question to answer is how selection is made. How is one mental event selected to occupy the focus of attention, and how are others relegated to the fringe of awareness? Two opposite answers have been offered to this question: *filter* theories involve the argument that all but the selected event are filtered or attenuated, whereas *amplification* theories contend that the most activated node automatically seizes the focus of attention. Filter theorists tend to look upon attention as a *cause;* amplification theorists look upon it as a *result.* Adherents of both theories have devoted a good deal of effort to determining where and how filtering or amplification occurs. Although they have usually used other terms, the question comes down to whether these processes operate in sensory analyzers, in perceptual analyzers, or in conceptual analyzers.

VOLUNTARY SELECTIVE ATTENTION

SHADOWING

At a noisy party, it is possible to focus your attention on a conversation across the room and ignore all the other voices. Imagine that one group of people is discussing long-term trends in the price of lettuce, and another group is gossiping about a friend. With remarkable facility, you can tune out the lettuce conversation and tune in to the gossip. You could easily do the reverse if you wished—attend to the talk about lettuce and ignore the gossip. The reason you would *want* to do this is beyond the scope of an elementary textbook. The ability for selective attention has been called the *cocktail-party phenomenon* (Broadbent, 1958), which Cherry (1953) was the first to study. Rather than doing his research at parties, Cherry devised another procedure that was not as much fun for his subjects but allowed him to be more systematic in his investigations. He simply tape-recorded two different messages, then, using headphones, played both messages at once, one message to each ear of his subjects. Their task was to *shadow*, or repeat back, one of the messages.

This task turned out to be fairly easy. Cherry's subjects could repeat one or the other of the messages without many errors. It was easy for them to switch attention from one ear to the other. It might appear that the basis for attention has to do with selection on a very basic level: people can direct their attention to what comes into one ear or the other. If this were the case, then people should not be able to disentangle two messages presented to the same ear. Cherry tried simultaneously playing two messages recorded by the same speaker to the same ear and found that his subjects could *not* disentangle them.

Spieth, Curtis, and Webster (1954) tried the same experiment, but they first put one of the messages through a band-pass filter, thus removing some of the frequencies in that message so that the two messages differed in voice quality. People could shadow one or the other message with ease. Spieth et al. also found that people can shadow on the basis of the location of the messages in space. In this experiment, different messages spoken by the same voice came from two separate loudspeakers. Egan, Carterette, and Thwing (1954) showed that people can also shadow on the basis of loudness; they can repeat *either* the louder or the softer message as directed. People can use ear-of-arrival as a basis for selective attention, or, when both messages go to the same ear, they can use other cues. All the cues used for shadowing are sensory as opposed to semantic. Perhaps people can focus attention only on the basis of such sensory cues.

Cherry's subjects had poor memory for the message they had repeated. The really interesting finding concerned their memory for the rejected message (the one they didn't shadow)—they remembered *nothing* from the rejected message. Even if the same word is repeated up to 35 times in the rejected message, it is not remembered (Moray, 1959). People apparently have no long-term memory for the rejected message. Do they notice anything at all about it? To find out, Cherry (1953) varied the rejected message. He tried playing the message backward to the rejected ear. The rejected message started and ended with normal English, with the middle section entirely reversed. When questioned afterward, a few subjects said there was something funny about the rejected message, but they couldn't say what! Most people noticed nothing at all. Next, Cherry changed the speaker of the rejected message from male to female in the middle part of the tape. People did notice and remember this. They also noticed if a 400 cycle-per-second tone was substituted for the voice in the rejected channel. These results are consistent with the hypothesis that subjects were filtering out the rejected message on the basis of purely sensory cues.

EARLY-SELECTION MODELS OF ATTENTION

Broadbent's Model

To make sense of these findings, Broadbent (1958) proposed a filter model of attention, as shown schematically in Figure 5-3. According to Broadbent,

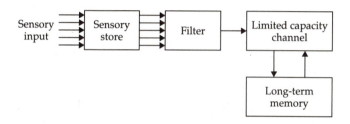

F I G U R E   5 – 3   Broadbent's early selection or filter model of attention. (From D. E. Broadbent [1958]. *Perception and communication*, p. 299. Copyright © Pergamon Press, Inc. Reprinted by permission.)

people have only a limited capacity to process information. Information arrives by means of sensory channels (e.g., vision, hearing, touch) and is retained for a very short time in what is now called sensory memory. The information decays and is lost forever unless it is selected for further processing. The selective filter picks out one type of information and passes it on. According to Broadbent, this filter selects on the basis of sensory attributes such as intensity, frequency, sensory modality, or location. It can select high-pitched signals, low-pitched signals, messages to the left ear, and so on.

According to Broadbent's model, only information that has reached the limited capacity channel (the equivalent of short-term memory) is remembered. Broadbent thought of short-term memory as a distinct *place* rather than as momentary activation of nodes—not only a place, but a small place. This is, he said, the bottleneck mentioned above. Only items that have occupied the focus of attention are stored in long-term memory. The model incorporates William James's (1890) observation that, unless something is specifically attended to, it is not remembered. In a shadowing experiment, some of the shadowed message gets into long-term memory, but none of the rejected message does. It can't, because none of it passes through the filter. In Broadbent's model, understanding of a message requires that it be "looked up" in long-term memory. For you to understand spoken English, you need to attend to it and "recall" what each word means. From the perspective of the Martindale model, Broadbent said that attentional selection takes place in sensory analyzers. For verbal material, the theory comes down to the assertion that we can select one or another input for attention only in the auditory analyzer; selection cannot take place in the speech analyzer or the semantic analyzer. For this reason, Broadbent's theory has been called an "early-selection" model of attention. Keep in mind that Broadbent was *not* using our model—he was using an information-processing model. He thought of short-term memory as a place distinct from long-term memory, not as a process that occurs in long-term memory.

Problems with Broadbent's Model

Hypothetically, unattended inputs are filtered out at the level of sensory analysis. Thus, no perceptual analysis of the rejected message is ever performed. This notion turned out to be wrong; the rejected message does in fact reach short-term memory. Cherry had asked his subjects at the end of the whole experiment if they remembered anything from the rejected channel. Norman (1969) tried another approach: he simply stopped the tape in the middle of the experiment and asked people what they had just heard. All his subjects were able to report the previous few words in both the rejected and the shadowed messages. Thus, information from the rejected channel was present in short-term memory. If we view short-term memory as momentary activity in a perceptual analyzer, this finding is contrary to Broadbent's model. The rejected message was supposed to have been completely filtered out in the sensory analyzer. Moray (1959) found that if a subject's name is mentioned in the rejected message, the person usually recalls that fact at the end of the experiment, so at least this item in the rejected channel has gotten into long-term memory. Although this finding seems trivial, recognition of one's name has to do with a perceptual or semantic rather than a purely sensory analysis of the message. It would not be very elegant to revise the model so as to have the filter select on the basis of pitch, intensity . . . and a person's name.

Later experiments showed that information from the rejected channel actually gets all the way to the semantic analyzer. McKay (1973) had people shadow ambiguous messages, such as "He is throwing stones at the bank." When the word *bank* occurred in the attended channel, either the word *savings* or the word *river* occurred in the unattended one. Later, subjects interpreted the shadowed message in accord with whichever word they had heard in the unattended channel.

Late-Selection Models of Attention

Several theorists proposed models that differed radically from Broadbent's filter model. There were four differences: (1) they deny the existence of an attentional filter that operates on sensory cues; (2) they deny that short-term memory is a "place" where stimuli wait prior to look-up in long-term memory (they argue that short-term memory *is* the temporary activation of cognitive units in long-term memory); (3) they hold that *all* incoming stimuli make contact with their cognitive units in long-term memory—however, only the most strongly activated nodes are attended to; and (4) they argue that the limited capacity attentional channel really comes *after*, rather than *before*, long-term memory.

Norman's Model

Early examples of such models are those of Blum (1961) and Deutsch and Deutsch (1963). We shall examine the later model proposed by Norman (1968), of which Figure 5-4 diagrams the major features. As you can see, attention occurs after rather than before long-term memory. According to Norman, initial analysis of stimuli is automatic. He postulates the kind of initial-feature analyses described in Chapters 2 and 3. Stimuli activate fea-

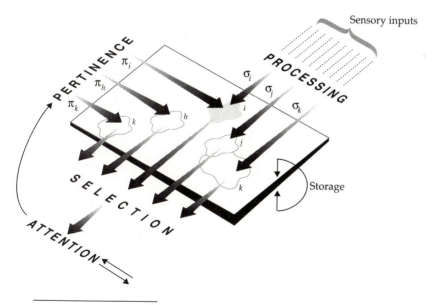

F I G U R E   5 – 4   Norman's late selection model of attention. (From D. A. Norman [1968]. Toward a theory of memory and attention. *Psychological Review, 75,* p. 526. Copyright © 1968 American Psychological Association. Reprinted by permission.)

ture detectors, which determine the "address" of the stimuli in long-term memory. Norman's long-term memory is equivalent to what we are calling semantic memory. To perceive something means that the cognitive units coding that thing have been activated in long-term memory. This temporary activation of traces in long-term memory *is* short-term memory.

Unless something else happens, the temporary activation in semantic memory will decay in a matter of seconds. One will have no episodic memory that the semantic memory nodes were activated. If we attend to something, then we will have an episodic memory of it. As to how the unit to be attended to is chosen, Norman says that it will be the most strongly activated unit. Sensory inputs activate units in long-term memory, which can also be activated by a "pertinence" mechanism. Norman's pertinence mechanism corresponds to two different phenomena: (1) some cognitive units have lower thresholds than others, and (2) expectations can prime (partially activate) cognitive units—priming makes them easier to activate. People hear and remember their own names in the unshadowed channel in a shadowing experiment. There is evidence that the unit coding a person's own name has a low threshold; for example, when Howarth and Ellis (1961) presented people with names that were difficult to hear because they were masked by noise, people correctly recognized their own names more often than other names. Sometimes activation from the pertinence mechanism can overwhelm activation from sensory input: we have seen that expectations can lead us to read a word we expect to see rather than the word that is actually printed. Norman said the pertinence mechanism helps to explain shadowing by priming nodes that are expected to occur in the shadowed message.

Norman's model has several points in its favor. It explains why some words in the rejected channel may be recalled and why they influence interpretation of the shadowed message on the basis of their meaning: everything in both channels reaches semantic memory. The model is consistent with the view of mind as a multileveled feature-analysis system. Basically, Norman's model states that we select an input for attention only in the semantic analyzer, not in the auditory or speech analyzer. Because the model also implies that all stimuli are processed to the deepest possible level, it has been called a "late-selection" model of attention.

Problems with Late-Selection Models

Treisman and Riley (1969) argued against late-selection models of attention. One problem is that late-selection models imply that people should be able to shadow just as well on the basis of meaning as on the basis of sensory cues, but this is not true. Shadowing without any sensory cues is extremely difficult (Johnston & Dark, 1986). One of Cherry's original experiments showed that it is impossible to shadow one of two messages spoken by the same voice and presented to the same ear, even if the content of the two messages is very different. Another problem is that the effects of content or meaning are quite small. The meaning of words in the unshadowed message influences shadowing, but the influence is slight.

TREISMAN'S ATTENUATION MODEL

Broadbent's early-selection model cannot account for the effects of meaning on shadowing performance, nor can late-selection models account for why the effects of meaning are relatively small. Also, they cannot explain why it is so easy to shadow on the basis of sensory cues and so difficult on the basis of semantic cues. Treisman (1969) proposed a compromise model of attention that resolves these problems. First, she argued that the selective filter *attenuates* signals rather than working in an all-or-nothing mode. This premise explains why some items in the rejected channel, such as a person's name, do manage to get through the filter. Second, she proposed that there is a series of filters: (1) sensory filters, (2) filters for specific sounds and words, and (3) filters for grammatical structure and meaning. These filters act in the sensory, perceptual, syntactic, and semantic analyzers. Filtering occurs at the earliest level at which the shadowed message can be discriminated from the rejected message. If two messages cannot be discriminated on the sensory level or the perceptual level, then filtering must take place in the semantic analyzer. This model accounts for all the findings fairly well; however, the "filter" has become quite complex. If it makes such complex analyses, then it has become indistinguishable from the activity of long-term memory itself—that is, there is no attentional filter as such. Attention must consist of attenuation in sensory, perceptual, and semantic analyzers, then after all this attenuation, one set of cognitive units will be left that occupy the focus of attention.

Treisman's model of attention fits with my view of the mind. Broadbent said that the basis for selective attention is filtering that can occur only in sensory analyzers, whereas late-selection theorists said that such filtering can be done only in the semantic analyzer. Treisman argues that attenuation can occur in any analyzer—sensory, perceptual, or semantic. This notion seems reasonable, since the structure of all analyzers is basically the same, and there is thus no reason to expect that attentional selection must be confined to only one analyzer. As we shall see, the lateral inhibitory structure of the analyzers can be used for the task of attentional selection.

THE CAPACITY OF ATTENTION

EVAPORATION OF THE BOTTLENECK

Recall Titchener's "wave" of attention: attention can be compared to a wave in the stream of consciousness. Early approaches to attention were devoted to looking for a "dam" or bottleneck in the stream of consciousness. Everyone knows we can't attend to very much at the same time, so it seems reasonable to ask where the bottleneck is. Broadbent's early-selection theory says the bottleneck is in sensory analyzers; Norman's late-selection theory says it is in the semantic analyzer. The most satisfactory theory says that the bottleneck is everywhere: according to Triesman, it is in all the analyzers.

If it is everywhere, however, the bottleneck metaphor breaks down. If someone says there is a dam blocking the stream of consciousness, it makes sense to ask where it is. To answer that it is everywhere along the stream is not satisfactory—there can be several dams along a stream, but not an infinite number. We would thus need another word to describe what we are talking about, which is what happened in the study of attention. Theorists stopped talking about filters and started talking about resources or capacity—attention is not caused by filters, it is caused by limited resources.

RESOURCE MODELS

Kahneman (1973) argued that the total capacity for mental "work" is limited. At any time, a number of different nodes can be activated. Some of the nodes correspond to perceptions and ideas, and others correspond to mental operations (e.g., decision processes). Activating a cognitive unit will require some of the limited capacity. Some cognitive units, such as those corresponding to perceptions, hypothetically require very little capacity, and other cognitive units, such as those corresponding to mental operations, require much capacity. Mental operations vary as to how much capacity they consume; the more difficult they are, the more capacity they need.

Kahneman identified capacity with cortical arousal. To perform any mental act, two types of input to a cognitive unit are required: (1) informational input from other cognitive units (e.g., vertical excitatory input), and (2) input from the arousal system. Convergence of these two types of input leads to attention. A cognitive unit is in focal attention when it receives enough of both types of input. The amount of arousal input corresponds to the intensity of attention. Subjectively, in the case of voluntary attention, arousal corresponds to a sense of effort, and in the case of involuntary attention, it corresponds to feelings such as surprise or interest. Kahneman held that there is one central pool of capacity, but later theorists prefer to believe that each analyzer has its own pool of capacity (Kinchla, 1980; Sperling, 1984).

WHAT OPERATIONS REQUIRE ATTENTION?

Perception is Effortless and Preattentive

Hypothetically, simple sensation or perception requires little effort or capacity. No inputs from the arousal system are necessary for us simply to see or hear—activation through inputs from other cognitive units seems to be quite sufficient. We are aware of such passive perception, but the activation usually fades quickly and leaves no long-term memory of its occurrence. At some point, processing ceases unless some input from the arousal system is present. When such input is present, deeper processing ensues. The units that benefit from such inputs are "in" short-term memory, and the most activated unit is "in" the focus of attention.

We have already examined some evidence for the effortless quality of perception. Reicher (1969) briefly showed his subjects either a single letter or a four-letter word, then showed two letters, and asked subjects which of them had just occurred. Performance was actually better for the four-letter word than for the single letter, which would not have been possible if recognition of each letter had required some attentional capacity. No more capacity is required to recognize four letters at once than to recognize only one.

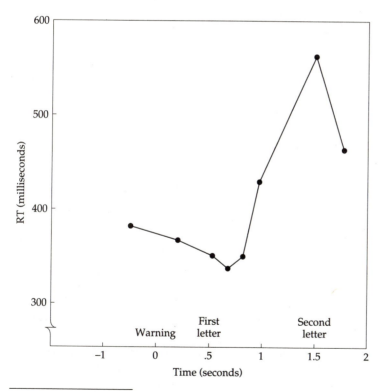

FIGURE 5 – 5 Reaction times (RT) for detection of probes in Posner and Boies's (1971) experiment. (From M. I. Posner and S. J. Boies [1971]. Components of attention. *Psychological Review, 78,* p. 403. Copyright © 1971 American Psychological Association. Reprinted by permission.)

Divided Attention

In a divided-attention task, one must do two things at the same time. If the two tasks draw upon the same pool of capacity, they should interfere with each other, whereas if they draw on independent pools of capacity, there should be no interference. Posner and Boies (1971) used such a technique. The primary task was letter-matching: one letter was shown, then another, and the task was to say whether the two letters were the same or different. This task is simple enough, but involves several operations: perceive the first letter, remember what it was, perceive the second letter, compare the two letters, make a decision, and give a report about the decision. The secondary task was to press a key whenever a noise was heard. The noise came on at unpredictable times. Reaction times for detecting the noise were recorded. The logic of the experiment was that if the two tasks did not interfere with each other, reaction time for detecting the tone should always be about the same. Posner and Boies's results are shown in Figure 5-5.

Reaction time to detect the noise was about the same between trials as when people were perceiving the first letter. This result suggests that perception requires no attention or capacity. After perception of the letter, reaction time for tone detection increased, because subjects would now be rehearsing or remembering the letter. Reaction time increased even more after the second letter was presented, when subjects would be comparing the letters and making their decisions. The letters were presented visually, whereas the noise was, obviously, an auditory signal. At first glance, the results suggest that auditory and visual analyzers share the same pool of capacity. If they didn't, the visual task should not have interfered with the auditory task.

But this initial conclusion overlooks something. When they have to maintain information for a short time, most people transfer the information to the speech analyzer and rehearse it, if possible. Consider what you do when you look up a new telephone number: you see it in the phone book, then to remember it, you repeat it over and over to yourself, either vocally or subvocally. In other words, you transfer it from the printed-word analyzer to the spoken-word analyzer. If Posner and Boies's subjects were doing this, then the noise and the letters would both be activating nodes in auditory analyzers—so their results don't definitely establish that auditory and visual analyzers share the same pool of capacity.

Later research has shown that different analyzers have their own pools of capacity, as they should, because they occupy different places in the brain (Robinson & Peterson, 1984). If visual stimuli are not transferred to the auditory analyzer, then visual and auditory tasks do not interfere very much with each other (Svenko, Jerneic & Kulenovic, 1983; Wickens, 1984b). It is fairly easy to attend simultaneously to auditory and visual messages; if it were not, people would not be able to understand television programs, where one must attend to both the visual action and to what is being said. If this were at all difficult, no one would watch television for relaxation.

When someone does something clumsily, a friend might joke that that person can't "walk and chew gum at the same time." But how, in fact, *can* we walk and chew gum at the same time? Both activities arise from activation of nodes in the action system. Because the nodes code very dissimilar actions, they must be remote from each other, and because they are remote, they don't exert much lateral inhibition on each other—hence, there is no interference. Can you talk and swallow at the same time? Don't try it, because you might choke. Talking and swallowing are similar, so the nodes that code them should be close together and should thus inhibit one another (Shallice, 1978). Similar actions interfere with each other, but dissimilar ones do not (Wickens, 1984b).

The same principle applies to other analyzers. Consider an experiment by Hirst (1986), where subjects were presented with words describing animals and plants. They had to press one key when they saw the name of a wild animal and another key when they saw the name of a vegetable. This task was fairly easy, because the nodes coding animals and plants are remote from each other in the semantic analyzer. Thus, we would not expect much inhibition, and no inhibition means no interference. In another experiment, Hirst's subjects had to press one key if they saw the name of one type of plant and another key if they saw the name of another type of plant. This task turned out to be rather difficult, as we would expect, because plants are all pretty similar to one another. The nodes coding them are close together, so we would expect a great deal of lateral inhibition. The subjective aspect of much lateral inhibition is confusion, hesitancy, and interference.

Automaticity

It is conventional to differentiate between controlled and automatic processes (Hasher & Zacks, 1979). Some mental processes, such as perception, are automatic and require no attention. Controlled processes, on the other hand, require a good bit of effort and attention—for example, doing long division without benefit of paper and pencil or a calculator. It would seem that the more we practice something, the more automatic it becomes. Shiffrin and Schneider (1977) gave subjects the task of saying whether certain letters (e.g., a "B" or an "M") appeared in briefly presented displays of letters. The displays were extremely brief, so this task initially required a great deal of effort. The subjects went through thousands of trials spread over a considerable period of time. Their ability to detect the letters improved to the point that subjects reported that the task required no effort at all, because the target letters literally jumped out of the displays at them. Unfortunately, the same letters also stood out when the subjects read a book, causing an unpleasant distraction.

Much of our behavior involves well practiced sequences of action. We can thus put ourselves on "automatic pilot" while we carry out routine behaviors, allowing us to focus our attention on less mundane matters while the action is being executed. This type of automaticity, however, is far from fail-safe. You have undoubtedly gone into a room to get something, only to find your attention drawn to the embarrassing fact that even while you are in the midst of searching for something, you have forgotten what it is. This sort of failure resulting from automaticity is carried to extremes in absent-minded people. Sir Isaac Newton devoted so much attention to weighty matters, such as how the universe works, that automaticity often got him into awkward situations. For example, when guests arrived, he would go to fetch a bottle of wine. Unfortunately, his study lay between him and the wine. When he failed to return, his guests would go searching, and find him, having totally forgotten they were there, puzzling over his equations. On other occasions, his attention would be called to the fact that he was walking down the street in his nightshirt—he would have automatically gone through his morning routine, with the exception of putting on his clothes.

INVOLUNTARY SELECTIVE ATTENTION

WHAT ATTRACTS ATTENTION?

Research on voluntary attention tells us little about which events normally draw attention. People in a shadowing experiment are told what to attend to, and they dutifully try to do so. It is not clear what everyday circumstances—other than eavesdropping at a cocktail party or studying while a radio is on—shadowing or divided-attention experiments simulate. We attend to both environmental and internal events throughout the day. What do we single out for attention? Or, it might really be better to ask what events *seize* our attention? This question is one of involuntary selective attention. Many answers have come from studies of cats and other creatures, but are quite relevant to human attention.

When Broadbent proposed his theory of attention in 1958, a quite different line of research had been going on for almost ten years concerning involuntary attention, the orienting reflex, and the reticular activating system. The reticular activating system has its origin in the midbrain and sends projections to every part of the cortex; it is equivalent to what we have called the arousal system. The anatomical existence of this system had been known for some time, but no one knew what it was good for until 1949, when it became clear that it is intimately connected with attention.

THE ORIENTING REFLEX

Animals, including humans, show a characteristic pattern of responses when they attend to something. Pavlov (1927) called this pattern the *orienting reflex*. When his dogs were confronted with something novel, they oriented themselves toward the stimulus. Ongoing behavior was arrested, and they did a sort of double take. Animals often prick up their ears and sniff when they display the orienting reflex. Increases in sensory sensitivity accompany this gross motor orientation toward the source of stimulation: the pupils of the eyes dilate, and there is a drop in the thresholds for detection of light and sound. Psychophysiological measures show a characteristic pattern: the EEG exhibits an arousal response, consisting of high-frequency, low-voltage brain wave activity. There is a decrease in respiration and heart rates (Lynn, 1966). Blood flow shows an interesting pattern: blood vessels to the limbs constrict, and those to the brain dilate. Presumably, this change facilitates cortical processing of the new stimulus (Sokolov, 1963). The orienting reflex occurs whenever attention is involuntarily drawn to a stimulus. People do not always show gross behavioral signs of the orienting reflex when they attend to something, although we usually orient at least our eyes toward whatever we are attending to (Posner, 1980). Try attending to something in the periphery of your visual field. You will find that it is almost impossible to keep your eyes from shifting toward the object so that you can get a good look. (You may have noticed this response when an attractive member of the opposite sex occupies the periphery of your visual field.) People also exhibit all the more subtle psychophysiological changes associated with the orienting reflex.

HABITUATION

What happens if the same stimulus is repeated over and over? Because novelty elicits the orienting reflex, we should expect decreases in the orientation reaction as the novelty of a stimulus decreases. A series of events called *habituation* occurs (Sokolov, 1963). The orienting reflex is elicited by the first ten to 15 repetitions of a stimulus. With every repetition, the orienting reflex decreases in intensity. After ten to 15 repetitions, it vanishes. Now, only the "localized" orientation response occurs, consisting of an EEG arousal response restricted to the cortical receiving area appropriate to the stimulus. On the other hand, the generalized orientation response is accompanied by EEG arousal across the entire cortex. The localized reaction also disappears over the course of 25 to 30 further stimulations. At this point, the organism often becomes drowsy and the EEG gives evidence of low arousal.

THE AROUSAL SYSTEM

Moruzzi and Magoun (1949) reported several surprising effects of electrical stimulation of the reticular system in cats. Stimulation led to awakening, if the cats were asleep, and to an orienting reflex, if the cats were already awake. Stimulation of the reticular activating system elicited an arousal or alerting response across the entire cortex. The usual slow alpha rhythm found when cats are just lounging was blocked, and brain waves resembled those seen when a cat attends to a stimulus. These results were amazing—stimulation of a very small region in the brain stem aroused the whole cortex. The reticular activating system seemed to be the control site for attention. This conclusion was strengthened by the finding that surgical destruction of the reticular system leads to coma and a sleeplike pattern of EEG waves (Lindsley, Bowden & Magoun, 1949).

Each of the senses is connected to a specific sensory receiving area in the cortex, and each also sends collateral fibers to the reticular activating system. If these collateral fibers are severed, stimuli still elicit activity in the cortical receiving areas via the direct pathways; however, the animal pays absolutely no attention to them (Lindsley, 1957). It appears that for a stimulus to be attended to, it must also activate the reticular system.

Sokolov (1963) presented cats with a series of 600-hertz tones that occurred at regular intervals. The cats habituated to the tones. After habituation was complete, one of the tones was omitted. The cats showed an orienting response to the *omission* of the tone! For an omission to be noticed, one must postulate that expectations are important; that is, the cats were habituating to the regular, expected tones and orienting toward any stimulus (or lack of stimulus) that violated this expectation.

SOKOLOV'S THEORY OF ATTENTION

Cortical Modeling

Sokolov (1963) proposed a theory to explain all the facts, as presented in diagrammatic form in Figure 5-6. According to Sokolov's theory, the cortex

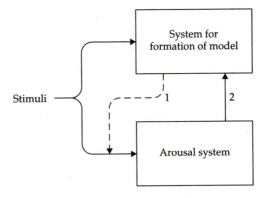

F I G U R E   5 – 6   In Sokolov's model of attention, sensory input goes to both cortical modules (system for formation of model) and to the arousal system. If sensory inputs match a preexisting model, inputs to the arousal system are inhibited via pathway 1. If there is a mismatch, the arousal system is not inhibited and activates the cortex via pathway 2.

compares all incoming stimuli with "models" or expectations. If the incoming stimulus matches a preexisting cortical model, the cortex *blocks* the reticular system and nothing happens; the reticular system does not activate the cortex, and the organism does not orient to the stimulus. On the other hand, if the stimulus is novel—if it does not exactly match any cortical model—then the cortex does *not* block the reticular system. The stimulus input activates the reticular system, the reticular system activates the cortex, and the cortical activation leads to orienting and attention.

The Match/Mismatch Rule

In Sokolov's view, habituation—the waning of attention—is caused by the gradual building of a cortical model to predict a situation. Consider the cats in his experiment. When they first hear the 600-hertz tone, it is a new stimulus. They are surprised and orient toward the novel stimulus. After a few repetitions, a cortical model, or an expectation to the effect that "a 600-hertz tone will occur every two seconds," is developed. The cats pay less and less attention the more times this model has been matched. Anything that fails to fit the model will elicit attention. "Anything" may be a 900-hertz tone, a mouse, or silence when a tone was expected.

Sokolov did not go into detail as to how the cortex matches stimuli with models. It is easy enough to see this as involving the types of feature-analysis systems I have described. The principle that Sokolov adds is a match/mismatch rule: if a percept exactly matches a set of cognitive units, nothing happens other than passive perception, whereas if a percept mismatches the "best-fitting" set of cognitive units, then the arousal system activates the cortex. This arousal response is accompanied by an orienting reflex, attention, and the construction of a new cortical model (a set of cognitive units that matches the percept).

Explanation of Voluntary Attention

Sokolov's theory of the reticular system seems to be similar to the late-selection models of Norman and others. Nothing in Sokolov's model, however, says that all stimuli need to be fully and completely analyzed. Unchanging aspects of the environment may so fully match cortical models at sensory and perceptual levels that semantic analysis is never carried out. Sokolov's model is consistent with Treisman's attenuation model of attention. It is not immediately apparent, however, how Sokolov could explain voluntary selective attention, in which there is no mismatch of inputs with expectations. Sokolov acknowledges that a perfect match between some stimuli and some cortical models does elicit attention, as when the stimuli are meaningful signals—an example would be the word *Fire!* The mechanism is a direct connection from the relevant cognitive units to the arousal system. Because any cognitive unit can potentially become a meaningful signal, it is necessary to postulate that all cognitive units have at least latent connections to the arousal system. This mechanism could be invoked to explain shadowing, wherein the message to be shadowed gains temporary pertinence or meaningfulness, and the relevant cognitive units are "temporarily" connected to the arousal system.

THE MECHANISMS OF SELECTIVE ATTENTION
LATERAL INHIBITION AND THE SEIZURE OF ATTENTION

None of the models we have discussed explain clearly exactly *how* the most activated cognitive unit is selected for attention. Triesman's model suggests that unattended inputs are attenuated, but does not specify how attenuation is accomplished. Late-selection models suggest that the most activated cognitive unit is selected for attention. But how is this unit located? What is it that does the selecting? Certainly, we cannot have the "mind's eye" looking over the cognitive units to find the most excited one. Deutsch and Deutsch (1963) suggest the analogy of trying to determine who is the tallest person in a room. One method would be to measure each person's height, write down the data, and then search through this list for the largest number. It would be more efficient to line everyone up and then lower a board until it touched someone's head—who would, of course, be the tallest one. But it is hard to fit this second method into the mind—what cognitive mechanism serves as the board?

Walley and Weiden (1973) proposed a theory of attention that goes a long way toward explaining how the most strongly activated unit is selected for attention. The appropriate analogy for their proposal is not Deutsch and Deutsch's board, but rather to have the strongest person in the room knock down all the others. Attention, Walley and Weiden argue, results from activation of a node that in turn inhibits surrounding nodes by means of lateral inhibition. The more activated a node, the more it will inhibit surrounding units. Walley and Weiden's argument is that there is no problem of having to *search* among units for the most strongly activated, because the most strongly activated unit will automatically inhibit other units. Attention is not an operation of selection at all; it is completely automatic. Attention is not the *cause* of anything, but the *result* of the competitive interaction of cognitive units. If one node is much more activated than its neighbors, it can quickly inhibit them. If a set of nodes are about equally activated, it should take longer for one of them to inhibit the others.

As long as one cognitive unit at a given level of an analyzer is appreciably more activated than others, it seems reasonable that it might be able to completely laterally inhibit activity of neighboring units. An intense or meaningful stimulus always seizes attention, presumably because the cognitive units coding such stimuli become quite strongly activated when the stimuli are present. In the case of voluntary selective attention, instructions—

for example, the instruction to shadow the message to the left ear and disregard the one to the right ear—could lead to priming, or partial activation, of units in the sensory analyzer dealing with inputs from the left ear. When inputs from the two ears arrive, the units coding those coming from the left ear will therefore be more activated than those coding inputs from the right ear. The result will be that the left-ear units can laterally inhibit the right-ear units. So far, so good—but how can we explain attention in cases where several cognitive units are about equally activated? Theoretically, each unit should laterally inhibit the other, and there would be no attention paid to either. But instead, any mismatch between expectation (a primed cognitive unit) and perception (a cognitive unit activated by an external stimulus) is a case where several cognitive units are activated. As we have seen, mismatches are actually potent elicitors of attention.

THE AROUSAL SYSTEM AND ATTENTION

All cognitive units receive nonspecific input from the arousal system. Hypothetically, this input is crucial in focusing attention. Empirically, attention is always accompanied by increased arousal, whether or not the attention is brought about by a mismatch. Kahneman (1973) notes that voluntary attention is always accompanied by a sense of effort. He conducted a number of studies showing that this sense of effort is the subjective aspect of physiological increases in arousal. For attention to occur, a cognitive unit must receive both informational input from other cognitive units and nonspecific input from the arousal system (Kahneman, 1973; Shallice, 1978).

It might not seem that indiscriminately adding activation to all the cognitive units in an analyzer by means of nonspecific inputs from the arousal system would be of any use. It would be useful, however, if inputs from the arousal system increase the activation of cognitive units in a multiplicative rather than an additive way. Multiplicative increase would increase the difference between the most activated cognitive unit and other less activated cognitive units. In turn, the most activated unit could now exert even greater lateral inhibition on neighboring units, further amplifying the difference in activation. Although he used different terms, Hull (1943) used the "behavioral law" that arousal multiplies rather than adds to the activation of nodes as the cornerstone of his entire theory of behavior. (We shall explore the reasons for the behavioral law in Chapter 6.) The important point is that, somehow or other, input from the arousal system allows one cognitive unit to become dominant over other neighboring units.

If this line of reasoning is correct, then an arousal reaction should be most likely when several cognitive units are nearly equally activated—because in this case, an exacerbation of differences in activation is most necessary. In a mismatch between perception and expectation, one node is activated by perceptual inputs, and another node is activated because of expectation. In the case of voluntary attention, more effort (and, hence, more arousal) is necessary to the extent that it is difficult to discriminate the stimulus to be attended to from other stimuli. The reason that novelty and disruption of expectation elicit arousal and attention is so that deeper processing can occur. Deeper processing allows the mind to see what "went wrong" and to construct a better cortical model. After the new model has been constructed, inputs exactly match existing cognitive units, and attention is no longer necessary.

GATED DIPOLES AND ATTENTIONAL RESETTING

Recall the mysterious stranger from Chapter 3. We left the two of you walking in the forest, busily establishing episodic memory traces. Let us say that it is a balmy summer night. You find yourself in a forest glade staring into each other's eyes. Some scripts for interacting with strangers call for comparing their eyes to stars. You see a bright star low in the sky and begin to formulate a proposition concerning the similarity of the stranger's glance to the light of the Morning Star. The features of the star do not fit with your expectations—it is too large, and it is moving too fast. This is a case of mismatch. We have seen that mismatches cause attention, arousal, and the formation of a new mental model.

Your situation is shown in Figure 5-7(a). The activated node on the upper level represents the Morning Star. It activates a set of feature nodes on the lower level. The actual stimulus is activating a quite different set of feature nodes. Following Sokolov, we also show the stimulus activating the arousal system; however, the arousal system is inhibited by the activated nodes on the two layers. Soon, though, there will be little activation on the lower level. Nodes coding the conflicting features will laterally inhibit each other, and they will no longer inhibit the arousal system. Thus, the arousal system will be disinhibited (Grossberg, 1980; Sokolov, 1963). The arousal system will bombard both layers of nodes with activation, as shown in Figure 5-7(b). The most activated nodes will benefit. But wait—the only activated node is the one coding the Morning Star, and it will become even *more* activated than before. It will then feed even more activation down to the nodes with which it is connected on the bottom layer. The next cycle through the process, these feature nodes will even further inhibit the feature nodes activated by the stimulus. Soon, a resonant feedback loop will be set up, so that even if a policeman shines a flashlight directly into your eyes, you will be seeing the star. Wish would destroy reality—but you know perfectly well that reality cannot be so easily evaded, so something is amiss. You are in a fix similar to the one described in the last chapter, where you were left confused as to whether you were seeing Julia or Claudia. Now we can describe how such mistakes are resolved.

We want the burst of arousal to turn *off* the most activated node rather than to increase its activation. How can this be accomplished by putting

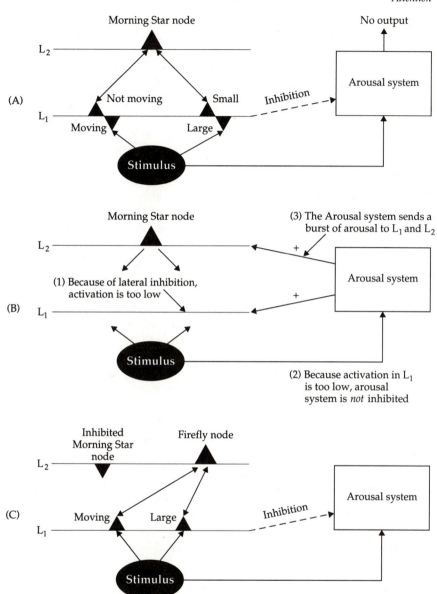

F I G U R E 5 – 7 How mismatches are corrected. In (A), expectation of seeing the Morning Star has caused top-down activation of the features "unmoving" and "small," but the stimulus has activated the mismatching features "moving" and "large." These mismatching features on Level 1 laterally inhibit each other, as shown in (B). Now the cortex cannot inhibit the arousal system, so arousal is sent to the cortex. The result, shown in (C), is that the Morning Star node is inhibited, which allows the feature nodes on Level 1 to activate another node—the one coding firefly—on Level 2.

arousal *into* the system? It is possible if cognitive units are composed of gated dipoles (Grossberg, 1980). Even though the on-cell (which codes the Morning Star) and the off-cell (which codes *absence* of the Morning Star) in a dipole pair will receive equal inputs from the arousal system, Grossberg has shown that the result will be that the dipole will be rebounded by a sudden burst of arousal. The on-cell will be shut off and the off-cell will be briefly turned on, which is exactly what we want. The reason for this surprising result is that the on-cell has been depleting its neurotransmitter substance in the process of "expecting" the star. Since it has been inhibited, the off-channel has stored up an excess of its neurotransmitter, and can thus respond more vigorously to the sudden onset of arousal. It gains the upper hand and inhibits the on-cell.

When a mismatch is detected, the arousal system sends equal amounts of activation to *both* the on-cell and the off-cell. Because it has stored up more neurotransmitter substance, the off-cell wins in this winner-take-all system. The off-cell inhibits the on-cell. Now, output of the on-cell is zero. Output of the off-cell is quite high. This corresponds to insight that the stimulus is *not* the Morning Star. Now, the feature nodes on the lower level can activate another on-cell on the upper level. It *won't* be the one coding the Morning Star, though. This unit is inhibited and out of the running. The competition at the Morning Star dipole will not last for long. The off-cell will rapidly deplete its transmitter substance. Also, the arousal system just sent a brief burst of activation. Soon, both members of the dipole will be back to their normal ration of activation. The members of the dipole will inhibit each other out of business.

The result of all the foregoing is shown in Figure 5-7(c). The Morning Star node is inhibited. The features activated by the stimulus can now activate a new node on the upper level. This node corresponds to the hypothesis that you are seeing a firefly. It will feed activation back to the lower-level feature nodes with which it is connected. If these nodes are the same as those activated by the stimulus, a state of reverberation will be established. You will see and attend to the firefly. If there is another mismatch, the process will begin again. Inspection of Figure 5-7(c) shows that you are probably confronted by a firefly. Top-down and bottom-up activation match rather well.

SUMMARY AND CONCLUSIONS

We began this chapter with the introspectionists' metaphor of the stream of consciousness and the wave of attention. This metaphor is not alien from the model we have developed; we have defined conscious awareness as the set of currently activated cognitive units and attention as the subset of these units that are most strongly activated. In perceptual and conceptual analyzers, consciousness generally "contains" only a few units. Attention is restricted to no more than one or two units. Thus, attention is extremely selective. This selectivity can be either voluntary or involuntary.

Voluntary attention has been studied with shadowing tasks, in which people are asked to repeat one message and ignore another. This task is fairly easy if the messages differ in sensory quality, which led Broadbent to propose a filter model of attention in which attentional selection occurs in sensory analyzers. Findings that unattended messages activate units in semantic memory, however, led Norman and others to propose that attentional selection occurs in the semantic analyzer. Theirs was something of an overreaction. We have settled on Treisman's attenuation model (which says that attentional selection can occur in any analyzer) as the one best able to account for the findings of shadowing studies.

Capacity models of attention contend that a fixed amount of arousal must be drawn upon to perform psychological work. Some activities, such as perception, require little or no arousal; others, such as decision making, require substantial arousal. As long as the pool of available arousal is not exhausted, attention can be divided among several tasks, especially when the tasks are carried out by different analyzers. Each analyzer may be said to have its own private pool of capacity.

Sokolov's theory of involuntary attention is compatible with the model of cognition we have developed. He holds that incoming stimuli are compared to preexisting cortical models. If stimuli match these models, nothing more than normal perception results. If a mismatch occurs, the arousal system is disinhibited and arouses the cortex. Orientation and attention result, and a new cortical model is constructed. Walley and Weiden argue that cognitive units "select" themselves for attention by laterally inhibiting surrounding units. Cognitive units are aided in this process by nonspecific inputs from the arousal system. Where attention is caused by mismatches between expectation and reality, Grossberg argues that inputs from the arousal system constitute a *reset wave*. Currently activated dipoles are rebounded or inhibited; if this were not the case, wish would destroy reality, and we would always perceive what we expected to perceive.

Primary Memory

ASPECTS OF AWARENESS

DISSECTING CONSCIOUSNESS

We could say that consciousness corresponds to the inventory of currently activated cognitive units in sensory, perceptual, and conceptual analyzers. Many of these nodes—corresponding to sensations and perceptions—are active because they are turned on by stimuli. Other nodes are active for other reasons: some may have been turned on by recent stimuli that are no longer present, and others may have been turned on because of their connections with nodes that are active or were recently active. We need a name for the part of consciousness that is *not* sensation or perception. William James (1890) called it "primary memory." Although this may not be the best term, primary memory might be defined as the contents of awareness minus sensations and perceptions. In the case of perception, we want to know how and why a set of nodes become activated. In the case of primary memory, we want to know what happens after nodes are activated. How long do they stay on? What turns them off? How many can be on at the same time? Why do they stay on if the stimulus they code has gone away?

SENSORY MEMORY VERSUS SHORT-TERM MEMORY

Of the two types of primary memory, the first is *sensory memory*. After a stimulus is presented, a sensory memory that is similar to a positive after-effect persists. This memory is very short; most estimates put the duration of sensory memory at under one second. Sensory memory is preattentive and automatic—no effort is required to maintain it. Loss results from decay or from masking by subsequent stimuli. There is a different sensory memory for each sensory analyzer.

The second component of primary memory is *short-term memory*. Short-term memory is the persistence of activation of nodes in perceptual or conceptual analyzers. Each perceptual analyzer has its own short-term memory, but people often transfer information to the speech analyzer to maintain it in short-term memory, regardless of which analyzer first processed the information. Short-term memory lasts about 20 seconds, although information in short-term memory can be maintained for longer periods by rehearsing it.

A good example of short-term memory is remembering a telephone number you have just looked up. It is easy to forget the number, so to counter this, you may *rehearse* it: you repeat it, aloud or covertly, over and over to yourself. The telephone number has been recoded from visual to phonetic form before rehearsal; whereas you looked at the number printed in a telephone book, you are rehearsing the digits in overtly or covertly spoken form. The capacity of short-term memory is quite limited. If a telephone number is unfamiliar, can you remember both the area code and the seven-digit number? Most people cannot. Some items in short-term memory are transferred into long-term memory. When we first use a new telephone number, we have to look it up every time we use it, but after a few times, we can retrieve the number from long-term memory rather than from the telephone book.

SENSORY MEMORY

ICONIC MEMORY

Visual sensory memory is called *iconic memory*. When a brief visual stimulus disappears, one continues to see it for a fraction of a second. An experiment by Sperling (1960) demonstrates iconic memory. Sperling presented an array of letters, such as that shown earlier in Figure 4–12(a), for 50 milliseconds on a tachistoscope. With such a brief exposure, no matter how many letters are shown, only four or five of them can be recalled by the *whole-report method*. The whole-report procedure simply asks subjects to recall as many letters as they can. The subjects reported that they saw all the letters quite clearly; in fact, they forgot the rest of the letters while they were reporting the first four or five. To avoid this problem, Sperling (1960) devised a *partial-report procedure*. By means of a prearranged signal, he indicated which row of the array his subjects were to recall. A high-pitched tone indicated the top row, a medium-pitched tone indicated the middle row, and a low-pitched tone indicated the bottom row. When onset of the tone coincided with offset of the visual display, people could recall any row with about 100 percent accuracy. Immediately after its termination, all nine letters of the display were "visible" to the subject.

Why can people report only four or five letters when the whole-report procedure is used? Sperling reasoned that there is a brief *icon,* or sensory memory. With the whole-report method, this icon has faded by the time four or five letters have been read, whereas the partial-report procedure lets the subject read any row of the icon before it fades. In this case, sounding the tone *after* the display is terminated should still be helpful—as it was, even when the lag was as long as 300 milliseconds. At short lags (up to about 100 milliseconds) subjects experienced the tone and the visual display simultaneously! They thought they were actually looking at a stimulus, rather than at a memory image of a long gone stimulus. Thus, iconic memory must last for around 100 milliseconds.

What is the purpose of iconic memory? It may serve the function of Selfridge's "Image Demon"; that is, it preserves a sensory "image" so that features can be extracted from it. A brief stimulus does not last long enough, so iconic memory prolongs it. Long-duration stimuli do not produce an icon that lasts very long (Haber, 1983)—because there is plenty of time for feature extraction, the icon is not needed. It may occur to you that iconic memory might smear your vision—when you move your eyes, the icon from the last fixation could blur the next scene. But it takes 250 milliseconds to move your eyes from one fixation point to another, and the icon has faded after about 100–200 milliseconds, so it is no longer present to make things messy at the new fixation point.

ECHOIC MEMORY

There is also sensory memory in the auditory system, where it is called *echoic memory* (Neisser, 1967). You are probably aware of this phenomenon, but have never thought about it. Say you are wrapped up in something really interesting, such as reading this book, when your roommate makes an inane comment out of the blue. As a reflex, you say "What?" You know he or she said something, but you didn't hear it—but as often as not, you *do* hear it quite clearly as soon as you have said "What?" What you have heard is an echoic memory.

Duration of Echoic Memory

Several methods have been used to measure the duration of echoic memory; we'll concentrate on just one. Suppose that we set up three loudspeakers, and three different sets of digits are simultaneously presented over the three loudspeakers. Thus, nine different digits are presented. If the whole-report method is used, people can correctly report four or five of them. People usually say they heard all nine digits and knew what they were. The problem was that they forgot the rest of the digits while reporting the first few. A partial-report procedure tests whether subjects are telling the truth or merely making an idle boast. After the digits are read, a light could be illuminated over one of the loudspeakers, with the subject's task to report the three digits that had been read over the loudspeaker. Crowder and Morton (1969) used such a procedure. If the light comes on immediately after the digits stop, memory is nearly perfect. The crucial question is how long one can delay light onset and still have it be helpful in recalling the digits. Crowder and Morton found that even if the light comes on two seconds after the digits stop, subjects are still quite good at recall, suggesting that echoic memory lasts for about two seconds. Even if the light comes on four seconds after the tone has gone off, light onset is still of some help in recalling the digits. Other methods of estimating echoic duration give a variety of results; most methods suggest that the duration is not quite so long, although all methods indicate that echoic memory lasts quite a bit longer than iconic memory.

What is the function of echoic memory? An important function has to do with speech perception. Although you are not conscious of it, how you hear earlier sounds in a word is strongly influenced by sounds that occur later in the word (Juszyck, 1986). Echoic memory allows this adjustment. If it lasts up to several seconds, shouldn't echoic memory smear earlier sounds? Not exactly; as indicated, it adjusts them, rather than smearing them.

The Stimulus-Suffix Effect

The stimulus-suffix effect was first observed by Dallett (1965). The experimenter reads a list of items (words, letters of the alphabet, or digits), and the subject must repeat the list. The average person can repeat a list of about seven unrelated items. Generally, the signal that the list has ended is simply that the experimenter stops reading. To produce the stimulus-suffix effect, an extra item is added to the end of the list. This item does *not* have to be recalled; the subject is told that the extra item merely signals that the list is complete. The presence of this redundant suffix item, however, impairs memory for the list. The suffix automatically takes up space in memory even though it does not need to be remembered. It especially interferes with memory for the last item on the list—a striking effect, for when there is no suffix, memory for the last item is virtually perfect.

The degree to which the suffix interferes with memory has little to do with its semantic similarity to the list items, but it is related to physical similarity (Crowder, 1978). A suffix spoken by a voice different from the one that read the list has less effect. There is also less effect if the list comes from one direction in space and the suffix from another, even if both are spoken by the same voice. The fact that sensory but not semantic similarity is important suggests that the suffix effect results from interference in echoic memory.

Crowder (1978) proposed a lateral inhibition theory of echoic memory. He suggested that the node coding the suffix laterally inhibits the nodes coding the last list items. Echoic memory consists of activity in an array of units that code information about the physical characteristics of auditory stimuli. These are nodes in the acoustic sensory analyzer, arranged according to time of arrival and "channel" (for example, spatial location), as shown in Figure 6–1. Stimuli that arrive through the same channel and are close together in time should inhibit each other.

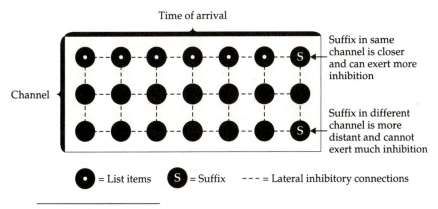

FIGURE   6 – 1   Crowder's (1978) lateral inhibition theory of the suffix effect.

When a list of items is read, many units are activated. All of them laterally inhibit each other. The last item (the suffix) has a special advantage, because no item follows it. It is inhibited by only one other item (the previous one). The unit coding the suffix is strongly activated and can mask the unit coding the last list item. Thus, two suffixes should do *less* damage than only one. The first suffix would itself be inhibited by the second suffix, and therefore could not inhibit the last list item as much. In other words, the unit coding the last list item should be *disinhibited*. This prediction is diagrammed in Figure 6–2. Crowder (1978) tested this hypothesis and found strong support for it: two suffixes hurt *less* than one.

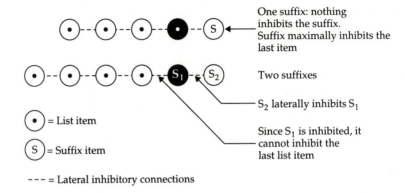

One suffix: nothing inhibits the suffix.
Suffix maximally inhibits the last item

Two suffixes

S_2 laterally inhibits S_1

Since S_1 is inhibited, it cannot inhibit the last list item

• = List item

S = Suffix item

- - - = Lateral inhibitory connections

F I G U R E   6 – 2   Why two suffixes exert less lateral inhibition than one suffix.

SHORT-TERM MEMORY

INFORMATION-PROCESSING   APPROACH

Psychologists who use the information-processing approach tend to describe short-term memory as a "place" in the mind containing about seven slots. The language of this place is phonetic. The slots hold speech sounds or words. To find something in short-term memory, it must be searched in some fashion; the usual implication is that the search is carried out by the Executive Processor. Early information-processing models usually held that there is another quite distinct place in the mind, that of long-term memory, which has a great number of slots in it. The language of long-term memory is semantic or conceptual, and things can be moved from one memory to another by rehearsal. There are a few shortcomings to this model. If short-term memory comes before long-term memory, we would not know the meaning of whatever was in short-term memory, because knowing the meaning requires looking up the information in long-term memory. The notion of the Executive Processor is also bothersome; it sounds too much like a homunculus (little person) that lives in the brain. These are not the concepts that information processing theorists have in mind; however, the terminology sometimes leads people to think this is what they mean. In any event, saying that the Executive Processor searches short-term memory complicates the situation, because we have to explain *how* the Executive Processor carries out this search.

There are many good reasons to think of short-term memory in the way we have described it. Recall the example of looking up a telephone number: the percept is visual, but most people retain it in short-term memory in a verbal form. If one had no more information than that, it would make sense to say that short-term memory is a place and that the code is verbal. Research shows, however, that each perceptual analyzer has its own short-term memory capacity. Remembering visual images and words simultaneously causes no interference (Peterson, Rawlings, & Cohen, 1977). One can also remember visually and auditorily presented letters simultaneously (Kroll, Parks, Parkinson, Bieber, & Johnson, 1970). There are many independent short-term memory stores—one for each perceptual analyzer.

NEURAL-NETWORK APPROACH

For our purposes, long-term memory is the entire neural network. Long-term memories are stored as connection strengths among nodes. Short-term memory, rather than being a separate place, corresponds to activation of some of these nodes. If the nodes stay activated long enough, the connection strengths among them will begin to change. This change is transfer from short-term memory to long-term memory. Transfer is speeded up by rehearsal. We shall consider rehearsal as corresponding to the setting up of a positive or resonant feedback loop among nodes, keeping them activated and changing their connection strengths. There are no real slots in short-term memory; it holds only about seven items because the activation available in any module of the network is limited. Trying to activate an eighth node causes the node to "steal" activation from the others. It will steal enough activation so that at least one of the nodes has so little remaining activation that we are no longer aware of what it codes.

If short-term memory does not have seven slots, the slots can't be searched. In addition, why search for what has not been lost? Short-term memory is the set of currently highly activated nodes in an analyzer. When the nodes are highly activated, one is conscious of them and thus does not need to search through them. Further, there is no entity to perform the search. *You*, the "I" that experiences and thinks and judges, *are* the neural network. To say that you search the network is the same as saying that the network searches itself—which it does. The process is hypothetically automatic and parallel. This view does not really conflict with the information-processing view; it merely involves stating things in a different, more useful, way. Information-processing theorists do not really think short-term memory is searched in a literal sense by a homunculus; however, it is easy to confuse their metaphorical use of the term *search* with a concrete search of a specific place carried out by some mental entity.

THE CAPACITY OF SHORT-TERM MEMORY

The Span of Immediate Apprehension

One of the first questions asked about what is now called short-term memory was about its capacity. How many items can it hold? In the 19th century, Sir William Hamilton (1859) introduced the concept of the *span of immediate apprehension*, the number of things one can apprehend in a single moment.

Hamilton suggested that one can say how many objects one sees in a brief glance as long as there are not more than about six objects to be seen. Jevons (1871), using himself as a subject, devised a method to test Hamilton's assertion. Jevons threw beans into a tray, quickly glanced at an area of the tray he had previously marked off, and made a quick judgment of the number of beans in that area. With three or four beans, he made no errors. Beyond three or four beans, the more beans, the more inaccurate he was. Erdmann and Dodge (1898) used a tachistoscope so that the length of "glances" could be more precisely controlled. When stimuli were presented for 100 milliseconds, they found that only four or five unrelated letters of the alphabet could be reported. These early studies, which used the whole-report method, give us an idea of the capacity of short-term memory rather than of sensory memory. The whole-report part of Sperling's (1960) study updated the earlier studies, and Sperling also found that people can report four or five items when the whole-report method is used.

Stimulus Qualities and Capacity

The foregoing studies used isolated, meaningless stimuli, whereas people perform a bit better with meaningful stimuli. In an influential review, Miller (1956) concluded that the span of immediate apprehension is 7 ± 2 items. The basic unit is what he called the "chunk." Say, for example, that one can remember seven unrelated letters. Chances are that one will also be able to remember seven unrelated three-letter words—but these seven words will be composed of 21 letters. Why does the unit change when the material to be remembered changes? Miller said the reason is that the unit of short-term memory is not the individual item but the meaningful chunk. Short-term memory can hold seven "chunks," which may be letters, words, or sentences. Much research supports this contention that the chunk is the basic component of short-term memory (Zechmeister & Nyberg, 1982). This view is consistent with the idea that short-term memory is the momentary activation of cognitive units. We can translate Miller's hypothesis into the contention that, on any level of a perceptual analyzer, about seven cognitive units can be active at once. If we were talking about the letter level, we would mean seven different letters; at the word level, we would mean seven different words.

Subsequent work suggests that the number 7 is not as "magical" as Miller thought, because the capacity of short-term memory is not constant. The deeper (more semantic) the level of processing, the smaller the capacity. Short-term memory can "hold" more shallow-level units than deeper-level units. Simon (1974) used himself as a subject and found that he could use short-term memory to recall seven one- or two-syllable words, six three-syllable words, four meaningful two-word phrases, and three meaningful longer phrases (e.g., "all's fair in love and war"). These estimates are probably somewhat generous, since Simon is a Nobel prize winner—the average person might not do quite as well.

THE FORM OF CONSCIOUSNESS

Short-Term Memory Capacity and Arousal

Samuel Johnson remarked that "nothing concentrates a man's mind like the prospect of being hanged" (Boswell, 1791). Psychological research is consistent with Dr. Johnson's conjecture. Easterbrook (1959) reviewed a number of studies of incidental learning and concluded that increases in arousal cause decreases in what he called the *range of cue utilization.* In other words, the capacity of short-term memory is decreased with increases in arousal, which is consistent with saying that more arousal causes more amplification of the already most activated cognitive units, resulting in greater inhibition of other units. Input from the arousal system affects the capacity of short-term memory. If arousal is high, a few things are strongly attended to, and every-

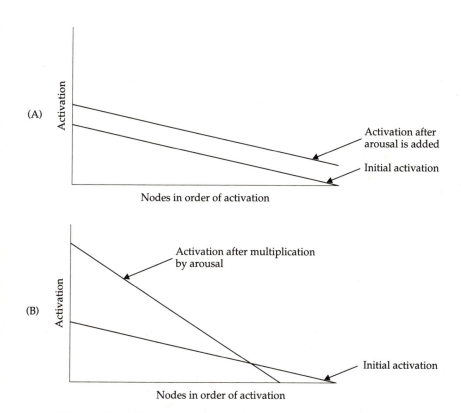

F I G U R E   6 – 3   As shown in (A), adding arousal to a set of nodes does nothing useful, because activation is merely increased by a constant amount in all the nodes. The miracle of multiplication is shown in (B): multiplying preexisting activation by arousal steepens the slope of the line; that is, it increases activation of more activated nodes and decreases activation of less activated ones.

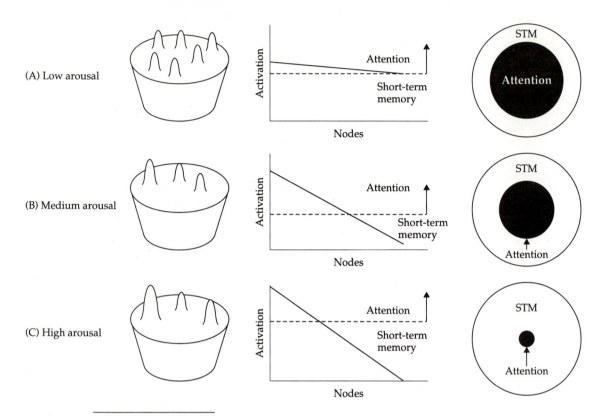

FIGURE 6-4 Effects of arousal on attention and short-term memory.
When arousal is low (A), almost everything in short-term memory is equally
attended to. As arousal increases, the focus of attention narrows (B and C). The
three columns represent three ways of drawing the same thing.

thing else is ignored. As arousal goes down, attention becomes defocused—
many things are attended to, but not very strongly. As arousal decreases,
attention spreads out so that it is finally equivalent to short-term memory.
This description is a cognitive restatement of Hull's (1943) "behavioral law"—
we should perhaps call it Hull's new, improved, updated, and restated law.

Speaking of behavior, that is what Hull was interested in. Hull had no
use for cognitive units, but he watched a lot of rats, and his experiments
showed that increasing arousal increases the probability of whatever behavior is most probable at the moment. Increasing arousal makes behavior
more stereotyped; on the other hand, decreasing arousal makes behavior
more variable—it increases the probability of less probable responses. Hull
said that any stimulus elicits a *habit-family hierarchy*. We would say that it
activates a set of cognitive units. The degree of activation of these units is
related to arousal.

Hull's behavioral law implies that arousal input multiplies the activation of currently activated units. Activation of a cognitive unit is a product

of stimulus input *multiplied* by input from the arousal system. Look at Figure 6–3(a). Adding arousal would not make the dominant response any more dominant—it would merely raise the entire curve, which could serve no useful purpose. Now look at Figure 6–3(b). This result is what we want: the more arousal, the *more* activated the more activated units are relative to less activated ones.

What does this have to do with short-term memory? Again in Figure 6–3(b), we see that as arousal increases, fewer and fewer units are activated; in other words, as arousal increases, the capacity of short-term memory decreases. But also note that the units that *are* in short-term memory are more activated the higher the arousal is. Why is the area beneath each line the same? There is only so much activation on any layer of a neural network. The activation is *normalized* (kept constant) by lateral inhibition.

Figure 6–4 diagrams in three different ways Hull's behavioral law as it regards short-term memory. In a state of low arousal, many nodes are activated to about the same degree. There is no real difference between attention and short-term memory, as would be the case if you were lying on the beach staring at the ocean waves and thinking about nothing in particular. If arousal is increased, some nodes become considerably more activated than others. With this increase, it makes some sense to draw a line between attention and short-term memory. If an attractive member of the opposite sex walked by, he or she would get more attention than the waves. You may have noticed that some passersby produce more arousal than do others. If we really increase arousal, only one or two nodes appropriate all the activation. Imagine that the person who is walking by has forgotten to put on a bathing suit. I daresay that such a sight will produce yet even more arousal—the node for the nude will consume your attention more or less completely.

The Yerkes-Dodson Law

We have not yet mentioned what short-term memory is good for, besides remembering telephone numbers. But evolution would not have created a telephone-number-remembering module. Short-term memory is used for *thinking*. Thinking involves seeing relationships among things. If only one cognitive unit could be activated at one time, you would not be able to think. You couldn't very well figure out how *A* and *B* are related if you forgot *A* when you thought of *B* and vice versa. There is a relationship among short-term memory, arousal, and task complexity, called the Yerkes-Dodson law. Yerkes and Dodson (1908) originally found that the relationship applies to *learning*. Hebb (1955) and others pointed out that it also applies to *performance* of things already learned.

The Yerkes-Dodson law has two parts. The first part states, reasonably, that a medium level of arousal is best for learning or performing any task. You don't do well at anything in a state of very low arousal, such as when you are asleep. On the other hand, you are not at your best when you are in a very high-arousal state of fear and trembling. The second part of the law is

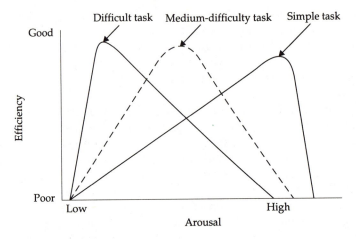

F I G U R E   6 – 5   The Yerkes-Dodson law. Efficiency of
learning and performance is an inverted-U function of arousal, and the
level of arousal needed for optimal efficiency varies as a function of
task complexity.

more interesting, as diagramed in Figure 6–5. In words, the simpler the task,
the higher the optimal level of arousal for learning or performing the task.
A very simple task is adding 1 + 1. We could judge efficiency at this task by
measuring reaction time required to give the correct answer. The higher your
arousal, the faster your reaction time would be. If your mind is still on the
beach, picture this situation: not one but two people have forgotten their
bathing suits. Being confused, they ask you how many of them there are. In
your high state of arousal, you could very quickly compute that there are
two of them. Your response would be quicker than if your arousal were lower.
Now, disregard the nudes. Let us say that you have brought your roommate
with you. He or she inquires as to how many seagulls are perched upon a
nearby rock. Even if there are but two, your answer will be slower in coming than your answer to the question posed by the nudes, even if you really
attempt to answer the question as quickly as possible.

Let us say that the nude strangers had posed a more complex question—for example, what is 666 divided by 17? Wouldn't you probably be
able to solve this problem more quickly if it had been posed by your roommate? When the nude strangers pose the problem, your arousal is too high,
and your attention is too focused. The Yerkes-Dodson law holds in other
situations as well: it applies to everything from clothed people making
decisions (Streufert, 1969) to rats making brightness discriminations under
water (Broadhurst, 1959).

Short-Term Memory and Normalization

The contents of short-term memory are normalized—meaning only that total
activation of the nodes on a layer is kept at a more or less constant level.

There are two reasons to say this: (1) if normalization didn't occur, activation could increase with no bounds—the network would blow up or melt down; and (2) there is much evidence that activation *is* normalized. Lateral inhibition automatically performs the normalizing as explained in Chapter 4.

Let's temporarily hold arousal constant: assume that each stimulus has the same intensity and that arousal is at a normal level. Consider remembering a series of numbers recited by a fully clothed psychologist. Each digit has about the same intensity. A three is not, after all, any more or less exciting than a five or a two. Here is our problem: we have one unit of activation to divide among all the nodes on a level. Let us wipe the slate clean and let the first stimulus arrive. Because all the other nodes are inactive, the node coding the stimulus can have all the available activation. Now, let a second stimulus arrive. The activation must be shared with the unit coding it. What makes the sharing occur? Grossberg (1978b) argues that we need what he terms a *short-term memory reset parameter*.

Activation of the two nodes is not really "reset." The two nodes exert lateral inhibition on each other, and the node coding the first item may have some advantage if it has been rehearsed. In our terms, rehearsal corresponds to setting up a resonant feedback loop between nodes connected by excita-

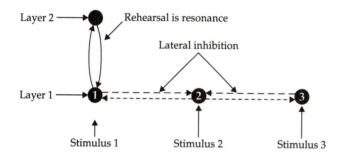

F I G U R E   6 – 6   Resonance and lateral inhibition compose short-term memory. Rehearsal corresponds to resonant positive-feedback loops. Lateral inhibition can cause items toward the middle of a list in short-term memory to be more poorly remembered than early or late items.

tory connections, as shown in Figure 6–6. The more the first node has been rehearsed, the more activated it will be; thus, the more it will be able to inhibit the second node. Now, consider what happens when a third stimulus arrives. Because the node coding the second stimulus is being inhibited by the node coding the first stimulus, it cannot effectively inhibit the node coding the third stimulus. Because the node coding the third stimulus has just been activated, it has a further advantage over the node coding the second stimulus.

SERIAL-POSITION EFFECTS

Shape of the Serial-Position Curve

The node coding the middle digit does inhibit the nodes coding the first and second digits; however, *both* of these nodes inhibit the node coding the middle digit. Thus, the units coding the first and last digits should usually be most activated, and the unit coding the middle digit should usually be least activated. The same is true if there are more digits, but other factors also come into play. The nodes coding the last few digits have a lot of the activation because they have just been activated—the *recency effect.* The nodes coding the first few digits have a great deal of activation because they have been rehearsed more and can easily be retrieved from long-term memory—the *primacy effect.* Nodes coding the middle digits are inhibited from both sides and thus come in last: the activation curve is *bowed.* If we assume that the probability of recalling something is a direct function of the degree of activation of the node coding it, then the memory curve should be bowed, too.

Suppose we present someone with a list of unrelated words. The task is to repeat back as many of the words as possible in any order after the whole list has been presented. This task yields quite stable serial-position effects. The probability that a word will be recalled is a function of its sequential order in the list. The *primacy effect* means that the first several items

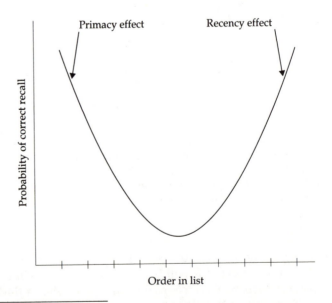

F I G U R E   6 – 7   A typical serial-position curve. Items in the middle of a list are poorly recalled, which may be in part because of lateral inhibition; however, there are other reasons as well. Items toward the beginning of the list have been rehearsed more often, and the nodes coding later items are more activated because they have been more recently activated.

on the list are fairly well recalled. Probability of recall decreases from the first to the second word, from the second to the third, and so on. Words in the middle of the list are poorly recalled. The *recency effect* means that the last several words on the list are also well recalled. Usually, the recency effect applies for the last four or five words on the list. (Recall that the span of immediate apprehension is four or five items.) A typical serial position curve is shown in Figure 6–7.

The Primacy Effect

What accounts for the primacy effect? Earlier items are rehearsed more often, and rehearsal leads to long-term memory; that is, given enough rehearsal, connection strengths will become strengthened. Some of the effect results from retrieval from long-term memory—that is why the span of immediate apprehension is only four or five, but short-term memory capacity seems to be about seven. The first word on a list can be rehearsed the most; the second word can be rehearsed next most; and so on. To test the idea that the primacy effect results mainly from rehearsal, Murdock (1962) devised an experiment in which he varied the presentation rate of the list to be remembered. A faster presentation rate should leave less time for rehearsal; thus, it should lead to worse memory for the first items. Faster rates of presentation did indeed cause worse recall of earlier items in the list.

The Recency Effect

If the recency effect is a direct result of the amount of activation of nodes, it should disappear if recall is delayed. If short-term memory does not last very long, then we should get the recency effect only if recall begins immediately after the list is presented. Glanzer and Cunitz (1966) tested this idea. They presented lists of words to be recalled, and subjects were asked to recall the words immediately, or after a delay of ten seconds or 30 seconds. During the delay, subjects had to perform mental arithmetic to prevent them from rehearsing the words on the list. The experiment showed a clear recency effect with immediate recall. There was a lesser effect with a ten-second delay, and the recency effect was completely wiped out by a 30-second delay.

Time-Order Errors

We can get a clearer idea of serial-position effects in short-term memory if we simplify matters and investigate memory for only two items. *Time-order errors* are found if people are asked to make judgments concerning, for example, the intensity of tones, the brightness of light flashes, or the size of objects. As Fechner (1860) first discovered, memory for such pairs is systematically distorted. As an example, we can present two tones to someone, calling the first tone *A* and the second tone *B*. We ask the subject if *B* was more intense than *A*. If the tones are considerably different, of course the subject will answer accurately. Our interest is in cases where the tones are identical in intensity. The subject's answer will depend upon the interval between the two tones. If the interval is more than 750 milliseconds, the second tone seems louder; if the interval is less than 750 milliseconds, the first tone seems louder (Hellström, 1985).

Why should this result occur? Subjects are not comparing perceptions; they are comparing memories. Time-order errors tell us about the time course of competition between two short-term memory images. Köhler (1923) explained the effect as follows. It takes some time for a cognitive unit (Köhler used the term *memory trace*) to achieve full activation. Once it is fully activated, its activation begins to decay. Look at Figure 6–8. If less than 750 milliseconds separates the tones, the node coding *A* is fully activated, so it can inhibit the node coding *B* (Figure 6–8[a]). We thus obtain a type of forward masking. At around 750 milliseconds, activation of both nodes is about equal, so the competition results in a tie (Figure 6–8[b]). If more than 750 milliseconds separates the tones, *B* competes against the decaying activation of *A*, so we have a form of backward masking (Figure 6–8[c]). Schab and Crowder (1988) suggest a somewhat similar explanation.

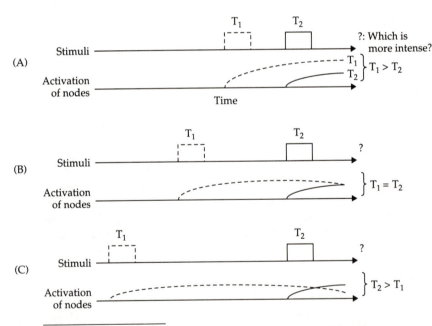

F I G U R E   6 – 8 Time-order errors. If the interstimulus interval (ISI) is less than 750 milliseconds, the node coding the first stimulus inhibits that coding the second stimulus (A). At 750 milliseconds, there is a draw (B); if the ISI is more than 750 milliseconds, the node coding the second stimulus inhibits the node coding the first one (C).

ACTIVATION EFFECTS

The von Restorff Effect

Serial-position effects and time-order errors can be seen as activation effects. If the nodes coding all items to be remembered are of equal strength, activation of a node will be a function of how long ago it was activated and how much it has been rehearsed. There are other ways to vary activation of nodes. Suppose I give you this list of names to remember: George Washington, Theodore Roosevelt, William McKinley, Greta Garbo, Abraham Lincoln, Millard Fillmore, Grover Cleveland. Which name are you most likely to remember? Probably that of Greta Garbo; this is the von Restorff (1932) effect—although it does not merely mean that Greta Garbo is hard to forget. The effect refers to the finding that an item on a list that stands out or is different from the others is better recalled. All the other names are those of U.S. presidents. If nodes are arranged according to similarity, the nodes coding these names should be close to each other and should thus exert

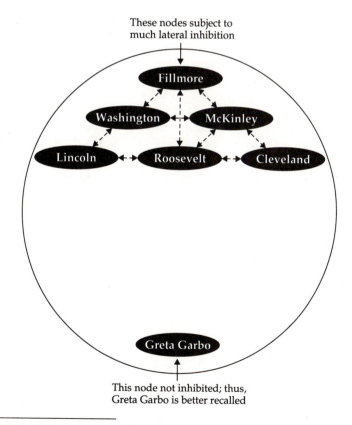

F I G U R E   6 – 9   The von Restorff effect: an item that is dissimilar to other list items is better recalled.

mutual lateral inhibition upon one another. The node coding Greta Garbo is way over in the actress section, so it is not subject to much of any lateral inhibition, as diagrammed in Figure 6–9. The Greta Garbo node should be fairly activated, so it should be well recalled.

Recall of other names on the list should also differ as to how well they are remembered. It is more likely that Lincoln will be recalled than that Grover Cleveland will be recalled, because the node coding Lincoln is probably stronger than the node coding Grover Cleveland—it is capable of greater activation and more resistant to lateral inhibition. You know more about Lincoln and have encountered the name more frequently. Nodes coding more familiar stimuli are stronger and, thus, easier to recall. Because of both this familiarity and the von Restorff effect, you would certainly recall if your own name had been included in the list.

Inhibition and Disinhibition Effects

A series of experiments by Deutsch sheds light on how short-term memory in general works. Deutsch (1970) selected people who had perfect performance in comparing two musical notes separated by a five-second blank retention interval. The first note and the test note were either the same or differed by one semitone. The task was to say whether the test note was exactly the same as the first note. The subjects were then given another memory task in which the retention interval was filled with six musical notes that they were told to ignore. These notes were close in pitch to the to-be-remembered note. The error rate was now 32.3%, which is not much better than the 50% error rate we would expect purely by chance. Activation of the nodes coding the interpolated notes laterally inhibited the node coding the to-be-remembered note.

In later experiments, Deutsch showed that amount of interference is a lawful function of the similarity between the to-be-remembered note and the interpolated notes. Deutsch (1972) used a five-second retention interval with six interpolated notes. Of these interpolated tones, all but the second were far removed from the to-be-remembered tone. The second tone was systematically varied from one the same as the first tone to a whole tone different. Results of the experiment are plotted in Figure 6–10. The "null" line indicates the number of errors in a baseline condition when this crucial note was also distant from the to-be-remembered note. The results show a facilitation effect (performance was better than in the baseline condition) when the crucial note was identical to the first one. There was more and more interference with greater difference between the test note and the interpolated note until interference reached a maximum when the interpolated note was two-thirds of a tone different from the to-be-remembered note. From that point, interference declined almost to the baseline level when the interpolated note was a whole tone different.

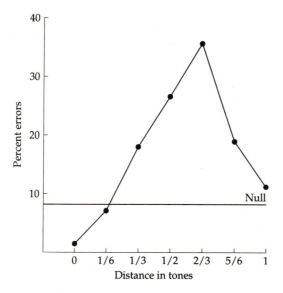

F I G U R E 6 – 10 Errors in pitch recognition as a function of the distance between the to-be-remembered note and a critical interpolated note. The "null" line indicates performance of a control group. (From D. Deutsch [1972]. Mapping of Interactions in the Pitch Memory Store. *Science, 768,* p. 702. Copyright © 1972 American Association for the Advancement of Science. Reprinted by permission.)

The analyzer for pitch contains an array of nodes subject to recurrent lateral inhibition (Deutsch, 1969). The amount of separation between nodes in this array is proportional to the difference in the frequency coded by the nodes: neighboring nodes must code frequencies about two-thirds of a tone different from each other. This model accounts for all the findings described so far. The reason for the interference effects found by Deutsch is as follows: the to-be-remembered note activates the node in the array that codes it, then each of the interpolated notes activates the nodes coding them. If these interpolated notes are similar to the to-be-remembered note, the nodes coding them will laterally inhibit the node coding the to-be-remembered note. The amount of inhibition will be a function of how close the nodes are. If one of the interpolated notes is two-thirds of a tone different, there will be maximal inhibition, because the two nodes are next to each other. If the interpolated note differs by more than two-thirds of a tone, there will be less inhibition, because the node coding the note will be further away. When the test note occurs, the subject responds "same" if activation of the node coding the to-be-remembered note is above some threshold level and "different" if activation is below this threshold. If the unit coding the first note has been inhibited, activation tends to fall below that threshold, and the subject will make a mistake.

The lateral inhibition model allows us to make another prediction. The crucial interpolated note laterally inhibits the to-be-remembered note and causes forgetting. So, if we inhibited the inhibiting note, we should be able to eliminate its damaging effect—as Deutsch and Feroe (1975) reasoned. Consider their design: the to-be-remembered note is presented, activating the relevant unit in the pitch analyzer. Then the interpolated sequence begins. All the interpolated notes except the second and the fourth are remote from the to-be-remembered note. The second note is always two-thirds of a tone distant from the to-be-remembered tone. The fourth note in the interpolated sequence varied from being identical to the second note to a whole tone removed from it. Consider what should happen when the fourth note is two-thirds of a tone distant from the second note (one-and-one-third tones distant from the note to be remembered). The fourth note activates a node that inhibits the node coding the second note. This second note node cannot now inhibit the node that codes the to-be-remembered note. Presentation of the fourth note should thus bring us back to where we started: memory for

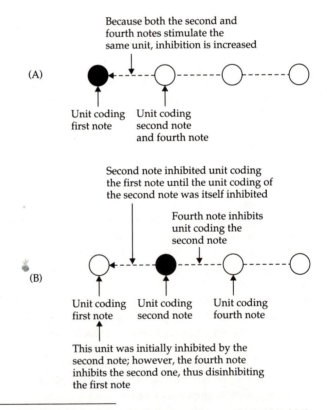

F I G U R E   6 – 11   In their experiment, Deutsch and Feroe (1975) were interested in two predictions: (A) What happens when the second and fourth interpolated notes are the same? (B) What happens when the fourth interpolated note inhibits the second?

the to-be-remembered note should be as good as under baseline condition, where the interpolated notes are all far removed from the test notes. On the other hand, consider what would happen if the fourth note were the same as the second note. This situation should intensify the interference, because the inhibiting unit has been activated twice. The sequence of events is illustrated in Figure 6–11.

Verifying these predictions would give strong evidence for lateral inhibition. Deutsch and Feroe's results conformed with all the predictions; for example, performance was even better than under baseline conditions when the fourth note was two-thirds of a tone removed from the second note, as predicted. These results could not be easily explained without postulating a lateral inhibitory mechanism. Note that we have also demonstrated another lateral inhibition effect in this section by repeatedly talking about nodes that code notes inhibiting nearby note nodes.

REHEARSAL

Unrehearsed material in short-term memory disappears in a matter of seconds. Rehearsal has two functions: (1) to maintain information in short-term memory, and (2) to transfer this information to long-term memory. How does it do these things? In our model, rehearsal consists of setting up a resonant positive feedback loop, which keeps the node coding the to-be-remembered item activated. Because long-term memory *is* the connection strengths between nodes, and because simultaneous activation of nodes increases connection strengths, the reverberation is bound to increase connection strengths.

Craik and Lockhart (1972) identify two different types of rehearsal. *Maintenance rehearsal* consists of mindlessly repeating items without thinking about them. Such rehearsal keeps material in short-term memory but does little to transfer it to long-term memory. *Elaborative rehearsal* consists of doing something with the new material, which involves processing it to a deeper level—for example, rehearsing items that belong to the same category, as people tend to do if the list to be remembered allows it (Rundus, 1971). We could produce maintenance rehearsal by giving some Spanish words to remember to people who do not speak Spanish. Since our subjects would have no units coding these words, about all they would be able to do is set up resonant loops between nodes on the phoneme and syllable levels of the spoken word analyzer (compare Wickens, 1984a). This process shouldn't be terribly effective. On the other hand, if the words were English, the resonant loops could be much more extensive and, presumably, effective. This situation corresponds to elaborative rehearsal.

The vertical excitation model of the mind suggests that stimuli will automatically be processed to the deepest possible level. Activation of units on any one level automatically activates units on the next deeper level; activation of units on the highest level of a perceptual analyzer activates semantic units, and so on. Maintenance rehearsal may be a rather artificial process. Left to their own devices, people would seldom do it, because of automatic vertical resonance, which corresponds to elaborative rehearsal. Be that as it may, we could certainly induce maintenance rehearsal by preventing deeper processing. The result, as you would expect, is that memory is worse than with elaborative rehearsal (Parkin, 1984).

LOSS FROM SHORT-TERM MEMORY

Prevention of Rehearsal

What causes loss of information from short-term memory? An experiment by Peterson and Peterson (1959) suggested that a passive process of decay might account for forgetting in short-term memory. The idea was that if rehearsal is prevented, information held in short-term memory will fade away in a few seconds. The design of their experiment was simple. On each trial, a subject was given three consonants to remember. The task was to remember the consonants for from three to 18 seconds. The retention interval was filled by having subjects do mental arithmetic—counting backward by threes from a specified number. The point of the mental arithmetic was to prevent rehearsal.

Peterson and Peterson's results are shown in Figure 6–12. As you can see, retention was about 50% after three seconds, but dropped to only about

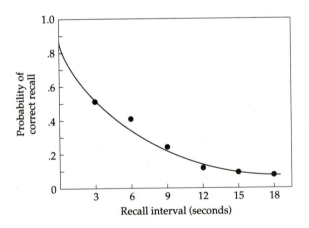

F I G U R E   6 – 12   Peterson and Peterson (1959) found that the probability of correct recall of consonant trigrams declines rapidly with lengthening retention intervals during which rehearsal is prevented. (From L. R. Peterson and M. J. Peterson [1959]. Short-term Retention of Individual Verbal Items. *Journal of Experimental Psychology, 58*, p. 195. Copyright © American Psychological Association.

10% after only 15 seconds! Amazingly, unrehearsed information in short-term memory fades away after about 15 seconds. It hardly seems quite right that we cannot remember the simplest things for even 15 seconds! But remember that rehearsal was prevented. Rehearsal is not prevented in everyday life, so we don't notice the transience of short-term memory. Nonetheless, there is no question that the effect is real; Daniels (1895) and Brown (1958) achieved essentially the same results, as have many experimenters since.

Interference

What accounts for these findings? One view is that the strength of short-term memory traces decays with time, a view favored by Peterson and Peterson (1959). Some loss from short-term memory must be the result of decay. Short-term memory is based upon activation of cognitive units, and if a cognitive unit is kept activated long enough, it fatigues. Fatigue and decay are the same thing. The alternative view is that forgetting is caused by interference. The reason for this alternative view is that there is not much direct evidence that passive decay causes forgetting in long-term memory, but there is substantial evidence that interference causes forgetting (see Chapter 7). There are two types of interference: *proactive inhibition* occurs when something already learned interferes with remembering something new, and *retroactive inhibition* refers to the finding that learning something new interferes with remembering something already learned.

In both retroactive and proactive inhibition, the amount of interference is a function of similarity. The more similar two items are, the more they interfere with each other. It is reasonable to ascribe the interference to lateral inhibition among the cognitive units coding similar items. Short-term memory consists of momentary activation of units in perceptual or conceptual analyzers. These units laterally inhibit each other in proportion to the similarity of the things they code. We should certainly expect to find interference effects in short-term memory, but whether they account for all forgetting from short-term memory is an empirical question.

Retroactive Inhibition

In the experiment described, the only possibility for retroactive inhibition would be that the mental arithmetic interfered with memory for the verbal items to be recalled. Peterson and Peterson chose the mental arithmetic task because they thought it would involve something (digits) distinct enough from the consonants that there should be no interference. But spoken numbers involves production of consonants. In place of the mental arithmetic task, Reitman (1971) substituted a nonverbal signal-detection task that was difficult enough so as to leave subjects with no time for rehearsal. In one condition, the task was to detect a pure tone of a given pitch. This task could be handled by the auditory sensory analyzer. There was no forgetting. In a second condition, the subjects' task was to detect the spoken syllable *toh* in a series of syllables of which most were *doh*. Otherwise, this task was similar to the signal-detection task in the first condition of the experiment. This task would have to be handled by the speech analyzer, but that analyzer was where the to-be-remembered consonants were being held. This task *did* cause decreases in recall. Although these results make it look as if forgetting of verbal material occurs only when the interpolated task is a verbal one, in a later experiment, Reitman (1974) found some evidence for passive decay. If retroactive inhibition is part of the cause of loss from short-term memory, then the reason that performance in the Peterson and Peterson paradigm is worse at 18 seconds than at three seconds would be that more interfering material has been interpolated in the longer retention interval.

Proactive Inhibition

Let us consider Peterson and Peterson's (1959) experimental procedure in more detail. Their subjects received 48 trials, eight at each of six different retention intervals. On each trial, subjects were given three consonants to remember. The results in Figure 6–12 are averages based upon all the trials. One possibility for the results is that proactive inhibition accounts for the forgetting. On all trials except the first one, the consonants presented on prior trials could interfere with retention of the consonants presented on that trial; if so, then the more prior trials, the worse performance should be. This possibility is in fact the case. Keppel and Underwood (1962) repeated the Peterson and Peterson experiment, but looked at trial-by-trial performance. Their results are clear: on the first trial, retention is nearly perfect at all retention intervals. Subjects can remember the consonants as well after 18 seconds as after three seconds, with no decline in performance. On the second trial, memory is worse; on the third trial, even worse, and so on. In other words, the so-called decay builds up gradually over trials. The results are consistent with the notion that forgetting results from proactive inhibition.

Release from Proactive Inhibition

Wickens (1973) tried a variant of the Peterson and Peterson task. On each of the first three trials of his experiment, people were given the names of three fruits to remember. As shown in Figure 6–13, performance got worse on each successive trial. On the fourth trial, some unfortunate subjects (the group labeled "control" in Figure 6–13) were given the names of three more fruits to remember, and their performance deteriorated even further. Luckier subjects were given three words from other categories; their performance improved. Shifting from one category to another leads to a *release from proactive inhibition*. Figure 6–13 shows the performance of subjects who were shifted to various other categories. The more distant the category, the greater

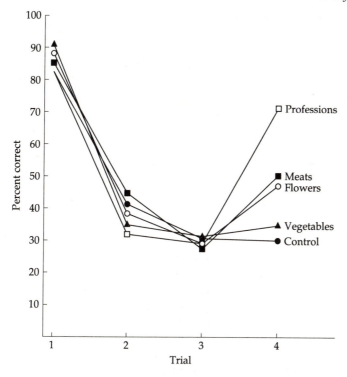

F I G U R E   6 – 13   Release from proactive inhibition. On the first three trials, subjects are given names of fruits to remember. Experimental groups receive names from another category on the fourth trial. The further removed this second category is from the category of fruits, the greater the release from proactive inhibition. (From D. D. Wickens [1973]. Some Characteristics of Word Encoding. *Memory and Cognition, 7,* p. 490. Copyright © 1973 The Psychonomic Society. Reprinted by permission.)

the release from proactive inhibition. Shifting to the category of vegetables leads to a small improvement in retention; shifting to the category of flowers leads to even more; and so on. If we assume that the cognitive units coding instances of a category are spatially near each other in the semantic analyzer, then shifting to a new category would involve a shift to a region where less lateral inhibition had built up. Recall should thus improve—the further away we move from the region of inhibition, the better performance should be.

RETRIEVAL

Sternberg's Experiment

Short-term memory consists of momentary activation of some of the cognitive units composing long-term memory. Once items are in short-term memory, how do we know what is there? This is not a particularly good question, but it certainly has a good answer, as provided by a classic experiment conducted by Sternberg (1966). On each trial, a subject was shown a string of from one to six digits, called the *memory set*. Then the subject was shown a single digit—the test item—and had to respond by pressing one of two keys to indicate whether the test item was part of the memory set. The trials took place so fast that the memory set was certainly being held in short-term memory; the question was how long it would take subjects to make their responses. Sternberg (1966) varied the size of the memory set, because the size could have different effects on the time necessary to search short-term memory—depending on exactly how the contents of short-term memory are searched.

Types of Memory Search

There are several ways a list of items can be searched. In a parallel or content-addressable search, all items are searched simultaneously—as seems to be what happens in perception and recognition. At any one level of perceptual analysis, all units are "searched" simultaneously; the stimulus automatically activates the unit that codes it. It is reasonable to expect that search of short-term memory might be parallel. If it were, then the size of the memory set should have no effect on reaction time. No matter how many items were in short-term memory, it would take the same amount of time to search them—if the time to "examine" each memory location is constant no matter how many items are in a list. If one uses a computer, the time is constant, but keep in mind that the brain is not a computer. Another possibility is that search through short-term memory is serial. If this were the case, then the more items in short-term memory, the longer the search should take. Sternberg found that reaction time *was* dependent upon the number of items held in short-term memory: the more items in short-term memory, the longer it took to make a response. Thus, short-term memory seemed to be searched in a serial rather than a parallel manner.

Evidence for Direct Access of Short-Term Memory

The idea of a serial search makes sense if short-term memory is a place with locations to be searched through. Does it also make sense if short-term memory is the momentary activation of units in long-term memory? Consider what happens in the Sternberg experiment. The memory set—say, digits 5, 9, and 3—is presented, and perception of it consists of activating the cognitive units coding 5, 9, and 3. Then the test digit—say, 9—is presented, activating the very same unit just activated by the 9 in the memory set. In what sense is a serial search supposed to take place? To say that the subject compares the test digit with the memory set is to say that the unit coding 9 is somehow compared to other units, including itself.

What must happen is this: presentation of the memory set activates some cognitive units; the more items in the memory set, the less activated any one node will be, because there is a limited amount of activation available—only enough to allow a few cognitive units to be simultaneously active. A positive test digit (a digit in the memory set) further activates one of these units. The subject responds "yes" if one unit is above some level of activation as compared to all the others: the unit activated twice will be more activated than the other units. The more items in the memory set, the more difficult this discrimination will be; thus, the longer discrimination will take. One reason is that the most activated unit (the one coding the positive test digit) must laterally inhibit other units until it is much more active than any other unit. At this point, the unit captures attention, and the subject responds "yes." In other words, short-term memory is searched in a parallel rather than a serial fashion. The more items in short-term memory, however, the longer the parallel search takes. There is not a serial search, but a parallel discrimination of amount of activation in a set of cognitive units that is slower the more units that are simultaneously activated. This direct-access theory was first suggested by Wickelgren and Norman (1966).

A consequence of the direct-access or parallel-search theory is that there should be serial position effects: items toward the end of the memory set are more recent, so activation of the units coding them should usually be stronger. If the test item corresponds to one of the later units, reaction time for a positive decision should be faster. Sternberg did not find this result, however; reaction time related only to list length, not to serial position of the test digit in the memory set. Sternberg presented the digits in the memory set at a rate of one per second. Then, a two-second delay intervened before presentation of the test digit. This presentation rate allows rehearsal of the memory-set digits, and the two-second delay allows time for the recency effect to disappear. If we presented the memory set at a faster rate and then immediately presented the test digit, we should find a clear recency effect. Decisions should be faster for items occurring later in the memory set. Wickelgren (1977) cites a number of studies finding exactly this effect, which the serial-search model cannot explain.

SUMMARY AND CONCLUSIONS

Perception consists of the activation of cognitive units in sensory and perceptual analyzers. Once activated, these units remain active for a period of time. This persistence is called *primary memory*. We may divide primary memory into *sensory memory* (persistence of activity in sensory analyzers) and *short-term memory* (persistence of activity in perceptual and conceptual analyzers). The function of this continued activity is to allow analysis at deeper levels of processing. Sensory memory allows feature detection by perceptual analyzers. Short-term memory allows the semantic and episodic analyzers to carry out the tasks of understanding and formation of long-term memory traces.

There is a separate sensory memory for each sensory analyzer and a separate short-term memory for each perceptual analyzer. People often maintain short-term memories in the speech analyzer, however, regardless of the origin of the stimuli giving rise to these memories. The capacity of sensory memory is rather large, but the capacity of short-term memory is restricted to a few items or "chunks." The duration of sensory memories is much shorter (less than a second) than that of short-term memories (around 20 seconds).

Loss from sensory memory may involve passive decay. There is evidence from studies of the stimulus-suffix effect that loss can also be caused by interference. Loss from short-term memory appears to result mainly from interference. Crowder and Deutsch propose lateral-inhibition theories to account for loss of information from sensory memory and short-term memory. These theories are consistent with the latticework model of the analyzers discussed in earlier chapters.

Experiments by Sternberg produced evidence implying that the contents of short-term memory are searched in a serial fashion. The more items held in short-term memory, the longer it takes to say whether a test item is identical to one of the stored items. The idea of a serial search through short-term memory loses its appeal if short-term memory is viewed as momentary activation of units in long-term memory. Sternberg's results can be explained in terms of the length of time necessary for one cognitive unit to seize attention by laterally inhibiting competing units.

Learning and Forgetting

LEARNING

Learning consists of modifying the connection strengths among cognitive units. Modification seems to happen by a process more or less identical to Pavlovian conditioning. You may have the notion that conditioning is a method for teaching stupid pet tricks to your dog, and that it doesn't have much to do with how people learn. After all, people learn without obvious rewards or reinforcements, whereas animals seem to need rewards to learn. It has long been known, however, that animals can learn without being reinforced (Tolman & Honzik, 1930). Attention rather than reinforcement seems to be the crucial ingredient for learning; reinforcement is simply a payoff to get the animal to demonstrate what it has learned (Spence, 1956). It is exactly the same with people. A plumber, for example, knows perfectly well how to unplug a drain, but will not demonstrate this knowledge unless given a reward.

You may also think that conditioning is a long, drawn out process. If it were, it would not be relevant to human learning, because people can learn without many repetitions. Well, conditioning does occur quickly—usually one trial for humans and only five or six trials for an animal (Rescorla, 1988). The mechanism is theoretically the same for people and animals. Speaking of mechanisms, behaviorist and cognitive explanations of learning used to be quite different, but that is no longer the case (Rescorla, 1988). Aside from minor details, modern behaviorist explanations (e.g., Rescorla & Wagner, 1972) and connectionist or neural-network explanations of learning (e.g., McClelland & Rumelhart, 1986) are identical.

To Be Conditioned Is to Develop a Theory

It is conventional to begin describing conditioning by discussing drooling dogs, because Pavlov (1927) discovered conditioning rather by accident while watching such dogs. He was originally interested in how saliva and gastric juices cause digestion. To induce salivation in a dog, Pavlov had a laboratory assistant spray meat powder into the dog's mouth. He noticed that a dog very soon began to jump the gun—that is, it started to salivate as soon as the laboratory assistant entered the room. This reaction is interesting on several counts: the dog had somehow learned to associate the laboratory assistant with meat powder.

What Pavlov learned is even more surprising. People have long noticed that one's mouth waters when one is anticipating a meal. Just the sight of a plate on the table can induce salivation. But nobody had attended to this fact the way Pavlov did. Pavlov disliked the communists who ruled Russia for an odd reason. He didn't really care if a czar or a commissar ruled Russia; what annoyed him was the way the communists had taken over. They had a revolution in 1917, some of it right outside his laboratory in Saint Petersburg. The shooting bothered his dogs, and his laboratory assistants neglected their duties and spent their time gawking out the windows watching the revolution. Pavlov simply could not understand this, because what he was doing in the laboratory was far more important than the commotion in the streets. He was discovering eternal laws, but the revolution would soon be forgotten—and he was right, in a way. You probably know that Lenin took over, but you have doubtless forgotten who was in charge before. In any event, Pavlov thought dog saliva was extremely interesting. Therefore, he attended to it very closely. It was thus that a drop of dog saliva revolutionized our view of mind.

One could argue that Pavlov did not discover anything, but that he himself was conditioned. Modern learning theorists emphasize that learning occurs when an organism discovers a discrepancy between the state of the world and the organism's representation of the world (Pearce & Hall, 1980). Learning consists of bringing expectation and reality into accord. Rescorla (1988) remarks that "organisms adjust their Pavlovian associations only when they are 'surprised.' " This statement suggests that conditioning and having an insight are more or less the same thing. To be surprised, one must be attending to or expecting something. No one attended much to saliva before Pavlov; thus, no one was conditioned in the way he was. To develop a conditioned response and to discover a regularity in the environment are the same thing. Rather than say that Pavlov developed a theory, we could say that he became conditioned; rather than say that Pavlov's dogs were conditioned, we could say that they were surprised by a relationship between laboratory assistants and meat powder and that they developed a theory to account for this relationship.

BASIC PRINCIPLES OF LEARNING

In case you have forgotten exactly what happens in conditioning, we shall review the basics in a practical context. Say you are trying to write a book about cognition. The last thing you want is people dropping by to chat when you are in the middle of a sentence about gated dipoles. It rather breaks the flow. What to do? One thing that will drive virtually anyone away is an Irish Setter. It is very friendly, and it drools all the time. It would crawl all over unwelcome guests and drool on them. The problem is that the thing will come and drool on you as soon as the guest is gone. A far, far better thing to do would be to buy a Doberman Pinscher and condition it to drool on guests. Let us say that we buy such a dog and name it Kerensky.

What we call the dog is irrelevant, but we should perhaps clarify why it is necessary to learn about how an animal learns. We need to understand simple learning before we can hope to explain complex learning. One of the cornerstones of the neural-network approach is that human learning is based upon principles similar to those that occur in lower organisms (Gluck & Bower, 1988). Of course, this is also a basic assumption of behaviorism. Information-processing psychologists doubted that this assumption is warranted; however, it turns out that animal learning is more complicated than early behaviorists had thought (Pearce & Hall, 1980) and that there are in fact many close parallels between human and animal learning (Estes, 1985; Turkkan, 1989).

Meat powder is an unconditioned stimulus (UCS), and drooling is the unconditioned response (UCR) to it—meaning simply that there is already a strong connection between the meat-powder node and the drooling node in a dog's neural network. To condition our dog, Kerensky, we need to connect a neutral stimulus—a conditioned stimulus (CS)—with drooling. For the CS, let us use the word *Kool-aid* as in "Would you like a glass of lukewarm Kool-aid?" Our ultimate aim is to get the dog to drool when we offer an unwelcome guest a glass of Kool-aid. It could be self-defeating to use words such as *beer* or *wine* as CSs, because they may lead the guest to expect a tasty UCS. In this description, we'll assume that as soon as your visitor sits down, you have Kerensky trained to put his paws on your guest's lap and stare him or her in the face. (Otherwise, the dog would merely stand in the middle of the floor and drool.)

Synchronization of CS and UCS

To condition the dog, we pair the word *Kool-aid* with meat powder a few times. We could get a friend to sit in a chair during training and hope that Kerensky will generalize his response to anyone sitting in the chair. Exactly

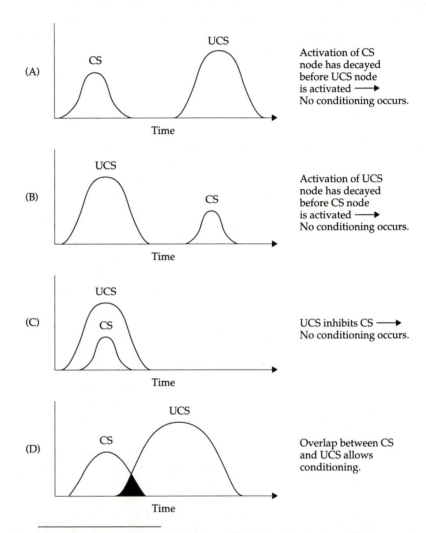

F I G U R E   7 – 1 Synchronization problems in conditioning. For conditioning to occur, nodes coding the CS and the UCS must be simultaneously activated. If the CS and UCS occur too far apart (A and B), there is no simultaneous activation. If the CS and the UCS are simultaneous (C), the UCS node inhibits the CS node. If the CS precedes the UCS by a short period (D), there is simultaneous activation, and conditioning occurs.

how we pair the CS and the UCS is crucial. This pairing is the *synchronization problem* (Grossberg & Levine, 1987). If the CS and the UCS are simultaneous, Kerensky will learn nothing, and if the CS follows the UCS, Kerensky will learn nothing. The CS must precede the UCS—usually, it should begin about a half-second before the UCS (Rescorla, 1988). Why is this? The nodes coding the CS and the UCS must be simultaneously active if the connection between them is to be strengthened. If the connection between the CS node and the UCS node is strengthened, then the CS (via its connection with the UCS node) will elicit drooling—the CS will set Kerensky to thinking about meat powder, and these thoughts will make him drool. A behaviorist would not phrase things this way, but our goal is to clarify what happens in conditioning rather than to elicit praise from behaviorists.

Figure 7–1 shows how to get the CS and UCS nodes simultaneously activated. If the CS precedes the UCS by too much time (Figure 7–1[a]), activation of the CS node will have decayed by the time the UCS node is activated. If the UCS precedes the CS by too much time (Figure 7–1[b]), activation of the UCS node will have decayed before the CS node is activated. Simultaneous presentation of the CS and the UCS (Figure 7–1[c]) creates another problem. A dog loves meat powder and couldn't care less about the word *Kool-aid*—in other words, the node coding the UCS is strong, so it will inhibit the weak node coding the CS. If the CS comes on shortly before the UCS, as in Figure 7–1(d), activation of the Kool-aid node and the meat-powder node will overlap. That is the situation we want, because the connections between simultaneously activated nodes are strengthened.

We must also note that mere contiguity is not enough. The CS must be an accurate predictor of the UCS (Rescorla, 1988). If you say *Kool-aid* just before you give Kerensky meat powder, you will condition him—although this is a big *if*. You cannot also go around saying Kool-aid and *not* give meat powder; the poor dog will never get the idea, because the word will not be a good predictor of the UCS. This circumstance is the point of the story about the little boy who cried "wolf." He kept saying "wolf" when no wolves were present, so no one got conditioned. When a wolf actually showed up, he cried "wolf," and nobody paid attention because the word was not an accurate predictor of anything.

OVERSHADOWING

Since we are devoting all this effort to conditioning Kerensky, we might want to build in a fail-safe system; for example, we could have two CSs, such as *Kool-aid* and a loud noise. Then, either *Kool-aid* or the loud noise or both together would produce drooling. You could greet your guest with feigned joy and say "How about some *Kool-aid*, good buddy," and simultaneously slap your friend on the back. Perhaps this combination will double the drooling. During training, *Kool-aid* and a loud noise will both precede the meat

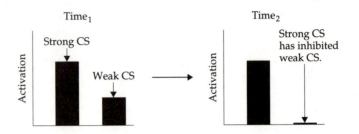

F I G U R E   7 – 2   Attempts to establish two CSs are doomed
to failure because the node coding the stronger CS inhibits the node
coding the weaker CS. Overshadowing occurs during initial conditioning: the potentially stronger CS inhibits the weaker one. Blocking
occurs after conditioning: the node coding the old CS is strong and
thus inhibits the node coding the new CS.

powder. In fact, this procedure is a prescription for disaster: you are likely
to get *overshadowing* (Staddon, 1983). The stronger CS will block the weaker
one, and Kerensky will become conditioned to drool in response to the loud
noise but not at all to hearing *Kool-aid*. As shown in Figure 7–2, the stronger
CS will laterally inhibit the weaker one; hence, only the stronger CS will be
activated when the UCS node becomes activated. Only the connection between the stronger CS and the UCS will be strengthened (Grossberg & Levine, 1987). You yourself show overshadowing whenever you ignore the irrelevant or weak aspects of a stimulus. When you read a book, you ignore
the typeface. For that matter, you ignore the exact phrasing of the sentences—
meaning usually overshadows other aspects of a verbal stimulus.

BLOCKING AND THE TURKEY/LOVE FIASCO

Because most of the guests you have are probably not stupid, they may dis-
cern (i.e., themselves develop a conditioned response) that whenever you
say *Kool-aid*, Kerensky drools on them. So perhaps you can recondition
Kerensky to respond to a new CS. Here is what to do during training trials:
as you say *Kool-aid*, simultaneously make a loud noise, then give Kerensky
his meat powder. A few of these trials and the dog should have it down pat.
The unwelcome guest arrives. You make not the slightest mention of Kool-
aid, but as you hand your friend his or her favorite drink, you make the
loud noise. Kerensky listens to you attentively; however, he does not drool
at all. The dog is not stupid; he is exhibiting *blocking* (Kamin, 1969).

   After one CS is attached to a UCS, another CS cannot easily be connected to the same UCS. Blocking and overshadowing occur for the same
reason. Figure 7–2 shows what happens. The cognitive unit coding the original CS becomes very activated, so it laterally inhibits the prospective new

CS. The node coding the new or redundant CS never becomes activated enough, so the connection between it and the UCS is not strengthened. On a descriptive level, the redundant CS is just that. If the original CS is a good predictor of the UCS, redundant predictors are ignored.

Grossberg and Levine (1987) provide an explanation for blocking. The circuitry is shown in Figure 7–3. The reason the CS node becomes so acti-

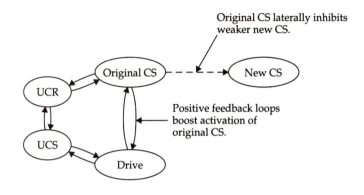

F I G U R E   7 - 3   Circuit showing why blocking occurs.

vated is that the connection from the CS node to a drive or emotion node (Bower, 1981) has been strengthened because the two nodes have been simultaneously activated. The connection from the drive node back to the CS node has also been strengthened, thus setting up a closed positive feedback loop. As also shown in Figure 7–3, the connections between the original CS and the UCS nodes have also been strengthened. Thus, there are several positive feedback loops serving to activate the node coding the original CS. The original CS node is thus able to inhibit the potential new CS node. As Grossberg points out, when you have a turkey dinner with your lover, you don't get cross-conditioned and want to have sex with the turkey and cook your lover. The reason is *blocking*. Even though the turkey and thoughts of sex may be in contiguity, no conditioning occurs. When you are thinking about your lover, your CS (lover)-Drive (sex) feedback loop keeps the turkey node inhibited, so it can't become activated enough to strengthen its potential connection with the sex node. By the same token, when you turn your attention to the turkey, the CS (turkey)-Drive (hunger) feedback loop inhibits the node coding your lover, so that its connection with the hunger node cannot be strengthened.

SECONDARY REINFORCERS

Early behaviorists assumed that the only real rewards are satisfaction of basic drives such as hunger, thirst, and sex. As we have just seen, if a CS

FIGURE 7-4
Circuit illustrating the basis for secondary reinforcement.

node is connected with one of these nodes, a closed loop is set up. Now, if the CS were used as a reinforcer, it would be what is called a *secondary reinforcer*. A secondary reinforcer does not work terribly well with animals; it soon loses its power, and the circuit collapses like a house of cards. A secondary reinforcer seems to work fine with people, however.

Figure 7-4 shows what is involved in establishing a secondary reinforcer. First the CS_1-Drive loop is set up by conditioning, after which we can set up the CS_1-CS_2 loop. If the human were a soldier, the drive could have to do with sense of self-worth. The CS_1 might be a little colored ribbon, and the CS_2 might be a bunch of heavily armed enemy soldiers. A soldier who has been conditioned correctly will take great personal risks to kill the CS_2. Part of the reason is that the soldier wants the CS_1—we can condition people to kill just to get colored ribbons. We cannot do that with a dog. Why? Your first guess might be that dogs are smarter than people, but we have other evidence that it is probably the other way around. All that is needed for conditioning is a closed feedback loop. Such a loop will cause nodes to become highly activated, causing the connection strengths of the nodes to increase. People are able to set up and maintain such feedback loops better than dogs and other creatures because we have more cortex to work with.

ATTENTION AND REINFORCEMENT

Do not infer that either basic drives or secondary reinforcers are necessary for conditioning; all we really need to produce learning is to get several nodes activated at the same time. The longer they are simultaneously activated, the more the connections between them will be strengthened. The more often they are activated at the same time, the more the connections between them will be strengthened. High levels of activation of nodes is the same thing as attention (see Chapter 5). Attention is caused by inputs from the arousal system. When we are surprised, the arousal system sends arousal to the entire cortex, and we attend to whatever surprised us. On their way to the cortex, fibers from the arousal system pass through centers in the midbrain that produce pleasure and displeasure (Berlyne, 1971). The displeasure centers do not become activated unless arousal is very high. Let's ignore them for now. The result of this circuitry is that—so long as arousal is not extremely high—attention will usually be accompanied by some pleasure, although the pleasure may be very weak. To get attention, we need arousal, and arousal produces pleasure. By definition, pleasure is reinforcing or rewarding. We learn when we attend, and attention happens to be accompanied by reinforcement. We could say that we learn when we are reinforced, but the crucial factor is probably attention or arousal. It does seem to be the case that we can learn without any conscious attention (Reber, 1989; Schachter, 1987). All that is needed for learning is to have two nodes simultaneously activated; however, learning is likely to proceed much faster the more activated the nodes are.

Latent Learning and Attention

We have already mentioned that animals can learn without reward, but this does not mean that they learn without attention. Tolman and Honzik (1930) had two herds of hungry rats that were placed in a maze. The lucky group always found food at a goal box. For the unlucky group, there was no food anywhere in the maze; they just wandered around the maze for a while every day for ten days. By that time, the lucky group had learned where to find the food quite quickly. On the 11th day and afterwards, everybody got food. By the 12th day, the unlucky group had caught up and knew how to get to the food as well and as fast as the lucky group.

The unlucky group had clearly learned its way around the maze—an example of *latent* or *incidental learning*. Until the 11th day, these rats had no particular reason to go to the goal box. What did the unlucky rats do for ten days? About the same as you might do if you were thrown into a strange prison with no explanation. You would probably not just sit lost in thought. You would look for an escape route. Finding none, you would check more carefully. You would look for the dangerous types of people who live in prisons. Finding none, you would still want to make sure you knew your way around in case any did show up. Even if you knew that you were perfectly safe, idle curiosity would lead you to explore the prison. Rats also explore mazes because of curiosity (Berlyne, 1960). Because all of this checking and exploring involves attention, there is nothing especially latent or incidental about this kind of learning.

Repetition and Learning

It seems obvious that more repetitions lead to better memory; however, this is only the case if one attends to whatever is being repeated. Here is a simple demonstration: get a piece of paper and draw the front and back of a penny. When you are finished, procure a penny and score your performance. You may be surprised to find that you don't remember what a penny looks like. Nickerson and Adams (1979) conducted an experiment exactly like this one. Except for one coin collector, none of their subjects could draw a penny correctly with no mistakes. In another part of their experiment, people were shown 15 plausible drawings of the front of a penny—plausible because Lincoln rather than someone else was shown, and typical American slogans appeared. Fewer than half the subjects picked the correct drawing. We see pennies all the time, but we don't attend to them, and inattention generally results in poor long-term memory.

GENERALIZATION AND DISCRIMINATION

Let us forget about people and get back to Kerensky. The dog has figured out that a sound pattern is a good predictor of meat powder; however, he is not sure exactly *what* about the pattern is crucial. Is it the exact word *Kool-aid* at an exact intensity? Is it any word beginning with /K/ or any word ending with /D/? Because of Kerensky's uncertainty, he will show a great deal of generalization; that is, he will drool somewhat in response to stimuli that resemble the word *Kool-aid*. If you say other words—such as *cook, calm, aid, raid,* and so on—and d*on't* follow up with meat powder, the generalization gradient will be much steeper (Grossberg, 1975). There will not be as much generalization, and Kerensky will drool more in response to *Kool-aid* than if no discrimination training (reinforcing *Kool-aid* but not similar sounding words) had taken place.

PEAK SHIFT AND BEHAVIORAL CONTRAST

Here is a stupid pet trick that is also a stupid people trick. Some visitors are more welcome than others, so we can give Kerensky some discrimination training. The word *Kool-aid* spoken loudly (say, at 70 dB) will be followed by meat powder; spoken softly (say, at 60 dB), it will not be. Saying *Kool-aid* at 70 dB is called the S⁺, and the word spoken at 60 dB is called the S⁻. This training will set up an e*xcitatory gradient* centered at 70 dB, meaning that, because of stimulus generalization, saying *Kool-aid* somewhat louder or softer will also cause some drooling. The excitatory gradient is shown in Figure 7–5(a). An *inhibitory gradient* will be set up around the S⁻. Because of generalization, *not* drooling will also be elicited by saying the word a bit louder or softer than 60 dB, also shown in Figure 7–5(a). Because the S⁺ and the S⁻ are close to each other, the excitatory and inhibitory gradients will overlap. Our goal was simple: if we say *Kool-aid* loudly, we want Kerensky to drool a lot; if we say it softly, we want Kerensky not to drool.

The result is not exactly what you would expect. Kerensky will exhibit a maximal amount of drooling if the signal is a bit *above* 70 dB (say, 75 dB). This is called *peak shift* (Hanson, 1959), which is also shown in Figure 7–5(a). The reason for peak shift is that in computing how much to drool, the inhibitory gradient (tendency not to drool) is subtracted from the excitatory gradient (tendency to drool). Note that the result, as shown in the figure, is to shift maximal drooling to a point beyond the S⁺. At 70 dB, there is a large tendency to drool, but also, because of generalization, some tendency not to drool. At 75 dB, there is a somewhat smaller tendency to drool, but hardly any tendency not to drool. Thus, the dog drools more if we say *Kool-aid* at 75 dB than if we say it at 70 dB.

Furthermore, Kerensky will drool *more* to a 75 dB signal than if we had done no discrimination training at all—that is, if we had simply conditioned

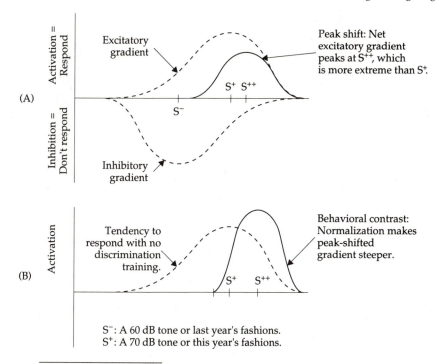

(A)

(B)

S⁻: A 60 dB tone or last year's fashions.
S⁺: A 70 dB tone or this year's fashions.

F I G U R E   7 – 5 Mechanisms of peak shift and behavioral contrast. Discrimination training sets up excitatory and inhibitory gradients. As shown in (A), propensity to respond is determined by subtracting the inhibitory gradient from the excitatory gradient. Because the gradients overlap, the result is peak shift: maximal responding is elicited by a stimulus (S⁺⁺) beyond S⁺ in a direction away from S⁻. As shown in (B), normalization produces behavioral contrast: S⁺⁺ elicits more of a response than did S⁺ before discrimination training. Note that S⁺ can be anything, from a 70dB tone to this year's fashions.

the dog to drool if he heard a 70 dB tone and not conditioned him not to drool to the 60 dB tone. This phenomenon is called *behavioral contrast* (Hanson, 1959), shown in Figure 7–5(b). Grossberg (1975) argues that behavioral contrast occurs because short-term memory activation is normalized or conserved—the amount of activation on any layer of an analyzer is kept about the same. In discrimination training, the inhibitory gradient is subtracted from the excitatory gradient, and the net result is smaller than if we had done no discrimination training (Figure 7–5[a]). Because lateral inhibition causes activation to stay more or less constant, the result is that the response gradient is taller: after discrimination training, there are fewer nodes activated, so each gets more of the available activation. Thus, Kerensky drools even more to a signal he has not been trained with than to a signal he was specially trained with.

A lot of stupid people tricks are based on this phenomenon. Fashion is one example. Look back at Figure 7–5 and read the other captions. Substitute last year's fashions for the 60 dB tone. People don't reinforce you for wearing them. Substitute this year's fashions for the 70 dB tone. You are reinforced for wearing them—people say you look nice. What happens when you go shopping? You drool most over things that are a little more extreme than this year's fashions in a direction away from last year's fashions—a case of *peak shift*. One human equivalent of drooling is spending money. You absolutely *must* have whatever peak shift makes you want—an example of *behavioral contrast*. Salespeople use this trick all the time without knowing that it has a name, and people fall for it all the time without knowing that it has a name. Now that you know about it, you will still fall for it, but you will know what to call it.

FORGETTING

EXTINCTION

Kerensky is not going to continue drooling on guests unless he is occasionally given refresher courses: pairings of the CS and the UCS. If you omit the refresher courses, the conditioned response will *extinguish*. Let us say that you train him and just let him drool. This approach will work for a while, but eventually he will drool less and less. He will have forgotten the conditioning. Here is something odd, though: assume that you are blessed for a week or so with no unwanted visitors, then one finally shows up and, from force of habit, you offer her *Kool-aid*. Kerensky will drool all over her—he has not forgotten at all. Forgetting must therefore involve active inhibition (Pavlov, 1927); if it were caused by passive decay of connection strengths,

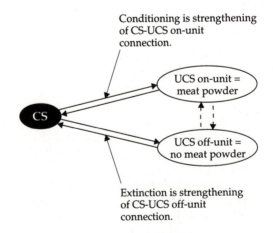

Conditioning is strengthening of CS-UCS on-unit connection.

UCS on-unit = meat powder

UCS off-unit = no meat powder

Extinction is strengthening of CS-UCS off-unit connection.

F I G U R E   7 – 6   Circuit showing why extinction occurs.

the conditioned response could not return in this way.

Here is what must happen. Whenever the CS is *not* followed by the UCS, Kerensky is surprised. Recall what happens when one is surprised: an attentional reset occurs, and units that are activated become inhibited. The more activated a unit is, the more it is inhibited. The companion off-units of formerly activated dipoles are activated for a brief period. During this period of activation, the connection between the CS unit and the UCS off-unit can be strengthened (compare Grossberg & Schmajuk, 1987); see Figure 7–6. The same thing happens every time the CS is not followed by the UCS. Each time, the connection strength between the CS unit and the UCS off-unit is strengthened a bit more. Finally, the CS becomes more strongly connected to the UCS off-unit than to the on-unit—which now means *no* meat powder and do *not* salivate. If we wait awhile, the new connection will decay quite a bit. Connection strengths seem to decay rather rapidly when they are first established. After this wait, the connection between the CS and the UCS on-unit will once more be stronger than the connection between the CS and the UCS off-unit. The conditioned response thus reappears.

After enough extinction trials, the connection strength between the CS and the UCS off-unit will be permanently stronger than connection strength between the CS and the UCS on-unit. Paradoxically, the connection between the CS and the UCS off-unit will *never* extinguish, because the meaning of this connection is that the CS predicts *nothing*. In our example, the meaning is now that the word *Kool-aid* predicts *no* meat powder. This expectation is never violated, so Kerensky is never surprised; no surprise means no attentional reset, and no attentional reset means no extinction.

EXTINCTION, REINFORCEMENT, AND HUMAN MEMORY

In our example, Kerensky's memory for drooling was rather fragile; it would extinguish if he were not frequently given booster shots. This situation doesn't seem to correspond to human behavior, although it corresponds quite well to *some* of our behavior. If you are used to saying hello to a classmate who then suddenly stops returning your greeting, what do you do? You say hello a few more times, become annoyed, then you too stop saying hello—this is an example of extinction. Animals in an experiment do exactly the same thing: they make some more responses, then they become frustrated and annoyed, and finally, they don't respond anymore.

People don't need periodic reinforcements to keep from forgetting facts such as that Napoleon lost the Battle of Waterloo—one does not need to pair the memory of Waterloo with food or sex to keep it from being forgotten. There are plenty of other reinforcers besides the real basics. The knowledge is in itself useful for understanding other things, and that is rewarding; in addition, people will think you are not very well educated if you forget about Waterloo, and that is *not* rewarding.

Here is a sad story about a man who didn't extinguish. Lenin's revolution was directed against Alexander Kerensky. After the revolution, Kerensky came to America and settled in Berkeley. (He died only a few years ago.) For decades, he spent almost every day in the University of California library. He had a single mission: to figure out *what went wrong.* Why didn't he extinguish? It is possible that learning and understanding and insight reinforce themselves: activation of cognitive units brings pleasure (Grossberg & Gutkowski, 1987; Martindale & Moore, 1988). Any kind of thought involves resonance among cognitive units, just as does emitting a conditioned response. As we shall see in Chapter 10, one way of looking at creative insight is that it consists of "discovering" a connection path among a set of nodes. The act of discovery is equivalent to establishing a resonant positive feedback loop that boosts the activation of the nodes in the loop. As we noted at the beginning of the chapter, conditioning and insight are more or less the same thing. Perhaps, then, Kerensky's failure to extinguish is not a sad story at all. Pavlov would tell you that to rule Russia is a small thing, but to understand is a big thing. Of course, the reinforcements that governed Alexander Kerensky were more subtle than those that governed our imaginary dog, Kerensky, but the basic principles are the same.

Interference Versus Decay

If you enjoyed the story about Alexander Kerensky, you may think everything about forgetting is settled: people don't extinguish the way animals do. If you didn't care for the story, you may think we have gotten ourselves into a corner; after all, people certainly do forget. Once we have learned something, it becomes harder and harder to remember it the longer we wait. The probability of being able to remember an item falls off very rapidly at first, then the rate of decline slows. The probability of correct recall continues to go down with the passage of time, but not as quickly as at first. You can easily demonstrate this fact to yourself: write down what you had for dinner last night, and rate how confident you are of this answer. Now do the same for the night before last, and so on. The further back you go, the worse your memory. The simplest explanation is that the strength of memory traces decays as time passes—the commonsense view of forgetting. The commonsense view is not necessarily wrong. A decay theorist would argue that decay is a gradual process in the nervous system that occurs independently of other activities, similar to the gradual loss of radioactivity in radium that goes on regardless of what is happening to the radium—whether it is buried in the earth, lying on the ground, or being carried about in your pocket. There is some evidence for decay of long-term memories, but decay does not seem to be the main reason we forget.

If forgetting is an autonomous decay process, then it should occur at the same rate no matter what is passing through a person's mind. In a classic experiment, Jenkins and Dallenbach (1924) taught their subjects lists of nonsense syllables, then the subjects either slept or carried out their normal activities for 1, 2, 4, or 8 hours. Recall was better at all intervals after sleep than after normal waking activities. Less goes on in the nervous system during sleep than during waking, so it must be that other activities in the mind, *not* a passive process of decay, cause forgetting. Why did the subjects who slept through Jenkins and Dallenbach's experiment forget anything at all? There is not a complete cessation of all mental activity during sleep. We do dream, and perhaps even this causes forgetting—in fact, retention of newly learned material is worse after sleep filled with dreams than after dreamless sleep (Yaroush, Sullivan, & Ekstrand, 1971).

INTERFERENCE THEORIES

The Jenkins and Dallenbach experiment led to almost universal abandonment of decay theories of forgetting. Later theories suggest that some form of interference causes forgetting. The idea behind these theories is that once something is entered in memory, other memory traces interfere with its retrieval. How this happens is explained in different ways by different theories: response competition, unlearning, and response inhibition. We can easily reformulate the last two in terms of Pavlovian extinction and lateral inhibition. The first theory is not true, so we don't need to reformulate it.

The Basic Data

Before we reformulate anything, let us see what we need to explain. One of the easiest ways to study human memory is with paired-associate learning. One gives a subject a list of paired items in the form *A-B*, usually words (e.g., *cat-mountain*) or nonsense syllables (e.g., *dix-fug*). The idea is for the person to learn all of the pairs on the list. Memory is tested by presenting each *A* item and asking the subject to respond with the correct *B* item. This technique is the same as establishing a set of conditioned responses: *A* is the stimulus and *B* is the response. There is no obvious UCS involved, nor is one necessary. All that is needed for conditioning is attention. If subjects in a paired-associate learning task are cooperative and pay attention, they will become conditioned. But simply teaching someone a list of paired associates will not help us study interference. Here is the most common way to study interference: first, subjects are taught an *A-B* list, then they are taught an *A-C* list. An *A-C* list is one in which all the *A* items have been re-paired with new (*C*) items; for example, this might be an *A-B* list: *cat-mountain, paper-green, stove-door, rug-ear*, and so on; and this might be the *A-C* list: *cat-floor, paper-truck, stove-red, rug-hill*, and so forth.

There are two paradigms for studying interference in memory. The more intuitively obvious one is the *retroactive inhibition* paradigm. Retroactive inhibition occurs when new material interferes with memory for old material. When one is young, one hears that learning Latin will do everything from improving our moral fiber to helping us learn other languages. Although Latin may help when you learn French, you can also be sure that French will destroy most of your memory for Latin—because of retroactive inhibition. If we are teaching paired associates rather than languages, we teach subjects the A-B list, then we teach the A-C list. Finally, we test for memory of the original A-B list. Before we can make any sense of what we find, we need a control group. This group also learns A-B. While the experimental group learns A-C, the control group does something equal in difficulty to learning the A-C list but which is otherwise as irrelevant as possible. Teaching them a C-D list, where the Cs and Ds are unrelated to the As and Bs, would be a good way to keep them occupied. The control group is then also tested on the A-B list. There should be minimal interference for the A-B list in the control group; on the other hand, learning the A-C list should interfere with retention of the A-B list in the experimental group. The basic finding is well established: the experimental group recalls the A-B list worse than does the control group. Furthermore, the more similarity between the B and C items, the worse the recall in the experimental group (Friedman & Reynolds, 1967). The basic principle of retroactive inhibition is that the more similar new material is to previously learned material, the more forgetting of the previously learned material it will cause.

The other type of interference effect is *proactive inhibition*. Here, prior memories interfere with subsequent memories. Proactive inhibition is the reason you can't teach an old dog new tricks. To study proactive inhibition, we would first teach subjects the A-B list and then the A-C list, just as in a retroactive inhibition experiment. The difference is that we would then test them for their memory of the A-C list. The proper control group would be one that engaged in a control task while the experimental group learned the A-B list. Then, the control group would also learn the A-C list and be tested on it. The finding is that the experimental group recalls the A-C list less well than the control group. Retention is again a function of similarity between B items and C items; the more similar they are, the more interference there is. The basic principle of proactive inhibition is that the more similar previously learned material is to new material, the more forgetting of new material there will be.

Response Competition

The earliest and most obvious theory of interference had to do with *response competition* (McGeoch, 1942). Consider learning in an A-B, A-C paradigm. If we test memory for the A-B list, we find retroactive inhibition; if we test memory for the A-C list, we find proactive inhibition. Perhaps the reason is that A words become associated with both B words and C words. To test memory, A words are presented; perhaps the A words lead subjects to recall *both* the B word and the C word, but they cannot remember which is correct. In other words, the subjects do not forget the A-B or A-C associations; they simply forget which list the association goes with.

This plausible theory has one clear implication: errors should usually be intrusions from the other list. Suppose we present the *A* items and ask our subjects to respond with the correct *B* items. When mistakes are made, they should consist of intrusion errors (giving the *A-C* association rather than the *A-B* association). Melton and Irwin (1940) tested this hypothesis and found that there were a few intrusion errors; however, no matter when memory for the *A-B* list was tested, intrusion errors did not account for much of the retroactive inhibition. Most of the mistakes were not *A-C* responses but *A*-Something-different responses. The longer the memory test was delayed or the more *A-C* trials there had been, the *fewer* intrusion errors there were, but the *more* forgetting there was. The response competition theory cannot account for these facts—it is a nice theory, but it is wrong.

Unlearning

Melton and Irwin (1940) proposed an alternative theory: that forgetting is like extinction in Pavlovian conditioning. In extinction, an association is actively inhibited. From this viewpoint, learning the *A-C* association causes the *A-B* association to be actively suppressed or inhibited. The node that chunks or connects *A* and *C* laterally inhibits the unit that chunks *A* and *B*, as diagramed at the bottom of Figure 7–7. Recall that when a conditioned

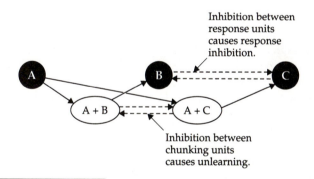

FIGURE 7 – 7   According to the unlearning hypothesis, forgetting occurs because of inhibition between chunking units. According to the response inhibition hypothesis, it occurs because of inhibition between response units.

response is extinguished, there is some spontaneous recovery if a period of time elapses (Pavlov, 1927)—the old association is still present, but the process of extinction has inhibited it. With the passage of time, some of this inhibition dissipates. We find the same thing in paired-associate learning. In an *A-B*, *A-C* paradigm, the original *A-B* associations spontaneously recover in strength with longer retention intervals (Underwood, 1948). The longer one waits before testing someone's memory, the more proactive inhibition there is (the worse the retention of *A-C*) and the less retroactive inhibition there is (the better the memory for *A-B* items).

Barnes and Underwood (1959) introduced a simple technique: they simply presented *A* to their subjects and asked them to recall both *B* and *C*. Barnes and Underwood first taught their subjects an *A-B* list, then an *A-C* list. Recall was tested after from one to 20 trials of the *A-C* list. The results were clear: the more *A-C* trials there had been, the fewer *B* responses could be recalled. The *A-B* associations had become genuinely unavailable. Note that the Barnes and Underwood experiment provides further evidence against the response competition theory. The supposedly competing responses are simply not present. We can reject the response competition theory of forgetting, but can we accept the unlearning theory?

Response Inhibition

The unlearning hypothesis is that it is the *association* between two items that is inhibited or forgotten, possibly by lateral inhibition between chunking units in memory: the chunking unit coding *A-B* and the chunking unit coding *A-C* inhibit each other. The more similar *B* and *C* are, the closer together these chunking units are and the more interference there is. But wait! Perhaps it is the *B* units and *C* units themselves that cause the problem. The more similar *B* and *C* are, the closer together the units coding them should be. Maybe we don't even need the chunking units to explain forgetting. Perhaps we could explain it simply by reference to inhibitory connections between the component units. Look at the top of Figure 7–7. The idea is that, no matter what happens with chunking units, the *B* and *C* units should inhibit each other in proportion to their similarity. Postman, Stark, and Fraser (1968) proposed that, during *A-C* learning following *A-B* learning, the *B* items are inhibited by the *C* items. This is the response inhibition hypothesis.

How can we tell if it is the association units or the item units that are inhibited? One possibility is to use the *A-B*, *A-C* paradigm, then give subjects all the *A* items and all the *B* items. Their task is simply to match the *A* and *B* items. If it were the *A-B* association (or the chunking unit coding it) that was inhibited, then providing the *B* items should not help much. The chunking unit tells which *B* item goes with which *A* item. On the other hand, if inhibition of the *B* units themselves were behind forgetting, this procedure should be quite helpful. Postman and Stark (1969) used an *A-B*, *A-C* paradigm, then tested memory for the *A-B* list in the manner just suggested. Subjects were given all the *A* and *B* items and simply had to match them. Subjects did very well on this task as compared to tasks where the *B* items have to be recalled; however, the results did show a trend toward forgetting some of the associations themselves.

Wickelgren (1976) reviewed a number of other studies using the same procedure that clarified the issue. Performance is always better with the matching task than with a recall task. Two explanations come to mind: (1)

some forgetting is in fact due to inhibition of the response items themselves, just as the response inhibition theory claims; or (2) presenting both the *A* and *B* units strongly activates the chunking units coding the *A-B* association. One could argue that in fact these chunking units are really responsible for forgetting, but presentation of both *A* and *B* is sufficient to release them from inhibition. It is unclear which explanation is correct. A second consistent finding of these studies is that there is always some evidence for unlearning the associations themselves. Even with the matching task, performance is not perfect. Thus, it is well-established that some forgetting comes from inhibition of chunking units coding associations.

Conclusions About Interference

Response competition cannot explain forgetting. Inhibition of one cognitive unit by another seems to be the main culprit, but it remains unclear exactly which cognitive units are inhibiting each other. The unlearning theory says that chunking units coding associations inhibit each other. The response inhibition theory says that the inhibition occurs between units coding the items that are associated. Present evidence does not allow us to reject either theory. The lateral-inhibition model of the mind would lead us to expect *both* types of inhibition, so probably both theories are true.

Decay Theory Revisited

It is also probably true that there is some decay of long-term memory connections. Inhibition theorists overlook a simple fact: if inhibition were the only cause of forgetting, the control groups in the experiments should have

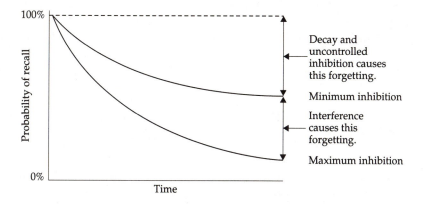

FIGURE   7 – 8   Forgetting curves. Some forgetting results from interference, but some may be caused by decay.

good memories for what they learned—but they don't. The simplest explanation would be that at least some forgetting in the control group is due to decay. Figure 7–8 shows two forgetting curves that summarize several different experiments. Both are exponential decay curves: the greater the amount of interfering material, the more forgetting there is; however, there is still considerable forgetting with minimal interference. It is reasonable to attribute at least some of this forgetting to decay. Wickelgren (1976) describes several lines of evidence that support the notion of long-term decay.

THE HEBB RULE

We have said that learning consists of changing connection strengths. As Hebb (1949) put it, "When the axon of cell A is near enough to excite a cell B and repeatedly and persistently takes part in firing it, some growth process takes place in one or both cells such that A's efficiency, as one of the cells firing B, is increased." Later theorists (e.g., Grossberg & Levine, 1987; McClelland & Rumelhart, 1986) have modified this rule in several ways, leading to what is usually called the Hebb Rule. First, we want a mechanism that will *decrease* the connection strength between A and B if they are *not* simultaneously activated. (In fact, Thorndike [1911] had already proposed the so-called Hebb rule and this modification long ago.) Next, we want to put a limit on how strong or weak a connection between two nodes can be; otherwise, we could end up with infinitely strong positive or negative connection strengths. It would also be a good idea to put a learning-rate parameter in: we don't want connection strengths to change too much on a single trial (otherwise, a network might see the Pope and learn that all men wear long gowns and attract large crowds, then it might see a policeman and learn that all men wear badges and arrest people). Finally, we should put a decay factor in to get rid of "mistaken" changes in connection strengths (Wickelgren, 1979b). We are not putting all these factors in just so the math comes out right, but because this is the way neurons seem to work (Levy, 1985; Singer, 1983).

A NEURAL NETWORK LEARNS ABOUT MEN, WOMEN, AND DOUGHNUTS

Let us consider a simple example based on neural networks investigated by Anderson, Silverstein, Ritz, and Jones (1977) and by McClelland and Rumelhart (1985). For the moment, disregard layers, lateral inhibition, and the like. Consider a neural network composed of only eight nodes. All the nodes are connected to all the other nodes. Assume that the nodes receive input about eight visual features; for example, one node might be a feature detector for legs, another for the presence of long hair, another for the presence of a sugarcoating, another for the presence of a beard, and so on. The more of one of these features that is present, the more activated will be the node coding it. Let us also assume that the nodes all send output to response nodes and that the network is in a dog's brain. Our ultimate goal is to get the dog to bark if a man comes to the door, be nice to women, and fetch doughnuts. To accomplish this training, we need to teach the dog to tell the difference between men, women, and doughnuts. A dog can learn to make these discriminations; the question is *how*. Any individual man, woman, or doughnut is characterized by a specific set of features. Presumably, all men will share some features, as will all women and all doughnuts. Note that we have no higher-order unitary percept nodes coding men, women, and doughnuts. We do not really need them: any stimulus will be characterized by a specific pattern of activation across the eight nodes. Given what we want the network to do, we need three response nodes: one for barking, one for being nice, and one for fetching things (in this case, doughnuts). Ultimately, we want to strengthen the output from one set of feature nodes to the barking node, output from another set to the being-nice node, and output from yet another set to the fetching node, but let us concentrate for now on the interconnections among the eight feature-detecting nodes.

For the network to learn, we need to take the dog around and show it specific men, women, and doughnuts. One possibility is to use the Hebb Rule to make the input from all other nodes to any one node equal to the input to that node from the visual system. This will allow *pattern completion*. The network will not have to see the entire stimulus to recognize it. If a node is not receiving any input one way or the other, the nodes that *are* getting input will automatically activate (or inhibit) it. Women usually have longer hair than men; doughnuts have no hair. We want the network to recognize a man, woman, or doughnut even when it is wearing a hat and the network thus cannot directly determine hair length. If a stimulus has a sugarcoating, we would want to strengthen the inhibitory connection between the sugarcoating node and the long-hair node (because the stimulus is probably a doughnut and, thus, does not have long hair). If a stimulus has breasts, we would want to strengthen the excitatory connection between the breasts node and the long-hair node. (Obviously, some women have short hair; this is just an example.) This wiring arrangement will also allow generalization: we want the dog to respond to things in general rather than only to the specific things it has seen. Any stimulus will produce a unique pattern of activation across the field of nodes. Recall, though, that we only want it to bark, be nice, or fetch things; thus, we don't care about the exact level of activation of each node.

If every node is connected to every other node, we have a matrix of 64 weights. The weights are adjusted after the network has observed its first stimulus. Let's let the network observe a second stimulus. Now let's do something that may seem ridiculous: change the weights by averaging together the weights for the second stimulus with those for the first stimulus. We'll keep taking such averages as the network is shown more and more stimuli. Intuitively, this should produce pure chaos; mathematically, that is not the case. If the stimuli (individual men, women, and doughnuts) were completely orthogonal (i.e., the features of each stimulus were completely uncorrelated with the features of all other stimuli), adding the weights together would produce no interference at all! The network would have a perfect memory for each stimulus. If the stimuli are not orthogonal, there will be some interference, but we *want* interference.

People are vastly different from doughnuts. We could say that people and doughnuts are orthogonal or independent: knowing the features that characterize a person doesn't allow us to say much of anything about the features that characterize a doughnut. The network will be able to store information about doughnuts and people with little interference. On the other hand, individual men are not orthogonal; that is, they tend to share features. Consequently, changing the network's weights to record its memory of one specific man will change or distort memories about other men. The network will automatically abstract *prototypes* of men, women, and doughnuts, even though the network has never seen the prototype. The prototypical man is the one who has the set of features a man is most likely to possess. The connection strengths among the nodes are influenced by each man the network sees; the network thus automatically extracts information about the average or prototypical man, as well as about the prototypical woman and the prototypical doughnut. Such knowledge of prototypes is a desirable property, because most concepts seem to be defined by prototypes (Rosch, 1975). The network will also remember individual instances and show *frequency effects*. The more often it is exposed to a stimulus, the more that stimulus contributes to the set of connection weights. As well as having abstracted the prototypical man and woman (neither of which the network has ever seen), it will also recognize me. It will have seen me frequently, so I will have contributed a lot to the weights.

Because of the way we built it, the network exhibits *pattern completion.* If shown part of the stimulus, the interconnections of the nodes will reproduce the entire stimulus; in other words, the network makes plausible *inferences.* If it doesn't see the length of a man's hair, it will infer that it is short, because the nodes that *are* activated by the man will automatically activate the node coding short hair. For the same reason, if it can't see, it may assume that a woman is wearing a skirt rather than pants. Of course, this would depend on which women the network had observed. Even though it sees only the top of a doughnut, the network will infer that the doughnut has no legs. If we connected the network to the arousal system, it would show *surprise*—it would be quite surprised to see a doughnut with legs. We would want it to do this, because surprise is what causes attention and large weight changes.

We have gotten the network to the point that it is likely to show one type of pattern of activation when it sees a woman, another when it sees a man, and another when it sees a doughnut. It is now necessary to get each pattern to activate one of the response nodes. This situation is similar to Pavlovian conditioning except that we want to connect eight nodes (CSs) with a single response unit. To do so, it would be necessary to provide "teaching" input to the response nodes so that their activation could be increased or decreased when they have made the right or wrong response to a pattern (Rumelhart et al., 1986). This teaching input might come from a UCS or drive unit if the neural network were embedded in a real organism. In other words, training would consist of Pavlovian conditioning. If the neural network were actually made up of only eight nodes, there would be massive overshadowing; that is, the most salient feature of men would elicit barking while other features were ignored, and so on. If, however, the network had, say, 8000—as it might in a human brain—there would still be overshadowing, but we could certainly connect a large number of nodes to a response unit. McClelland and Rumelhart (1986) and Rumelhart and McClelland (1986b) deal with the details of how this process can be accomplished.

SUMMARY AND CONCLUSIONS

Learning leads to long-term memories by adjusting the connection strengths among cognitive units. If two nodes are activated at the same time, the connection between them is strengthened. If one node is activated while another is inhibited, an inhibitory connection between them becomes strengthened. Attention helps learning to occur because attention involves high levels of activation of cognitive units. One of the main causes of attention is surprise. When we are surprised, we learn: we adjust connection strengths so that our neural network provides us with a better model of reality.

Animals and humans learn in much the same way, but, of course, people can learn more complicated things. Some learning principles are not intuitively obvious; examples are overshadowing, blocking, and peak shift. These phenomena are natural consequences of the structure of neural networks. Another consequence of the structure of neural networks is that they automatically abstract concepts. Merely showing a network examples of categories is enough to allow it automatically to compute an average of these examples, called a prototype that defines or examplifies the concept.

As soon as we have learned something, we promptly begin to forget it. Some forgetting is probably caused by passive decay of connection strengths, but much is caused by active inhibition. The memory remains, but it is inhibited by other memories. A dog that has been conditioned to do something when it hears or sees a stimulus may forget what it is supposed to do. This situation, extinction, is caused by learning *not* to emit the behavior. When the same thing happens in people, we call it unlearning.

Long-Term Memory

DISSECTING LONG-TERM MEMORY

Psychologists agree that there are several different types of long-term memory. *Semantic memory* contains general knowledge, such as the knowledge that ducks quack. Semantic memory is not time-tagged, which means (1) you don't remember when you learned this crucial fact, and (2) there is no sequence to general knowledge. A duck quacks, and that's it. *Episodic memory* contains specific knowledge that is time-tagged. Some theorists would restrict this type of memory to one's autobiographical knowledge. You know when things happened to you, and you can remember the sequence in which they happened. Other theorists put any historical knowledge in episodic memory; for example, it would be a good place to keep your knowledge about Abraham Lincoln's biography. *Procedural memory* is knowledge about how to do things. Some of this knowledge concerns output to the motor system; examples range from how to climb stairs to how to play the piano. Other procedural knowledge is more mental—for example, how to multiply numbers or how to make logical deductions.

Some psychologists argue that these three types of memory are merely aspects of a single long-term memory system (Anderson, 1985; Hintzman, 1986; McClelland & Rumelhart, 1985). Others say there are three distinct long-term memories—one for each type of memory (Tulving, 1985). Some evidence tends to support the view that there is just one long-term memory (McKoon, Ratcliff & Dell, 1985; Watkins & Kerkar, 1985), whereas other evidence supports the view of structurally separate memory systems. People with amnesia lose their episodic memories, for example, but have no semantic memory deficits (Graf & Schachter, 1987; Shimamura & Squire, 1989), and episodic but not semantic memory deteriorates as a person ages (Mitchell, 1989). In some cases of brain damage, the patient has no problem learning new procedural memories, but is unable to acquire new semantic or episodic memories (Squire, 1982). Finally, the pattern of blood flow to the brain is quite different in tasks requiring access to semantic versus episodic memories (Wood, Taylor, Penny & Stump, 1980). If there are three separate long-term memory analyzers, they are richly interconnected. Most of our general knowledge (semantic memory) is abstracted from specific experiences (episodic memory). On the other hand, it is difficult to remember specific experiences (episodic memory) if one doesn't understand (semantic memory) what is going on. For convenience, we shall treat semantic, episodic, and procedural memories as separate systems.

SEMANTIC MEMORY

The semantic analyzer is a vast dictionary in our minds. The meanings of all the concepts we know are stored in this dictionary. Encyclopedia might be a better description, since we keep all our general knowledge there. Activation of a semantic unit corresponds to experiencing the meaning of a concept. Semantic units are connected to spoken-word units, as well as to image units and to printed-word units. These connections are not always one-to-one affairs; many concepts cannot be expressed by a single word or image—for example, *The Middle Ages*. But simply saying that there are semantic units does not explain anything; to explain how we know the meanings of things, we have to consider how semantic units are connected to or defined by other semantic units. The knowledge is actually in the connections rather than in the units.

THE SEMANTIC ANALYZER

The structure of the semantic analyzer is similar to that of other analyzers (a diagram was shown in Figure 3–4). The idea is that units coding specific concepts (e.g., *mallard*) are connected to and defined by units coding basic-level concepts (e.g., *duck*). These are, in turn, connected to and defined by superordinate units (e.g., *bird*). Finally, the latter are connected to "super-superordinate" units (e.g., *animal*). This arrangement is consistent with the model suggested by Rosch et al. (1976).

The vertical excitatory connections in the semantic analyzer define cognitive units on one level in terms of units on other levels. Units on the same level should be related in a lateral inhibitory fashion. Lateral inhibitory connections code what a semantic unit *does not* mean. The lattice structure of the semantic analyzer provides a way of coding what a concept *is* (e.g., a *mallard* is a *duck* is a *bird*) and what it *is not* (e.g., a *mallard* is *not* a *merganser* or a *pintail duck*). This is only a bare skeleton for defining the meanings of things; we know more about a concept than what it is and what it is not.

Network Models of Semantic Memory

Hierarchical network theories of semantic memory let us flesh out our skeletal model. The most influential of these was first proposed by Collins and Quillian (1969) and later modified by Collins and Loftus (1975). In their theory, semantic memory is composed of a hierarchy of cognitive units and relations among the units. The units code concepts, and the relations are of different types, meaning that they are *labeled* in some way. One type of labeled relation codes superordinate relationships. These connections are what we have called vertical excitatory relations. Other types of relations code attributes, such as *has, can,* and so on. An example of a hypothetical portion of semantic memory was shown in Figure 1–1(b).

Stored Versus Inferred Knowledge

One attribute of the semantic memory system postulated by Collins and Loftus is its cognitive economy. Does a canary have wings? Of course it does. Have you stored the knowledge directly via the linkage *canary* $\xrightarrow{\text{has}}$ *wings*? If so, this is not a terribly efficient method, because you would have to have such a link between the cognitive unit coding every bird and the node for *wings*. It makes more sense to store this fact only once, with the concept of *bird*, rather than to store it for each of the birds you know about. Collins and Loftus say that this is the case; we do not really *know* that a canary has wings. We *know* that a *canary* $\xrightarrow{\text{is a}}$ *bird* and that a *bird* $\xrightarrow{\text{has}}$ *wings*. From this we *infer* that "a canary has wings." When asked if a canary has wings, you can reply that it certainly does; however, this knowledge is not represented in your semantic memory by a direct link between the two concepts.

If we must infer some knowledge (e.g., "a canary has wings") but other knowledge is stored directly (e.g., "a canary is yellow"), then the inferred knowledge should take longer to retrieve. Questions concerning knowledge that is stored directly (e.g., "a canary is yellow") should be answered faster than questions that require inference (e.g., "a canary has wings"). The longer the inferential chain, the longer it should take to answer the question. It should take longer to answer "true" to the statement "a canary has blood" than to the statement "a canary has wings." To answer the first question, you have to traverse three links: canary $\xrightarrow{\text{is a}}$ bird, bird $\xrightarrow{\text{is an}}$ animal, and animal $\xrightarrow{\text{has}}$ blood. To answer the second one, you only have to traverse two links: canary $\xrightarrow{\text{is a}}$ bird and bird $\xrightarrow{\text{has}}$ wings. Collins and Quillian (1969) found evidence to support these predictions. People were shown a large number of statements of the types described and had to respond "true" or "false" as soon as possible to each statement. The length of time to respond correctly to statements was as Collins and Quillian predicted. Reaction time was quickest when the relevant information was directly accessible from a semantic unit; when one intervening node had to be traversed to find the information, reaction time was longer. It was longer still for sentences that called for traversing two intervening nodes.

Spreading Activation

In their revision of the original theory, Collins and Loftus (1975) proposed a spreading activation theory of semantic memory. Thinking about a concept means activation of the node representing that concept. When a node in semantic memory is activated, the activation spreads along all the connections this unit has with other units. Subjectively, spread of activation corresponds to understanding the meaning of a concept. Objectively, spreading activation explains performance in question/answer experiments. When a statement such as "a canary has wings" is presented, activation spreads from the activated units—canary and wings—in all directions. In the case of a true sentence, this activation will converge; activation from canary will reach wings, and vice versa. The activation should not only converge; it should also resonate. Canary is connected to wings and vice versa, so a positive feedback loop is established, which should boost the activation of both nodes. When the activation passes some threshold, a person will respond that the statement is true. The further apart the nodes, the longer it takes to respond.

If activation spreads in semantic memory, then other kinds of priming effects should also be observed. Activating a superordinate unit—for example, bird—should automatically activate subordinate units such as canary, robin, duck, and so on. If we asked about a canary on one trial, people should be able to answer the question faster if they had just answered a question about a bird on the prior trial than if they had not. The reverse should also be true: activation of any subordinate should automatically activate the relevant superordinate. Rosch (1975) has done several experiments that provide clear evidence for this kind of vertical facilitation.

Finding Falsehood

Is a duck a toasted cheese sandwich? How do you know? It hardly seems reasonable to think that you know that a duck is not a toasted cheese sandwich by reference to directly stored knowledge. It does not seem likely that there is a *not* relation between the semantic units coding *duck* and *toasted cheese sandwich*. We would need to have a *not* connection between *duck* and virtually every other node in semantic memory. There are few things that a duck *is* or *has*, but there are millions of things that a duck *is not* and *does not have*. The same is true for all the other entries in semantic memory. It is not likely that every semantic unit would be connected with almost every other semantic unit by *not* relationships. Some kind of inference process must be used to disconfirm false sentences.

Contradictions

Glass and Holyoak (1975) considered this question. False statements involve contradictions. We can respond "false" as soon as we find the contradiction. Consider the statement "all ducks are geese." Both *duck* and *goose* are connected by *is a* relations to the superordinate node *bird*. According to the Glass and Holyoak theory, two nodes connected by the same relation to the same superordinate node are different things. Thus, *duck* $\xrightarrow{\text{is a}}$ *bird* and *goose* $\xrightarrow{\text{is a}}$ *bird* imply that a duck and a goose are *not* the same thing. This notion is diagrammed in Figure 8–1. The statement is contradictory, so we know it is false. Now consider the statement "all ducks are dogs." This is not true either, but the contradiction occurs at a deeper level: *duck* $\xrightarrow{\text{is a}}$ *bird* does not contradict *dog* $\xrightarrow{\text{is an}}$ *mammal*, but *bird* $\xrightarrow{\text{is a}}$ *animal* contradicts *mammal* $\xrightarrow{\text{is an}}$ *animal* (see Figure 8–1). Because the contradic-

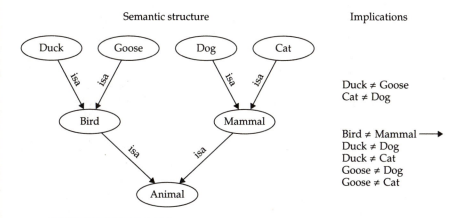

Semantic structure   Implications

Duck ≠ Goose
Cat ≠ Dog

Bird ≠ Mammal ⟶
Duck ≠ Dog
Duck ≠ Cat
Goose ≠ Dog
Goose ≠ Cat

F I G U R E   8 – 1   Illustration of Glass and Holyoak's contradiction theory of how we determine the falsehood of sentences.

tion is deeper, it should take longer for spreading activation to converge on the contradictory link. This is what Glass and Holyoak (1975) found, although they do not explain exactly *how* a contradiction is discovered. We can safely say, however, that contradictions do *not* produce resonance. In our example, *duck* and *goose* activate each other via the *bird* unit, but *duck* and *goose* also laterally inhibit each other, so no closed positive feedback loop is set up. Because there is no loop, activation does not reach the threshold needed to produce a response of "true."

Responding to Ridiculous Assertions

What about ridiculous false sentences, such as "A duck is a toasted cheese sandwich"? Such sentences can be disconfirmed even more quickly than highly contradictory statements such as "A duck is a goose" (Glass, Holyoak, & O'Dell, 1974). Probably the strategy is that we wait a decent—but very short—interval for activation to spread; if there is no convergence or resonance at all, then we respond "false." Thus, we can reject ridiculous assertions very quickly. On the other hand, if there is some convergence of activation, then an "evaluation" must take place to determine if the summation is contradictory. In other words, we have to wait for activation and inhibition to cancel each other out.

Salient Counterexamples

Glass and Holyoak (1975) also discuss some other rules for finding falsehood. Consider the statement "All birds are chickens," which can be disconfirmed by finding a single *salient counterexample*. The duck would suffice. Activating the *bird* unit causes spread of activation to units connected with it. One of these would be the *duck* unit. We have already established that a duck is not a goose; you can pursue this line of reasoning to establish that a duck is not a chicken, either. Thus, if a duck *is* a bird and it *is not* a chicken, it can't very well be that *all* birds are chickens. The idea is not that such ratiocination actually occurs, but that a salient counterexample leaps into the focus of attention because the unit coding the superordinate activates the unit coding the counterexample. Rather than resonance, we get a combat between lateral inhibition and activation. When the decent interval has passed, activation is too low, and thus the subject responds that the statement is false.

Holyoak and Glass (1975) found evidence that the longer it takes to find a salient counterexample, the longer it takes to disconfirm a false statement. It takes less time to disconfirm the statement "all generals are ducks" than to disconfirm the statement "all generals are dead." If, for example, when we think of generals, we might think first of Rommel. When the *general* node in the semantic analyzer is activated, activation automatically spreads to the nodes coding individual generals. As soon as one has thought of Rommel, he or she can disconfirm the first statement on the grounds that Rommel was not a duck. He was called the Desert Fox. If he were even remotely similar to a duck, I suppose that he would have been called the desert duck. So far, nothing has come to mind that will allow us to disconfirm the second statement, although that takes only a bit more time. By the time that instant has passed, we may have thought of Patton, Napoleon, and Grant, but they, like Rommel, are dead. Perhaps the semantic unit coding Colin Powell has by now been activated, so we can disconfirm the second sentence. General Powell is chairman of the Joint Chiefs of Staff, and to occupy that position, one must be alive.

STRENGTH OF EXCITATORY CONNECTIONS IN SEMANTIC MEMORY

When we turn our thoughts to generals, some come to mind before others—as is the case whenever one thinks of any category at all. Take a moment to write down the names of all the pieces of furniture you can think of. Sixty or so will be sufficient. Whether or not you were able to think of sixty pieces of furniture, you probably thought first of items such as *chair, sofa,* and *table.* These items came easily to mind. If you compare your list to those of others in your class, you will find that almost everyone else also thought of these items first. After a while you started to scrape the bottom of the barrel; you would be down to items such as *lamp* and *hassock.* In the end, you probably got to some rather questionable pieces of furniture, saying to yourself "technically speaking, a *rug* is furniture" or "very loosely speaking, a *telephone* is furniture."

When people are asked to list items that belong to a category, some items are produced by almost everyone. Usually these items are also produced first. Other items are produced by many people, and some are thought of by just a few. Items thus differ in the probability that the category name will elicit them (Battig & Montague, 1969). Rosch (1975) asked people to rate items from several categories as to how well the item represented their idea of the category. This kind of rating is called a *typicality* rating. For items from the furniture category, *chair* and *sofa* were tied for first place as being of highest typicality. Of the items Rosch used, *telephone* got the lowest typicality rating. The typicality ratings in Rosch's experiment correlated highly with the probability that an item was produced as an instance of the category by Battig and Montague's subjects.

What happens if we ask people to respond as to the truth or falsity of statements such as "a chair is furniture" or "a lamp is furniture"? The higher the typicality of the subordinate, the more quickly the question is answered (Rosch, 1973). The connections between a superordinate category node and its subordinate instance nodes must vary in strength. The higher the typicality of a subordinate, the stronger the connection between it and the superordinate node. More activation spreads along these strong connections, thus accounting for why we think of more typical instances before less typical instances. It also accounts for why we can more quickly verify that these more typical instances are category members.

LATERAL INHIBITION IN SEMANTIC MEMORY

Is there any evidence for lateral inhibition in the semantic analyzer? We expect units on the same level to laterally inhibit each other in proportion to their similarity. The inhibitory bonds have no content; their function is not so much to store information as to sharpen discrimination. There are also plenty of *excitatory* connections among units on the same level; examples are *cat* $\xrightarrow{\text{eats}}$ *mouse* or *cat* $\xrightarrow{\text{fears}}$ *dog*. These excitatory connections make lateral inhibition harder to demonstrate in the semantic analyzer than in other analyzers. In general, the extent of our knowledge about relationships between most coordinates (e.g., *duck* and *robin*) is that they are similar (connected to the same superordinate) but not identical. This nonidentity is the relation coded by lateral inhibitory connections.

Production of Category Instances

When people are asked to think of category instances, the instances are produced in bursts or "scallops" at a negatively accelerated rate (Gruenewald & Lockhead, 1980): a number of examples are produced, then there is a pause, then another set of examples is produced, and so on. Over time, the rate slows; the scalloping is consistent with the oscillatory pattern of activation in networks with inhibition (Wilson & Cowan, 1972), because networks with no inhibition *cannot* produce oscillations. The negatively accelerated rate of production is consistent with a gradual buildup of lateral inhibition. If there were no lateral inhibition, production would speed up rather than slow down across time. Each retrieved example would add to rather than subtract from activation of other category examples.

Brown (1981) reported a set of studies that examined buildup of lateral inhibition in semantic memory. In one study, the task was to produce examples of a category (e.g., a bird, the name of a state). On each trial, the subject was given a letter of the alphabet and asked to produce a category example beginning with that letter. Reaction time increased across trials, in contrast to the case for subjects who had to produce instances from *different* categories on each successive trial. In another experiment, subjects had to name pictures of common items from the same category. Again, reaction time increased across trials.

Brown's results suggest that lateral inhibition is fairly weak in semantic memory, so it takes time to build up—thus explaining why many studies have not found evidence for inhibition. In fact, facilitation is often found. In a lexical-decision task, if *cat* is the prime and *dog* is the target, the general finding is that reaction time to say that *dog* is an English word will be facilitated (Henderson, 1985). Brown's results suggest that inhibition rather than facilitation would be found if one used four or five primes from the same category.

Part-List Cues

Consider a task in which people are given a list of items belonging to several different categories to remember. At the time of recall, subjects are provided with an example of each category as a retrieval cue. Hypothetically, the units coding examples of a category laterally inhibit each other; therefore, using category examples as cues in a recall task should inhibit recall. The cues should activate cognitive units that laterally inhibit the cognitive units coding the words to be recalled—exactly as Slamecka (1969) and a number of subsequent experimenters have found. The more instances that are given as cues, the *worse* performance becomes (Roediger, 1973). Giving more examples causes more lateral inhibition, and more inhibition causes worse recall.

Mach Bands in Memory: Inhibition by Category Priming

Some evidence for lateral inhibition comes from a series of studies by Rosch (1975). The crucial finding was that category priming speeds up reaction times for decisions about high-typicality category instances but slows down reaction times for decisions about low-typicality category instances. People first saw a category prime: the name of the category was presented. They then had to judge whether two words were exactly the same (physically identical) or different. If the words were high-typicality members of the category, the category prime facilitated reaction time, whereas the category prime had an inhibitory effect on low-typicality members. This effect is hard to explain without postulating some lateral inhibition. No matter how weakly a subordinate unit is connected to a superordinate unit, a superordinate prime must *activate* the unit. We need lateral inhibition to explain why the category prime can slow down rather than speed up reaction time.

The lateral inhibition explanation of the effect Rosch found treats it as an analog of visual Mach bands (Martindale, 1981). If a light (cf. activated superordinate unit) is shined onto (cf. a superordinate-subordinate connection) an ommatidium (cf. subordinate unit) in the eye of the horseshoe crab, the result is that the ommatidium is activated, but surrounding ommatidia are inhibited (Ratliff, 1965). Recall from Chapter 2 that the ommatidia are interconnected in a lateral inhibitory network. Activation of a unit is the net product of the excitation and the inhibition impinging upon it. If very small amounts of light are allowed to shine on surrounding ommatidia (cf. units of low typicality), they will still be inhibited by the strongly illuminated ommatidium (cf. units of high typicality): excitation will be overwhelmed

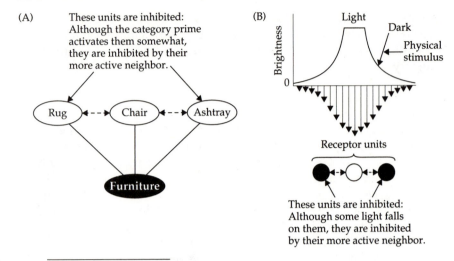

F I G U R E   8 – 2   The Rosch category-priming inhibitory effect (A) is similar to the reaction of a horseshoe crab's eye to a fuzzy patch of light (B). In both cases, weakly activated units are laterally inhibited by more strongly activated units.

by lateral inhibition. This is diagramed in Figure 8–2. The explanation of Rosch's results rests upon the idea that category primes activate nodes coding superordinate categories. These nodes in turn excite nodes coding subordinate instances of the category. The higher the typicality of an instance, the stronger the connection between it and the superordinate. Activation of a superordinate unit activates high-typicality instances *more* than low-typicality instances. The activated instance units laterally inhibit each other. The more activated a unit, the more it inhibits neighboring units. High-typicality units will be more activated, so they will inhibit low-typicality units more than they are inhibited by low-typicality instances. The net result for units coding low-typicality instances will be inhibition. Thus, reaction times to questions about these instances will be slowed down.

FORGETTING SEMANTIC INFORMATION

Material in semantic memory is relatively immune to forgetting. One reason is that much of it is overlearned. Every day we relearn the fact that people have noses. Another reason is that there is less interference in semantic memory than in episodic memory. You eat dinner every day, so what you ate when quickly becomes confounded. Once you have learned that ducks quack, there is not much to interfere with this knowledge. Nothing else quacks, and ducks do not do much besides quack. Until you started reading this book, you didn't have much occasion to think about ducks, and no thinking means no interference.

There is some forgetting in semantic memory. We certainly don't recall every fact we have ever learned. Bahrick (1984) extensively studied almost 800 peoples' memories for Spanish. Some of the subjects had just completed an introductory Spanish course, and others had taken a course anywhere from one to 50 years before. The subjects had not spoken, heard, or read Spanish since they had finished their courses. The last thing they expected was that Bahrick would show up and give them an extensive test on their knowledge of Spanish—but he did, and he found that some forgetting occurred for the first six years. After that, memory was fairly stable and remarkably good. He argued that memory for Spanish was in a "perma-store" just waiting to be recalled and apparently immune to forgetting.

EPISODIC MEMORY

According to Tulving (1985), *episodic memory* contains information such as what you did last weekend, what words were on the previous page of this book, and so on. In large part, episodic memory is a record of what has happened to *you*. It is also a perfect place to put other stories, too: the plots of novels, jokes, gossip about friends, and so on. Episodic memory is coded in the language of semantic memory. It differs from semantic memory, though, in that it keeps track of the temporal order of events. Semantic memory contains the basic elements of knowledge, and episodic memory is made up from these elements. Semantic memory is like a dictionary containing the meanings of all of the words and images you know. Episodic memory is like a novel or a movie that puts these concepts together in particular ways.

Reconstruction Versus Veridical Memories

It might seem simpler to propose that episodic memory consists of an archive of visual "pictures" and a "tape recording" of everything we have ever heard. Actually, the majority of people think memory is like this (Loftus & Loftus, 1980), but there are reasons to doubt this conception. The first thing I can remember in this life is the last thing many people in the 1940s saw before they died. I was staring straight into the face of an officer of the dreaded German SS. I was very young at the time. My mother was holding me in her arms while she talked to the man, so I got a very good look at the face of evil. His face is not in the memory, though. *I* am in the memory. The memory consists of the officer, his men behind him, and my mother holding me in her arms. This could not be an exact memory, because my mind did not leave my body to get a good snapshot of the event. But it is certainly a memory rather than a pure construction—that is, it is not just something that I was told happened to me. After I figured out how to talk, I asked about what was happening. People were surprised that I remembered the event, but confirmed that the memory was quite accurate. Clearly, the memory is a *reconstruction*.

If you sift through your own memories, you will find yourself in some of them—that is, the memories are not in the perspective from which you experienced the events. This suggests that the image we conjure up when we remember is a reconstruction. When an event occurs, we remember it as a proposition—an abstract description of the action in the event, who did what to whom, and so on. When we have to recall the event, we retrieve the

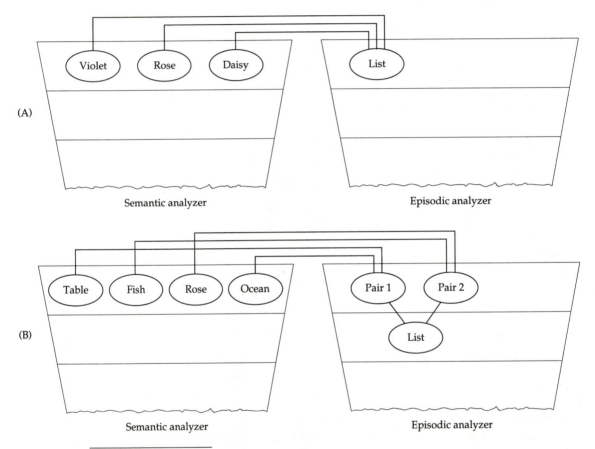

F I G U R E   8 – 3   Use of the episodic analyzer for simple memory tasks. (A) In a simple list-learning task, units coding each list item are hypothetically connected to an episodic chunking unit. (B) In a paired-associate list-learning task, each pair is hypothetically connected to an episodic chunking unit, then each chunking unit is connected to a deeper-level chunking unit coding the fact that the pair was on the list.

abstract proposition, then we *reconstruct* the memory on the basis of the proposition. This reconstruction often takes a visual form, but that does not mean the memory was stored this way; it may be that the abstract proposition coding the memory is merely expressed in a visual form.

STRUCTURE OF THE EPISODIC ANALYZER

The cognitive units at the highest level of the episodic analyzer are connected to units at the highest level of the semantic analyzer. These connections "define" the episodic units and can also be used to "realize" or express them. Cognitive units in the episodic analyzer can be connected to units in any of the other analyzers, although they seem to have an elective affinity for units in the semantic analyzer and for units in visual perceptual analyzers. A node is set up at least temporarily for each event that happens to a person. What good does this do? Episodic memory is good for remembering associations among cognitive units. Semantic memory contains the basic nodes. Learning a completely new word or concept requires constructing a new entry in semantic memory. All we have to worry about with episodic memory is making associations among these preexisting nodes.

Let us consider a few of the things people can remember. One of the simplest tasks used in laboratory experiments is to ask someone to remember a list of words—for example, *violet, rose, daisy, lily, iris.* Figure 8–3(a) shows how this might be done. The units in semantic memory coding these flowers are all connected to a unit in episodic memory. The episodic-memory unit codes the concept "words on the list I just learned." In a paired-associate task, one gives a subject a list of word pairs. The task is to remember which word goes with which. Figure 8–3(b) shows how this might be done. This time, chunking nodes representing the pairs are set up on the top layer of episodic memory. The list unit is on the next lower level. Why would we have a separate analyzer devoted to remembering lists of unrelated words? We do not have such an analyzer, but we can *use* episodic memory to perform such a task—although that could hardly be what it was designed for. In real life, we seldom have to remember lists of unrelated items, and when we do have to, we simply write them down.

EVENT UNITS

Any event can be coded as a proposition (Anderson, 1985). An event can be remembered as shown in Figure 8–4, which uses an event unit at the highest level of the episodic analyzer connected by labeled associations to units in semantic memory. An event can be thought of as the minimal chunk of experience, consisting of an action, an agent who performs the action, and so on. A proposition is an abstract description of an event. (We shall discuss this topic further in Chapter 9.) The episodic unit is a chunking node that

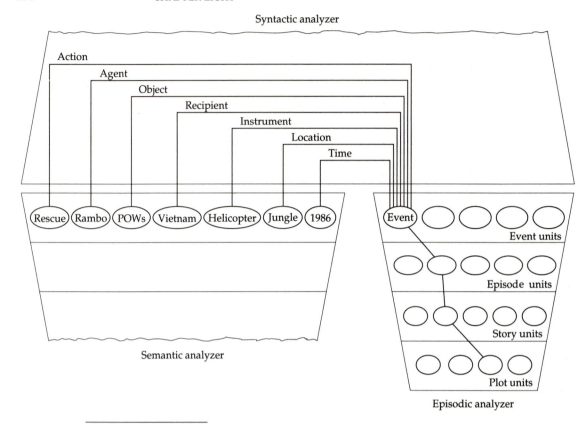

F I G U R E   8 – 4   Coding an event as a proposition. In this case, the event concerns Rambo rescuing POWs in the jungle from the Vietnamese in 1986 with the aid of a helicopter.

codes the proposition. There would be one propositional unit for each event that a person can remember. When one hears a sentence, syntactic analysis must occur before one knows the agent, object, and so on. The analysis takes place in a syntactic analyzer interposed between episodic and semantic memory. This analyzer attaches the "labels" to the associations between semantic and episodic memory, as we shall see in Chapter 9.

Episode, Story, and Plot Units

So far, we have accounted for only one level of the episodic analyzer. What units do we find on deeper levels? Episodic memory is designed to remember meaningful sequences of events. Another term for a meaningful series of events is a story. Mandler and Johnson (1977) suggest that events are chunked together by *episode units*. The most basic episode is one that chunks together three events: a *beginning event* that causes a *development event* that causes an *ending event*, also illustrated in Figure 8–4. Although he was talking about literary stories, Todorov (1971) suggested something similar: an episode is about an initial state of *equilibrium* that changes into a state of *disequilibrium*, which in turn changes to a final state of *equilibrium*. Rather than disequilibrium, we could use the term *mismatch*. Recall that mismatches attract attention, suggesting that we remember events that attract our attention. Recall also that if we do not attend to something, we seldom remember it. A story can have more than one episode, so we can place story units on the next lower level. It has been remarked that all stories are really just variants of a few basic plots, so we can put plot units on the bottom level. That is speculative, but I dislike blank spaces. I didn't forget all my Latin. Such a distaste is called *horror vacui*.

WHAT IS REMEMBERED?

Speaking of horror, what was I doing staring into the face of an SS officer? My mother was giving him orders. If you know anything about the SS, you are probably bracing yourself for a sad story about my mother. There were only a handful of women in Germany who would dare to give orders to *anyone* in the SS. Don't worry; my mother is alive and well. Here is the entire episode: she gave her orders to the officer, he relayed them to his men, and they carried them out. I could have described each of these three events by a lot of propositions rather than by only one. If these extra propositions didn't convey any extra information, your memory for the episode would be no better or no worse (Mandler & Johnson, 1977).

MY MEMORIES OF THE THIRD REICH

If we want to study memory, my own story is too short, which makes it too easy to remember. I'll provide some more details—all true, but that doesn't matter. Our interest is in your episodic memory rather than mine. The story may strike you as unpleasant, but keep in mind that I was very young, so I took no part in what I observed. I did not even understand most of what I saw and heard. In fact, my mother had authority to give orders not only to SS officers but also to Wehrmacht (regular army) officers. The Third Reich was a strange and bizarre place. The orders were always the same. They were always orders to kill: where to kill, what to kill, and how to kill—always orders to kill. That was the only kind of orders she had authority to give or wanted to give. Death had dominion there, but I did not know that. I remember only the jokes and laughter that came after the orders had been given. I did not understand the jokes, but I liked the laughter. My mother wanted her area cleansed of undesirable species; this was so the superior species could thrive. In some regions, this was done from the air with poison mist. In this case, it could not. The good and the bad were intermixed. The only thing to do was to send soldiers through the area and have them kill the undesirables. Undesirables were killed where they were found. It would have been a waste of time and effort to send them to the concentration camps. No one suggested it. Hundreds of thousands were killed. Nobody bothered to keep an accurate count. The job would be done only when all of the other species was killed. In the Third Reich, Jews and Russians were not considered to be humans; they belonged to another species altogether. In the future, some of them might be used as slaves. Because of the war, they had to be eliminated in some regions. Because of historical reasons, many Germans lived in Russia; they belonged to the master race and were citizens of the Reich. Russians and Jews had to be killed so these Germans and those who came after them could thrive. In any case, this is the way it was done in Russia. Because some of the soldiers were untrained, they had to be told exactly what to do. Many were not even Nazis. Some could not even tell the difference between a German and a Russian. It was said that they were like city boys who couldn't tell the difference between the crops and the weeds; they learned quickly though. Everyone thought that this job was reasonable and necessary, and no one felt the slightest guilt at all about it. The enlisted men did especially not like to do it. There was not much danger, because most of their enemy were unarmed. Many undesirables were very young. Of course, they had to be killed, too. Otherwise, they would grow up and reproduce someday. They were hacked to death. It would have been a waste of ammunition to shoot them. In fact, this was forbidden. It was tedious work. It is tedious to kill from dawn to dusk. That is why the enlisted men did not care for it. If the enlisted men let anything undesirable live, the officers screamed at them and often struck them. I remember seeing this. The soldier had to go back and kill whatever he had missed. The officers did little killing but, occasionally, they killed merely to pass the time. Everyone was just following orders. Nobody ever had the slightest regrets for any of this, and almost everyone was actually glad to be there. The only exceptions were a few SS men who would rather have been killing Americans instead.

Assimilation to Schemas

Now that you have read the story, we can make some observations about episodic memory. There is general agreement about several aspects of episodic memory. Verbatim memory for my story would be poor. You remember the gist rather than the exact wording (Alba & Hasher, 1983). When you hear or read a story, you assimilate it to a schema (Bartlett, 1932; Thorndyke, 1977). Another way of saying this is that you filter it through semantic memory. If you know nothing at all about World War II, the story may not have made much sense to you, so your memory for it would be poor. Bransford and Johnson (1973) had subjects read a story containing 18 ideas. The story was purposely vague. If people were not told what it was about before reading it, they recalled very few of these ideas. The story was really about how to wash clothes. If people were told this before the story, it made perfect sense. In this case, people remembered much more about it. I told you that my story was about cleansing the land. That should have helped you to remember it.

If you do know about World War II, you interpreted the story in light of this knowledge. If we tested your memory for the story, we would probably find that you had automatically filled in missing information that is plausible but that I didn't mention (Glenn, 1978). The longer we waited, the more likely this would be (Dooling and Christiansen, 1977). Did the officers like to kill Russians and Jews? I didn't mention anything about it, but you probably inferred that they must have. The longer we waited, the more likely that this inference would turn into a "memory." When you remember something, you integrate it with what is already in memory (Anderson, 1985). This can help recall, but it can also distort it. Did the Nazis do their job better? I didn't say so, but you may think so. Was my mother anti-Semitic? I didn't say so, but you probably think so (Sulin & Dooling, 1974).

People do not completely confuse real memories with inferences, reconstructions, and the like. Reder (1982) argues that in real life we do not attempt exact recall; we make plausible inferences. Did killing make any of the soldiers sick to their stomachs? Of course not. I didn't say that, but you made a plausible inference. After several days had passed, Reder found that people were faster at making a plausible inference than at saying whether a specific statement was or was not in a story such as mine.

EYEWITNESS TESTIMONY

Merely asking leading questions may distort your memory (Weinberg, Wadsworth, & Baron, 1983), and the longer we waited, the more likely this would be the case (Loftus, Miller, & Burns, 1978). Why were the children clubbed to death? Why were the soldiers always struck twice if they were remiss? It is likely that answers to these questions might be incorporated into the memory even though they were not in the original story.

Loftus (1979) has shown that how questions are asked can produce memory distortions with rather serious consequences. Eyewitness testimony is given considerable weight in a courtroom; however, because memory is fallible, so is eyewitness testimony. Say, for example, that you see a car go through an intersection without stopping. If you are asked how fast the car was going when it ran the stop sign, you may add a stop sign to your memory even if there wasn't really a stop sign in the original memory. Nazis are still being tried for war crimes 45 years after World War II ended. Would I be a reliable witness after all these years, or could my testimony be swayed by the way I was questioned? For reasons you will quickly discover, I would be a quite worthless witness.

DEMONSTRATION THAT MEMORY INVOLVES ASSIMILATION TO SCHEMAS

You may have misunderstood my story. I forgot to mention several details, and I also mentioned some completely irrelevant ones. Thus, you may have assimilated my story to the wrong schema. Step back and look at the big picture. If my mother had been in charge of genocide in Russia, am I likely to bring this up in the middle of a book on cognition? I admit that I led you down the garden path, so don't feel bad if you fell for it. My story is true enough, but it happened in Colorado. Perhaps the title of my story was rather misleading, but Hitler said, "Where a German is, there is Germany." This was not just idle chit-chat. So far as he was concerned, we *were* in the Third Reich. The Germans were prisoners of war. To help them pass the time, the army let us use them as farm laborers. The desirable species was sugar beets, and the undesirable ones were just what I said—weeds. One gets rid of them the same way in Russia as in America—people go into the fields and chop them out; it would be silly to shoot them. In any event, prisoners of war do not get to keep their guns. As for why my mother was giving the orders, that's simple enough. The Germans couldn't understand English, so she was telling them what to do in German. There were a couple of American soldiers hanging around with rifles to emphasize the desirability of getting rid of the weeds rather than wandering off in the direction of Berlin, but they weren't all that necessary. As I mentioned, almost everybody thought this was a fine place to be while the Third Reich declined and fell.

STORIES, MEMORY, AND AFFECT

People spend a lot of time reading out the contents of episodic memory. This is possibly what most people do most of the time when they are talking. These readouts are usually not indiscriminant core dumps beginning at an arbitrary time; rather, they are retrievals of memories that fit deeper-level story or plot schemas such as "my memories of the Third Reich," "embarrassing events occurring on dates," and so on. People spend a lot of time telling each other stories. Memory retrieval in real life is quite different from memory retrieval in the laboratory.

Here is another story: my pen just ran out of ink. I filled it. I resumed writing. This is quite true. My word processor is a fountain pen. The story has beginning, middle, and end events. Would you care to hear an expanded version? Shall I remember this for long? The answer to both questions is, of course, no. Unless an episode arouses some affect or interest, people do not even consider it to be a story (Brewer & Lichtenstein, 1982). They are not likely to remember the episode very well either. When we share our memories with others, we try to make a good story.

Brewer and Lichtenstein (1982) developed a structural-affect theory of stories. Remember, only a narrative that involves some affect is viewed as a story, which puts some restrictions on content. Ink doesn't cut it; blood does. According to Brewer, a story involves a discrepancy between event structure and discourse structure. *Event structure* is the sequence of events as they actually occurred, whereas *discourse structure* is the order in which the events are told. Three main devices can be used to make memories into stories. *Surprise* involves withholding something in the event structure. In my Third Reich story, I withheld several crucial events: where the story happened, and what was actually being done. *Suspense* involves relating a crucial event early on and not explaining the outcome until later. In the short version of my story, my mother's giving orders to the SS would have led to suspense, but I ruined the suspense by immediately telling the outcome. *Curiosity* involves letting the reader know that something is being withheld but not giving the information. I used that technique, too. Who was my mother? Why didn't she get shot in Siberia for pulling such a stunt? I don't have the right kind of name to be on the Eastern Front watching Mom and the SS kill Russians. All these details were supposed to make you curious.

MEMORY FOR SEQUENTIAL ORDER

Though we occasionally get confused, we remember the sequential order of events. If we could not, we should be unable to remember our own life histories. Estes (1972) proposed a lateral inhibition theory of memory for serial

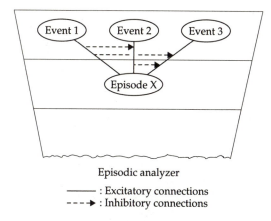

FIGURE 8 – 5 Estes's (1972) asymmetrical inhibition model of memory for serial order applied to episodic memory.

order. The notion is that asymmetrical lateral inhibitory connections allow us to code the temporal relations among events. As shown in Figure 8–5, a deeper-level chunking node in episodic memory is connected in an excitatory fashion with a set of units coding events. Suppose it is necessary to recall the events in a specific order, as it would be if they were components of an episode. Activating the episode node activates all the event units; however, the unit coding each event laterally inhibits units coding all later events, as shown in Figure 8–5. Thus, when the episode node is activated, the unit coding Events 1, 2, and 3 are activated. The unit coding Event 1, however, inhibits the units coding Events 2 and 3, with the result that only Event 1 is available to consciousness. After recalling it, activation of the unit coding Event 1 is automatically squelched. Squelching the activation of Event 1 causes disinhibition of the unit coding Event 2. Event 2 is then recalled, and the unit coding it is deactivated, allowing recall of Event 3. This system

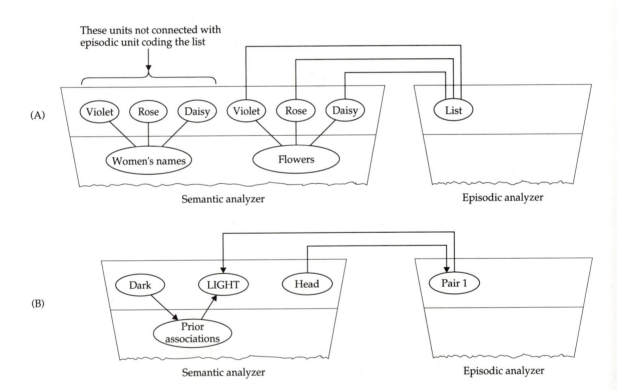

F I G U R E 8 – 6 Encoding specificity. (A) shows an example with list learning: the retrieval cue, "women's names," will be ineffective if a person thought of the list of words as names of flowers during learning. (B) shows an example in paired-associate learning: only "head" is an effective retrieval cue for Pair 1, even though "dark" is strongly associated with "light" because of prior learning.

works perfectly only if all the event nodes are equally strong. If a later one is especially strong (interesting, striking, or whatever), it may not be inhibited enough; therefore, it will become activated too early. This situation happens all the time. When one has some important news, he or she tells the good part first and then goes back and fills in what led up to the event. Someone who is good at telling stories can do the reverse—leave out earlier events to build curiosity or evoke surprise.

ENCODING SPECIFICITY

Do you recall the example of remembering a list of women's names? If not, you may be a victim of encoding specificity (Tulving, 1985). A different retrieval cue may help. Do you recall the example of remembering a list of flowers? The list was composed of *violet, rose, daisy, lily*. The problem is shown in Figure 8–6(a). Because of encoding specificity, using "a list of women's names" as a retrieval cue does not help in recall.

The encoding specificity principle means that what is understood at the time of input is what is stored in episodic memory (Tulving & Thomson, 1973). When people are taught a list of words in an experiment, they remember not just the list but the list plus context. If they are taught the list in one room and tested in another room, they remember it less well than if they are tested in the same room (Smith, Glenberg, & Bjork, 1978). The greater the difference in context, the greater this effect is. Godden and Baddeley (1975) taught some scuba divers a list of words 20 feet under the ocean; other divers learned the list on the shore. Recall was best if the scuba divers were tested in the situation in which they learned the list. *State-dependent learning* is related to encoding specificity. If one learns something while smoking marijuana, for example, he will remember it better when he is smoking marijuana than when he is not (Eich, Weingartner, Stillman, & Gillin, 1975).

Thomson and Tulving (1970) taught people a number of lists of words under three conditions:

1. Strong cues (highly associated words) accompanied each list word during learning (e.g., dark-*light*).
2. Weak cues (weakly associated words) accompanied each list word (e.g., head-*light*).
3. No cues accompanied each list word.

Whichever type of cue was present at input was also present at the time of recall. On a crucial trial, the subjects were given a different set of cues at the time of recall than they had been given at the time of learning. Giving strong cues at the time of recall did *not* help at all if weak cues had been present during learning. Recall in this condition was no better than in the control condition where no cues were given at the time of recall.

Figure 8–6(b) shows how encoding specificity might work. Learning the pair head-*light* consists of establishing the association shown in the figure. Only presentation of the word "head" allows retrieval of the node marked Pair 1. Presentation of the word "dark" should activate the cognitive unit coding "light" because of their prior association. Maybe it does, but it is evidently Pair 1 (head-*light*) that was learned and stored in episodic memory. The encoding specificity principle says that it is not just the list words that are stored in episodic memory, but the list words in the experimental context. It is not "light" that is stored in episodic memory, but "light" in the context of "head." Thus, "light" in the context of "dark" is not recognized as being on the list. If this is correct, even showing a subject the word *light* should not lead it to be recognized as being on the list. That sounds farfetched, but it is exactly what happens.

Flexner and Tulving (1978) report a number of experiments that demonstrate encoding specificity. People first learned a list of paired associates (e.g., *head-light*). Then they were given a set of words that included all the response words on the paired-associate list. The subjects were asked to go through the set and circle the words they recognized as being on the original list. They recognized very few of the words. Then, a recall test was given. The first member of each pair on the original list was presented, and the subject had to give the correct response. This time, most of the response words were correctly recalled, including many of the same words people had just failed to recognize!

This result is quite odd, because a recognition test is usually much easier than a recall test. As Flexner and Tulving (1978) put it, "Why should a perfectly normal and intelligent person not be able to recognize a familiar word that he has studied only a short time before and about whose presence in the list he is perfectly well aware as judged by his ability to produce it in response to the list cue?" It is difficult to explain these findings with the theory that episodic memory consists merely of "marking" units in semantic memory. If that were the case, people should instantly recognize list words when they are shown to them. Tulving and Thompson (1973) argue that encoding specificity is evidence that episodic memory is a system separate from semantic memory.

PROCEDURAL KNOWLEDGE AND ACTION

Procedural knowledge may be vaguely described as knowledge about how to do things. A procedure can be a motor skill such as walking or climbing stairs, or it can involve some thought and some action, such as playing a sonata on a piano. It can also be purely mental, such as solving logic problems. Lashley (1958) argued that the mechanisms of thought and action are identical "save for the lack of facilitation of the final motor path" in the case of thought. If Lashley is correct, then it makes sense to put knowledge about all these procedures in the same analyzer.

THE STRUCTURE OF ACTION

Miller, Galanter, and Pribram (1960) suggest that the basic building block of action is the feedback loop, which allows not only "left-to-right" sequencing but also hierarchical control. These researchers call the basic unit of action the TOTE (Test-Operate-Test-Exit) unit; they say that "action is initiated by an ʻincongruity' between the state of the organism and the state that is being tested for." A TOTE unit is shown in Figure 8–7: we test for the presence of some desired goal or state of affairs. If it is present (percept and goal match), we "exit" from the test; if it is not present (percept and the goal mismatch), then we operate (perform some action). After this operation is performed, control returns to the test unit. Control returns to the test unit so that we can determine if the goal has been met. Another test takes place for a congruity or match between the desired goal and the present state of affairs. If there is a match, control exits from the test unit, and if there is a mismatch, the operation is performed again.

Operation of a TOTE unit may be illustrated with the spine-tingling procedure of hammering a nail into a board. The goal is to have the nail flush with the board. We test for this goal; if the nail is flush, we can exit. If it is not flush, then we must perform the hammering operation. After hitting the nail with the hammer, control passes back to the test unit—that is, we check to see whether the nail is flush. If it is, we exit; if it is not, we hammer again. Sequencing in a TOTE unit involves feedback: we check the results of an action rather than merely perform the action. Control passes back and forth between perceptual and operational units.

Miller et al. (1960) locate the origin of action in a mismatch between a mental model (the goal) and perceptual input, which is exactly what Grossberg (1988a) and Sokolov (1963) say causes arousal and focused attention (see Chapter 5) and what Rescorla (1988) says causes learning (see Chapter 7). We saw earlier in this chapter that a mismatch is the stuff of which stories are made. A mismatch between internally activated cognitive units (goals, expectations, or desires) and externally activated cognitive units (percepts) leads to arousal and attention, resulting in action aimed at reducing the mismatch. There are two ways to remove a mismatch. Grossberg, Rescorla, and Sokolov talked about mental actions (building a new model) to bring about a match: we fix our mind so it accords with reality. Miller et al. talk about overt actions undertaken to bring about a match: if we don't like reality, we can try to fix the world so that it matches our mental model.

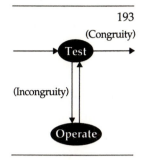

F I G U R E 8 – 7 A TOTE (Test-Operate-Test-Exit) unit. (From G. A. Miller, E. Galanter, and K. H. Pribram [1960]. *Plans and the structure of behavior*, p. 26. Copyright © Holt, Rinehart, & Winston. Reprinted by permission.)

The Action System

Propositional Nature of Action

Shallice (1978) argues that there are cognitive units that correspond to general actions such as hammering. He says that, in addition to perceptual, conceptual, and motor systems, the brain contains an action system. The action units in this system control general procedures such as hammering, and there must be at least one action unit for each action we can perform. Shallice says there would have to be one action unit for each action that can be described by a verb referring to an intentional act (e.g., *eating, walking, throwing, handing,* etc.). Input to action units comes from cognitive units in perceptual and conceptual analyzers: the hammering unit will not be activated unless a hammer, nails, and a board are actually present. An action unit along with its inputs may be seen as coding a proposition: the action unit defines the action (e.g., hammering); and the inputs define the components of the proposition, such as instrument (e.g., hammer), recipient (e.g., nail), location (e.g., board), and so on.

Executive Ignorance

Output from action units goes to the motor system, which controls the exact details of the action in question. The details include the specific muscular contractions necessary to execute the action. Shallice holds that the action system follows a principle of "executive ignorance": the action unit does not know about or control the details of an action—somewhat as a powerful business executive might tell a subordinate to build a factory in a country where there is cheap labor. The executive does not want to know about or be bothered with petty details of exactly how or where this factory gets built. The idea of executive ignorance corresponds well with conscious experience: we are conscious of deciding to execute an action, but we are not conscious of the details. Look at some object in front of you and decide to pick it up. You are conscious of this decision. The decision corresponds to activation of an action unit. The next thing you know, you have picked up the object, with no consciousness of whatever processes intervened between activation of the action unit and the motor behavior brought about by this activation. We consciously decide to pick something up, but we do not consciously pose ourselves questions such as "Is the velocity of my hand decelerating at the proper rate?" The complex details of action are taken care of by the motor system completely outside conscious awareness.

Sensorimotor Memories

What is learned and remembered when one learns how to execute a procedure is an abstract proposition rather than concrete sensory and motor details. Try writing something with your nonpreferred hand, or try writing with the pen between your teeth. You may not be skillful at these tasks, but you can certainly do them. If your memories for how to write were specific, you would be *completely* unable to write in unusual ways. You have learned an abstract procedure for writing that can be *realized* in a variety of ways. This abstractness of learning seems to be generally true of motor behavior.

A rat in a maze learns an abstract proposition about getting to the goal box; it does *not* learn specific motor responses. Say that one trains a male rat to run through a maze to get to a rat singles bar where there are some interested lady rats. What would happen if the maze were flooded with water? If the rat had learned a specific set of motor responses, it would be at a complete loss. If it had learned the general "idea" of how to get to the goal box, it could express this idea just as well by swimming as by running. What does the rat do? It swims (MacFarlane, 1930). Gleitman (1955) carried this line of research to its logical conclusion: he put his rats in little "limousines" that carried them through mazes. At the goal box, the rats were given a reward that they seemed to enjoy quite thoroughly. What did they do when placed in the maze with no limousine? The same thing you would do—they walked to the goal box.

Structure of the Action System

Shallice's contention that the action system is hierarchically arranged suggests that it is a multilayered system like the other analyzers we have discussed. At the top level are the action units that receive input from perceptual or conceptual units and send output to motor units. They are also connected in an excitatory fashion with units at the next lower level of the action system. These deeper-level units code more general plans of action.

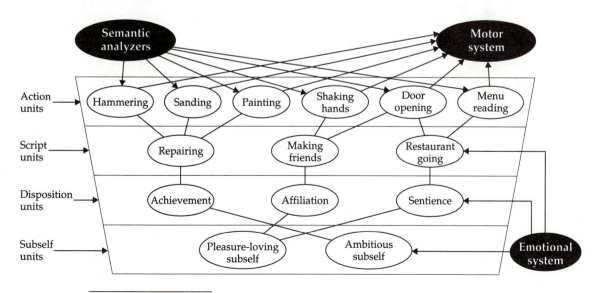

F I G U R E 8 – 8 The action system.

In Figure 8–8, various units—such as hammering, painting, sanding, and so on—are connected to a deeper unit labeled *repairing*. Other units at this deeper level code other general categories of action such as *making friends*, *going to a restaurant*, and so on. Schank and Abelson (1977) refer to such sequences of actions as *scripts*.

In elaborating Shallice's theory of the action system, we can postulate several deeper levels (Martindale, 1980). Below the level of script units is a layer of disposition units. Each disposition unit is connected to a large number of script units. Murray's (1938) list of 20 or so basic motives might be seen as an approximation of the "alphabet" of the action system. An example of a disposition unit would be what Murray called the *need for achievement*. The disposition unit coding achievement is strongly connected to scripts involving achievement (e.g., *repairing*) and less strongly connected or not at all connected to scripts that do not involve achievement (e.g., *going to a restaurant*).

Hypothetically, at the deepest level of the action system are subself units, the "distinctive features" of the action system, each of which is connected to a set of dispositional units. The reason for postulating such units has to do with observations pertinent to *social psychology* (people often exhibit quite different "selves" in different situations), *personality psychology* (people sometimes exhibit sudden conversions from one coherent self to another), and *abnormal psychology* (patients sometimes exhibit multiple personalities). You have probably noticed that one part of you sometimes carries on a covert running commentary about what another part of you is doing, especially when you find yourself in an unusual and uncomfortable situation where your usual subself must turn over control of behavior to an unpracticed and "alien" subself. As you politely carry on about your rich uncle George's prize rose bushes, a partially inhibited subself gives you its comments on your obsequious, self-serving hypocrisy. The partially inhibited unit can produce covert or inner speech. Fortunately for you, only the dominant subself is activated enough to produce overt speech or action. This is consistent with the idea of a set of subselves existing in a lateral inhibitory network.

The action system is a "bureaucracy" for controlling behavior. The currently active subself activates a set of disposition units, which activate a set of script units. The script units activate a set of action units. This vertical activation is subjectively felt as intention, volition, or will. Unless stimuli are very strong or actions are extremely habitual, action units need *both* vertical activation from deeper-level units in the action system as well as stimulus input from other analyzers before they become activated enough to unleash the behavior they control. One function of the vertical excitation is to assure that one does not do things out of character. If vertical excitation were not present, behavior would be completely under the control of external stimuli: a stimulus would activate an action unit, and this unit would

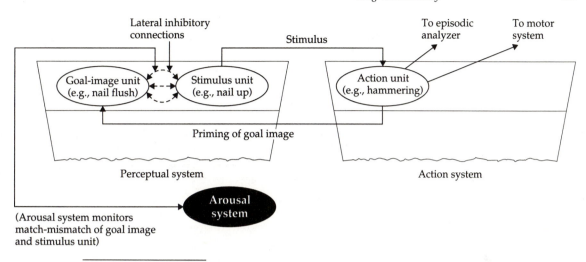

FIGURE 8–9 Relationships among action units and a dipole coding stimulus and goal image.

unleash the behavior it controlled. The vertical structure of the action system gives one at least some say in things; it gives the currently activated subself, disposition, and script units some control over action.

Connections to Other Analyzers

Besides sending output to the motor system, the action system must also send outputs back to perceptual and conceptual analyzers. As the TOTE model suggests, action units are intimately connected with "test" or goal units. As shown in Figure 8–9, an action unit must activate perceptual units coding its expected outcome. This priming serves to keep attention focused on relevant perceptual inputs. Partial activation makes it likely that the units will be more activated by incoming stimuli than units coding stimuli not relevant to the task at hand. Without priming, we would be continually distracted—any stimulus more intense than the one involved in ongoing activity would seize attention.

An action is often intended to transform a perceptual state (e.g., *nail up*) into its opposite (e.g., *nail flush*). The percept (*nail up*) that initiates an act is the opposite of the percept coding the goal state (*nail down*). It is not unreasonable to suppose that full achievement of a goal state causes full excitation of the unit coding it (*nail down*). This unit inhibits whatever unit (*nail up*) initiated action. As shown in Figure 8–9, gated dipole units would be useful in this situation. Failure to achieve the goal leads to reactivation of the unit initiating the action (*nail up*), causing reactivation of the action unit. There is an opponent-process relation between units coding the stimuli eliciting actions and the stimuli coding the expected effects of these actions. Inhibition between these opposing units may be important in attending to the mismatch that leads to action in the first place.

AVALANCHE CIRCUITS

Most scripts and procedures must be executed in a specific serial order. When you go to a restaurant, you are not supposed to ask for the check before you order. Playing a sonata on the piano sounds much better if one plays the notes in the right order. These facts are obvious, but it is not obvious how one stores knowledge about serial order and executes actions in the correct order. We can adapt Estes's (1972) theory of memory for serial order to explain this (see Figure 8–5). Consider going to a restaurant. The script unit is activated and activates all the component action units. They are connected in an asymmetrical lateral inhibitory manner. Until the first act is emitted, it inhibits subsequent actions. After it is emitted, the unit coding the first act is deactivated, and the second action unit is now partially activated. When stimulus conditions are right, the second unit will be fully activated and unleash whatever motor behavior it controls. When one is ready to order a meal, the ordering-unit is partially activated; it does not become fully activated unless the appropriate stimulus (a waiter or waitress) is present.

Serial order information is not closely coupled to speed of execution (Grossberg, 1978a). When you go to a restaurant, you can execute the script quickly or slowly. Say you go because you are hungry. You will attempt to get to the eating part of the script as fast as possible. After you have eaten a bit, you are not as hungry. If your companion is interesting, you may slow down or interrupt the restaurant script so that you can interweave or interpolate the chatting script—the relative strength of the deeper-level disposition units has changed. If you are starving, you eat fast; if you are socializing, you eat more slowly or not at all.

Once you have started to execute a script, you do not necessarily have to finish it. Say you are chatting in a restaurant and trying to keep the waiter from dumping your dessert on top of your half-finished meal when it is brought to your attention that the restaurant is burning down. In such a case, one would probably not finish the meal and pay the bill before fleeing, because being surrounded by flames should strongly activate the flee-burning-building script. The unit coding this script does two things: first, it laterally inhibits other script units (explaining why you don't finish your meal); second, it activates the action units with which it is connected (explaining how you get out of the restaurant). Of course, if you panic under fire, you may make a mess of the script—you may freeze, try to execute actions in the wrong order, and so on. In such cases, activation overwhelms inhibition or vice versa. Most of us do not have a well learned flee-burning-building script, so it must be pieced together in the heat of the moment. Because panic is not the optimal situation for innovation, your neural network may malfunction; consequently, you may not get out of the restaurant.

SUMMARY AND CONCLUSIONS

There are three types of long-term memory. Semantic memory contains general knowledge. Episodic memory contains specific memories arranged in temporal order; in large part, it contains memories of what has happened to a person. Procedural memory contains knowledge about how to do things—anything from how to solve logical syllogisms to how to climb stairs. These three types of memories may reside in three separate analyzers.

Semantic memory is arranged hierarchically. The vertical connections contain information about subordinate-superordinate relationships. Lateral inhibitory connections allow discrimination; without them, we might confuse ducks and geese. Spread of activation and inhibition in semantic memory allows us to retrieve meanings. True statements set up resonant feedback loops—that is how we know that ducks quack. False statements do not set up such resonance, accounting for how we know that a duck is not a toasted cheese sandwich.

Episodic memory is also hierarchically arranged. Event units code specific events in the form of propositions. They are connected to episode units. The connections allow us to recall which events occurred together. Lateral inhibition allows us to remember the sequential order of events. When we retrieve an episodic memory, it sometimes looks like a snapshot of the past, but episodic memories are probably reconstructions. Some peculiarities of the "snapshots" make us pretty sure of that. When we establish episodic memories, we assimilate them to schemas—we filter the events through semantic memory. This process is usually quite helpful, but can cause problems if we use the wrong schema, as the story about the people working in a field was meant to demonstrate. If one picks the wrong schema, the wrong thing will be remembered.

Procedural knowledge is our memory for how to behave. We learn general actions rather than specific behaviors, and the actions are organized into scripts. An example is the script for what to do at a restaurant. An action is usually emitted only if a stimulus elicits it and the action unit is partially activated by deeper-level script or disposition units—unless both sources of activation were necessary, we would blindly follow any order we were given. When we become conditioned, we adjust our mental model of the world to fit reality. The action system allows us to turn the tables: when we act, we adjust reality to fit our mental model of the world.

Language

THE POWER OF LANGUAGE

Language accounts for virtually everything mankind has accomplished. Without it, we would still be wandering around grunting and grubbing for roots and berries. Someone who thought of an innovation would not have been able to tell anyone else. Knowledge would not have accumulated, and we would not be masters of the earth. Animals are unaware that we are in charge; because they have no language, we can't explain this to them. Nobody ever tried to stop a rabbit from crossing a national border, because it would not understand. It doesn't understand about paying taxes or joining the army, either. There is, or course, a down side to language and civilization.

Language is powerful. Its power can be direct, as in a military order, but it can also be indirect. Some feminists argue that the English language perpetuates sexism; for example, "one . . . he" constructions (e.g., "If one has a pen, he has power") imply that the only people worth talking about are men. Feminists insist that we ought to change the language to fix these problems. Much of the opposition to their suggestions has nothing to do with sexism but comes from purists of both sexes who say that the suggested changes are awkward or that they violate the rules of "the Queen's English." Because of its power, we take an interest in language.

THE GLORY OF LANGUAGE, WITH A NOTE ON ITS ORIGIN

If you have ever been called a "Young Turk," you probably understood what was meant, but you may not have known that this phrase is a *dead metaphor*—one that used to be a figure of speech but is now just a phrase with a specific meaning. The Young Turks were a bunch of young people who lived in Turkey. In the early part of the century, Turkey was ruled by a sultan who seemed unaware that the date was 1920 rather than 1620. Led by Kemal Atatürk, the Young Turks took over. They started to modernize and fix everything, including the Turkish language (Heyd, 1954). Turkish was filled with words borrowed from Arabic and Persian, and the Young Turks wanted to eliminate foreign words, because pure Turkish should be the language of Turkey. Removing Arabic or Persian words from English would not be difficult, but eliminating them from Turkish would be like trying to rid English of words of French derivation—almost half our words would change.

Atatürk didn't realize how interested people are in language. He had opened a Pandora's box. Every day, Turkish newspapers printed lists of words derived from Arabic or Persian (Heyd, 1954), and good neologisms derived from Turkish were invited. They poured in. Fixing the language became a national obsession, and everyone had a different opinion. Family members argued about what to call tables and chairs. A national committee picked winning words, and newspapers were required to print at least two articles every day in pure Turkish—although no one knew what the new, pure Turkish words meant. Rather than becoming purified, the Turkish language was heading toward chaos.

Several fortunate discoveries were made. Many supposedly offensive words had really been Turkish all along: Arabic had borrowed them from Turkish, and they were later borrowed back from Arabic. The second discovery was more stupendous. We wouldn't have civilization without language. Where did civilization begin? In central Asia. Who lived there at the dawn of time? The Turks! That meant that Turkish was the *Ursprache*—the first language from which all other languages are derived. It was thus pointless to purge Turkish of "foreign" words, because these words had all been borrowed from Turkish in the first place. Had it not been for the Turks, there would have been no other languages. This discovery is called the *Sun theory* of the origin of language—because the first word uttered by a human being was doubtless uttered by a Turk, who looked up at the sun and said "Ah." This theory does not seem at all plausible to linguists, who bring up picky objections based upon data and evidence. We don't know if Kemal Atatürk really thought the Sun theory was plausible, because we have only his verbal behavior to go on: he proclaimed it a brilliant discovery. All the foreign words could stay, because they were really Turkish anyway. Most Turks readily agreed that this was at least a convenient theory; once again, they knew the words for tables and chairs. And now that we know where language come from, we can ask what it is.

LANGUAGE VERSUS COMMUNICATION

WHAT IS LANGUAGE?

Language allows people to communicate with one another. But we cannot define language simply as a mechanism for communication, because animals communicate with each other. Do they do so by means of language? It would seem not, if we look at what is involved in human language. According to linguists, language is defined by several features (Hockett, 1960):

1. Language is composed of *arbitrary semantic units*. In spoken language, the semantic units are words. With a few exceptions, there is no connection between the sound and sense of words. We can call a duck a duck or a *canard* or a glog; as long as everyone agrees, it doesn't matter. Arbitrary signs with a specific meaning do not differentiate language from animal communication. Squirrels have several "words" for the concept of "predator in the neighborhood" (Horwich, 1972). Vigorous tail flicking means minimal danger (e.g., a kitten); a loud chucking sound means maximal danger (e.g., a predatory cat or any dog); a throaty growl means an unfriendly squirrel. These signs are arbitrary. Ravens have an even larger vocabulary. They even have specific names for their own mates (Tinbergen, 1951). The relationship between sound and sense is also arbitrary in raven talk.

2. The units of languages are *discrete*. Words are obviously discrete, whereas a squirrel's chucking sound is not discrete but continuous. Loudness and length of the chucking sound give information about the degree of danger. Honeybees can tell each other where to find honey by doing a "dance" (von Frisch, 1967). The angle at which they perform the dance signals the angle with respect to the sun in which to fly to find the pollen. Bees don't carry the angle out to many decimal points, but the angle of the dance is continuously variable.

3. Language has what Hockett (1960) called *displacement*. It does not have to be elicited by a stimulus that is present. I can talk about Turkey

more or less out of the blue, but a squirrel has no way of saying "Imagine a world without dogs."

4. Language has *productivity*. It allows us to produce novel utterances. If you make a sentence long or odd enough, you can be pretty sure no one has ever said it before. Animal communication systems do not allow this, because their vocabulary is too limited. Technically, animal communication that is continuous rather than discrete can be productive: ants tell other ants where food is by marking the path with a pheromone or scent trail (Wilson, 1975)—and one could go so far as to say that there are an infinite number of lengths, directions, and places to put these trails.

5. Language is *iterative* and *recursive*. By iterative, we mean that, at least in theory, a sentence could go on forever. One can join two sentences into one by leaving out the period and sticking in "and," or "while," or something, and one could keep on joining sentences together forever. By recursive, we mean that (again, in theory) one can make an infinitely long sentence by embedding clauses in it; for example:

The duck shot the hunter.

The duck, who had a gun, shot the hunter.

Hunters do not fear such a scenario because ducks have no language. No animals do. No animal communicative system allows iteration or recursion. Even the first sentence above involved iteration in that several words were strung together. Ducks have a word for danger and a word for duck, but they can not combine them to say anything new.

Animals do not have languages, but perhaps they could learn language. It would be best to test this idea with apes, since they are more intelligent than other animals. Several experimenters have unsuccessfully tried to teach chimpanzees to talk (Kellogg & Kellogg, 1933). The efforts were doomed to failure, because apes' vocal tracts do not allow production of speech sounds (Lenneberg, 1967). Later experimenters tried to teach language to chimpanzees using sign language (Gardner & Gardner, 1969) or colored shapes (Premack & Premack, 1983). It seemed to the experimenters that the apes did learn language, but others disagreed. The experimenters may have conditioned the apes inadvertently to make responses that made it seem as if they had learned language. Linguistic chimps do pretty well if they are tested by their trainers, but they don't do nearly so well if they are tested by a stranger who does not know the sign system being used (Tartter, 1986). Such a person cannot give any subtle reinforcements. B. F. Skinner was dubious about these chimpanzee experiments. He conditioned pigeons to do the same kinds of things that linguistic apes can do and concluded that you can say that apes can learn language if you want to, but then you have to say that pigeons can, too (Epstein, Lanza, & Skinner, 1980). Nobody is willing to say that. There is no conclusive evidence that chimpanzees can learn language (Sebeok, 1984).

GRAMMAR

OVERVIEW

A grammar has three parts: *syntax*, *semantics*, and *realization rules* (Jakobson, 1956). Syntax describes the rules for how to put the units words in a language together. Semantics describes the meanings of the units, as we learned in the last chapter. Realization rules describe the rules for expressing the units. In the case of spoken language, this part of grammar is called *phonology*, which describes the rules for putting speech sounds together.

There are several types of grammar. Prescriptive grammar (that which is taught in high school) tells what some of the rules are supposed to be; one follows these rules or is branded a barbarian. Of course, if you follow some of the more obscure rules, most people won't understand what you are talking about. Descriptive grammar is what it sounds like: it describes the rules people in a speech community actually follow. A complete grammar of English will never be written, because the rules are so complicated that they will never all be discovered, let alone written down (compare Chomsky & Halle, 1968). How do we speak, then? As it is seemingly not by reference to explicit rules, the rules must be known *implicitly.* Everyone agrees that speakers of a language cannot explicitly state most of the rules of the language; for example, speakers of English consistently use the simple present tense (e.g., "I walk") and the present progressive tense (e.g., "I am walking") in different contexts. Although we "know" the rule, as evidenced by the fact that we follow it perfectly, you will probably agree that most of us could not even begin to explain it. Some theorists argue that we *do* know explicit rules that are stored as propositions (e.g., Pinker, 1984). The problem is that these propositions are in an analyzer that we can't consciously access. A great deal of slow and unconscious thought would be needed to explain how the rules are applied. The alternative view is that the rules are in the connection strengths among cognitive units—an analogy would be the rule that makes a honeycomb take the shape it does (Bates, 1979). The shape is caused by the properties of wax. The bees do not know the rule, nor does the wax know the rule, yet the rule gets followed.

Some linguistic rules seem easy to state. To form a plural in English, you add an "s" to the end of the word . . . unless you do something else. In German, it is the other way around: one does just about anything *except* add an "s" to form a plural. There are exactly 12 German words that are made plural by adding an "s" . . . if you don't count the other ones that are also made plural by adding an "s." Most books omit the second part of the rule, apparently because the author wants the student to think that German has at least one exceptionless rule. To put an English verb into the simple past tense, one adds "-ed" to it—if it is a regular verb. If you stop and think, this is a spelling rule rather than a speaking rule. The past tense of a word such as *look* is spelled by adding *ed*, but is pronounced by adding a *T* sound. This rule covers only some verbs; there are rules for the others, but they get rather complicated. Bybee and Slobin (1982) list nine classes of English irregular verbs; however, two "classes" should really be called "miscellaneous," because they are just lists of exceptions. You don't learn explicitly all the ways to form an English past tense; rather, you pick up this knowledge automatically. The point of these examples is that linguistic rules are so complicated that it is not plausible that they could be stored as lists of explicit propositions; they must therefore be implicit in connection strengths.

Survival in the Prison-House of Language

Language has been compared to a prison-house (Jameson, 1972): everything that is not forbidden is compulsory. Because we are totally unaware of most of the rules, they do not have to be enforced. Our neural networks do the enforcing. There are millions of rules on the phonological level; for example, it is absolutely forbidden to begin an English word with more than three consonants—you don't get put in jail if you try, you just produce a non-English word that nobody understands. People don't even try to produce such words because there are no connections in the neural network that allow their production. On the semantic level, there is some choice. There are several words you can use to express the concept "man." Most of these are ruled out by context. If the person is present, one probably can't use "turkey," or a lot of other possibilities. It doesn't occur to people to call a man a table, because connections in the semantic part of the neural network rule this out. Again, the rule is implicit in the connection strengths.

Some syntactic rules are so well learned that no one bothers to mention them. In a simple declarative sentence, you are forbidden to put the object before the subject; you can't say "The duck shot the man" and expect people to understand that you meant "The man shot the duck." Again, it does not even occur to people to make this mistake. The wiring of the analyzers involved in speech production automatically prevents it. The reason for teaching some prescriptive syntax in schools is to try to ensure that you say what you intend to say and understand what others say. A problem arises, however, if speakers are using different rules. If you speak standard colloquial American English, "I will go to Europe" and "I shall go to Europe" mean the same thing, except that only snobs and professors would say it the second way. If you are talking with someone who uses standard British or "Queen's English," the statements have different meanings. The first is an emphatic promise, and the second is what you meant: a prediction about the future. Suppose the speaker of standard British replies that "you shall finish college before you go to Europe." This is not a casual prediction stated in an odd way. You have received a direct order. The person has the authority to give the order and the power to enforce it. If he meant to use the future tense, he would have used "will" rather than "shall." This rule is simple: to express the future tense, one uses "shall" for the first person ("I", "we") and "will" for everybody else. To be emphatic or give a command, one flips things around. It is a nice, British sort of rule: you don't have to raise your voice to give orders or emphasize a point. But if the rule is so simple, why don't most people learn it? One reason is probably that connection strengths in the syntactic analyzer cannot be changed by an act of will. We learn syntax implicitly—by listening to what other people say—rather than explicitly—by doing what school teachers tell us to say.

LANGUAGE COMPREHENSION

PHONOLOGY

Components of Speech

Before people can understand spoken language, they have to hear the words. This is not as simple as it seems to be. Recall from Chapter 3 that several levels of analysis in the spoken-word analyzer are involved. The analyzer is

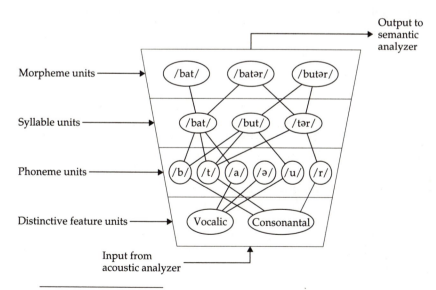

F I G U R E   9 – 1   The spoken-word analyzer. Only a few sample nodes are shown.

shown in Figure 9–1. Rather than words, we should talk about *morphemes*. *Free* morphemes are root words that have a meaning on their own; examples are words like *duck, go,* etc. *Bound* morphemes have meaning only when they are combined with a free morpheme; for example, *S.* By itself it has no meaning, but if it is attached to the end of a free morpheme, it changes the free morpheme's meaning. In English, it usually changes the meaning of a noun from singular to plural. *Ducks* is really two morphemes: *duck* is the free one, and *S* is the bound one. Other examples of bound morphemes are *-ing* and *-ed.* Adding *-ing* to the end of a verb produces a *gerund*; now the verb can be used as a noun—for example, *go* is a verb, and *going* is a gerund.

Morphemes are made up of *syllables*, and syllables are made up of *phonemes*. A phoneme is the smallest particle of sound that makes a difference in meaning. Depending on how one counts, there are 35 to 45 phonemes in English—examples are the sounds /k/ and /d/. Changing the /k/ in *keep* to /d/ gives a word with a totally different meaning, *deep*. There are many ways to pronounce /k/: for example, the /k/ sound in *keep* is different from the /k/ sound in *cool*. In English, this difference in sound makes no difference in meaning, so we can barely hear it. In English, the two ways of saying /k/ are *allophones*. In Arabic, the two /k/ sounds are phonemes; thus, Arabic has words with completely different meanings that sound exactly the same except for the pronunciation of the /k/. The name *Qhadaffi* is one of these words. Colonel *Qhadaffi* is a nuisance to the American government for a variety of reasons, the least of which is that we can't pronounce his name correctly. In English, /r/ and /l/ are phonemes, but in Japanese they are allophones of one phoneme—they are interchangeable and are not used to distinguish words, which is the reason that Japanese have trouble pronouncing them when they learn English. Because they sound very similar to the Japanese person, he or she has trouble producing the sounds that we insist are different.

Distinctive Features

Phonemes are made up of distinctive features. A phoneme is defined by the presence of some of the features and the absence of others. Distinctive features are produced by the position of the vocal apparatus. One distinctive feature is *vocalic* versus *consonantal*. Vowels are vocalic, meaning that they sound somewhat like musical notes. Several frequencies are present, but they do not change while the vowel is being produced, as shown in Figure 9–2(a). Consonantal means that the frequencies *do* change during pronunciation—an example is shown in Figure 9–2(b). Both vowels and consonants are made up of several bands of frequencies: the lowest is called the first *formant* (F1); the next higher is the second formant (F2); and the third highest is the third formant (F3).

Consider English vowels. We can break them down as shown in Figure 9–3, which shows only pure vowels, although most English vowels are *diphthongs*—a combination of two vowels. The vowels vary along two di-

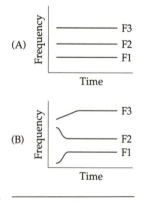

F I G U R E   9 – 2
Formants of vowels (A) and consonants (B).

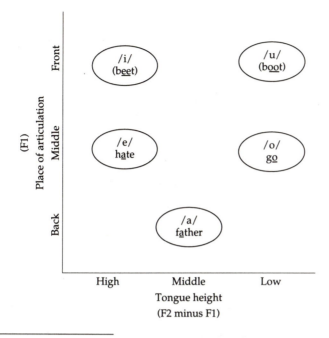

F I G U R E   9 – 3   The features of pure vowels. The precise
point in each circle where a vowel is pronounced varies from person to
person and from word to word.

mensions or features. These features can be defined in two ways: how the
vowel was produced, or the sound pattern of the vowel. The *y*-axis corresponds roughly to where in the mouth the sound is produced. The vowels
/i/ and /u/ are pronounced toward the front of the mouth, vowels /o/
and /e/ are produced in the middle, and /a/ is produced toward the back.
The *x*-axis corresponds roughly to how high the tongue is; for example, try
to say /a/ while you raise your tongue. You will end up saying something
that sounds more like /i/. The dimensions also correspond to the formants
of the vowels (Lass, 1984). The *y*-axis corresponds to the frequency of F1,
and the *x*-axis corresponds to the difference between F2 and F1. Note that
each vowel has a region of space. The frequencies of F1 and F2 do not have
to be exact, but merely in the ball park. If they are in the ball park, we hear
the right vowel.

　　Distinctive features define consonants, too. Let us consider only the
consonants shown in Figure 9–4, all of which are called *stop* consonants,
because there is a complete stoppage of the airstream when they are produced. Such is not the case with nonstop consonants such as /m/ or /l/.
Stop versus nonstop is a distinctive feature. Two distinctive features divide
the consonants shown in Figure 9–4. Those on the left are *voiced,* whereas
those on the right are *unvoiced.* These are somewhat unfortunate terms, as
all of them are voiced in the sense that we can hear them. Voiced consonants

Voicing

Place of articulation		Yes: early voice onset time	No: late voice onset time
	Front (bilabial)	b	p
	Middle (alveolar)	d	t
	Back (velar)	g	k

F I G U R E   9 – 4   A distinctive feature system for describing stop consonants.

involve *early* voice onset time, whereas voice onset is *late* with "unvoiced" consonants. Put your fingers on your throat and say *ba, da,* and *ga.* Note that vibration begins immediately with these voiced consonants. Now try *pa, ta,* and *ka.* There is a brief delay before vibration begins with these unvoiced consonants. Place of articulation refers to where the stoppage of air takes place. Pronounce the syllables again. The air is stopped at the lips with the bilabial phonemes (*bilabial* means *both lips*). In the case of /d/ and /t/, the tongue stops the air at the *alveolar ridge*—the place your tongue is when you say *da* or *ta. Velar* consonants are pronounced with the back of the tongue against the *velum*—the back part of the roof of the mouth. We could find distinctive features that define the rest of the phonemes. If we did so, we would discover that we need only about ten of them to define all the phonemes in English (Jakobson, Fant, & Halle, 1963; Chomsky & Halle, 1968).

The Silence of Sounds and the Sounds of Silence

From our discussions of speech perception in earlier chapters, we know that it is not just a bottom-up process. Only about half of English words can be identified correctly if they are taken out of context and presented in isolation (Pollack & Pickett, 1964). Spoken English sounds like a discrete series of words with pauses between each one, but it is really a continuous string of sounds (Liberman, 1982). In German, in which words can be very long, there are pauses between morphemes—at least in theory. French has rules for how to *elide,* or put together, separate words, but in English, we just elide everything. Pauses in spoken English may be longer within a word than between words. We hear "imaginary" pauses between words because of top-down expectations.

   We also do the reverse: a brief silence in a word can make us "hear" a phoneme (Liberman, 1982). Stop consonants (e.g., /p/ and /t/) do involve a very brief silence. If a brief silence follows the /s/ in *say,* the word is heard as *stay* or *spay.* The misheard silence can work its way into how a word is pronounced. Most of us pronounce "something" as "sum*p*thing" (Lass, 1984), because the brief pause after /m/ is heard as a /p/ even if a /p/ is not inserted by the speaker. Such context effects also allow us to mispronounce phonemes; for example, the same sound will be heard as /t/ or /d/ if context suggests that the word must be *tip* or *dip* (Ganong, 1980). The same thing happens even if context does not clarify matters until several words later (Samuel, 1981). The nonword *eel (where * is a vaguely speechlike sound) is heard as /m/ if the sentence is, "It was found that the *eel was on the table." It is heard as /p/ if the sentence is, "It was found that the *eel was on the orange."

SEMANTICS

Meaning and Context

After we have segmented a stream of speech into words, each word is automatically looked up in semantic memory. Many words have several meanings; for example, "bug" can be an insect or a secret listening device. The nodes coding *both* meanings are activated when the word is heard, even if context completely determines which meaning is correct (Swinney, 1979). Swinney had people read prose passages. Occasionally, a lexical-decision task was interposed; for example, he had people read a passage that should have primed the listening-device interpretation of bug. If the lexical-decision task occurred within 400 milliseconds of "bug," both senses of the word had been primed: a decision about "ant" was speeded up (because *bug* activated *insect* and *insect* activated *ant*). A decision about *spy* (because of activation of *listening device*) was also speeded up. After 400 milliseconds, only the *spy* decision was facilitated. The node coding *insect* had by then been inhibited.

The correct meaning of a word is determined in part by syntax. One problem, however, is that syntax is also determined by semantics—for example, any verb can be used as a noun. Following the rules, one does this by adding -*ing* to make a gerund—for example, "*Reading* is fun." If one is bent on destroying one's language, one doesn't bother: a recent favorite is "This book is a good *read*." Almost any noun can be used as a verb. We could say of people who use *read* as a noun that "they are *quisling* their language." (Quisling was the name of a Norwegian traitor.) At least the military follows some rules when they make verbs into nouns and nouns into verbs: "They prioritize their assaults on the fortress of language."

Meaning Is Metaphorical

You understood the previous sentence even though it was *metaphorical*. Language is not really a fortress that can be attacked. It is generally thought that metaphors are ornaments for spicing up language. If you think it through, it turns out that language is almost entirely metaphorical (Hobbs, 1983; Lakoff, 1987; Lakoff & Johnson, 1980). Many of these metaphors are spatial. *Look back* at the last sentence. I asked you to think things *through.* I told you that something *turned out.* We bring *up* topics. We *put* them *on the table.* If you could argue with me, Lakoff and Johnson (1980) point out that we would have a war: you might try to *attack* and *shoot down* my arguments. I would try to *defend* them by trying to *demolish* your *position* and *counter-attacking.* Lakoff's argument is that if we took all the metaphors out of language, there would be virtually nothing left.

Some words that do not appear to be metaphorical were at one time; they are now dead metaphors. Asch (1958) argues that every adjective used to describe personality traits is a metaphor: it either is or once was used to describe inanimate objects. "Sweet" can be used to refer to either people or candy; "aggressive" is derived from a word meaning *to go out.* Some of the transfer must have gone the other way—from personality to objects

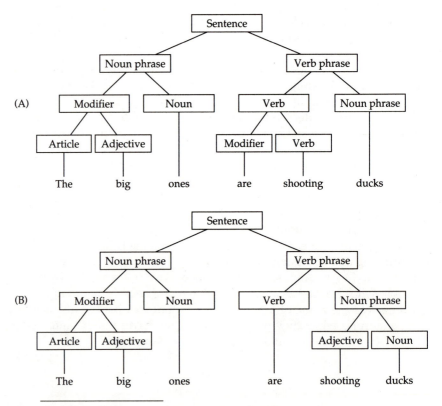

F I G U R E   9 – 5   Alternate tree diagrams of the same sentence. In (A), some people are shooting ducks, whereas in (B), the ducks are doing the shooting.

(Martindale & Martindale, 1988). "Sad earth," for example, is an archaic expression for densely packed soil; "sad" was probably first used to describe people and got transferred to soil because "heavy" is a metaphor for "sad."

SYNTAX

Surface Structure

You may have learned about making tree diagrams of sentences in high school, a practice that helps in *parsing,* or dividing a sentence into its component parts. Let us say we have a sentence "The big ones are shooting ducks." The sentence as expressed is the *surface structure.* We can divide it as shown in Figure 9–5(a). We first divide the sentence into a noun phrase and a verb phrase. We further divide the phrases as shown in the figure. Note that the verb phrase is itself divided into a verb and another noun phrase. If the ducks were doing the shooting, we would diagram the sentence as shown in Figure 9–5(b).

Does this type of diagram tell us anything useful? Yes, because phrases are the basic constituents of sentences. When we speak, we tend to pause between phrases, thus helping the listener to parse the sentence. If we do not pause, the listener hears a pause anyway. Fodor and Bever (1965) had people listen to sentences with embedded clicks and asked where the clicks occurred. People heard the clicks at the nearest phrase boundary, regardless of where they really were, suggesting that we automatically segment sentences into phrases when we hear them. There is other evidence for this. Jarvella (1970, 1971) had people listen to long prose passages, and when the passage ended, they had to write down what they remembered. Verbatim memory for the last sentence was quite variable. People correctly remembered the last phrase about 80% of the time. They had a correct verbatim memory for the third to the last phrase only 10% of the time. Jarvella's results suggest that we forget the exact wording of a phrase as soon as we have parsed and interpreted it.

Deep Structure

Chomsky (1957) argued that phrase-structure syntax does not describe language adequately. Consider these sentences:

The duck ate the telephone book.

The telephone book was eaten by the duck.

The meanings are identical, but the surface structure is completely different. Chomsky's idea is that a common *deep structure* underlies both sentences. A grammar should describe the deep structure and the *transformation rules* that are applied to it to arrive at the surface structure. In our example, the deep structure would be something like "Duck eats telephone book." To get the first sentence, a past-tense transform is applied; to get the second sentence, both a past-tense transform and a passive transform are applied. Do people understand sentences this way? If they do, the more transforms that have been applied to the deep structure, the longer it should take to understand the sentence. Is this the case? Not really. Of the many experiments on this topic initially seemed to support Chomsky's ideas; however, when factors such as sentence length are taken into account, the results are not in line with predictions derived from Chomsky's theory. Fodor, Bever, and Garrett (1974) reviewed this line of research.

Case Grammar

How do people understand sentences, then? Fillmore's (1968) case grammar provides a better answer than Chomsky's transformational grammar. An abstract proposition is the deep structure, consisting of an action and a number of cases. Fillmore's idea is that a spoken or written sentence is an expression or realization of an abstract proposition. A proposition has a limited number of *cases*. The most important of these are as follows:

Action: The action defining an event, usually described by a verb (e.g., Rambo *rescued* the POWs).

Agent: The person or thing that performs the action in question (e.g., *Rambo* rescued the POWs).

Object: The thing that is affected by the action (e.g., Rambo rescued *the POWs*).

Recipient: The person or thing that bears the brunt or receives the effect of the action (e.g., Rambo rescued the POWs from *the Vietnamese*).

Instrument: The thing by means of which the action was brought about (e.g., Rambo rescued the POWs with *a helicopter*).

Location: Where the action took place (e.g., Rambo rescued the POWs in *the jungle*).

Time: When the action took place (e.g., Rambo rescued the POWs in *1986*).

We could combine the information given in these examples as follows: *rescue (Rambo, POWs, Vietnamese, helicopter, jungle, 1986)*. All we have done is put the components of the event together in a specific order: *action (agent, object, recipient, instrument, location, time)*. This proposition can be expressed in several ways; here are two possibilities: "Rambo rescued the POWs from the Vietnamese in the jungle with a helicopter in 1986." "In 1986, POWs in the jungle were rescued from the Vietnamese by Rambo, who used a helicopter to do so." A proposition does not have a one-to-one relationship with a specific sentence. Active and passive are two equivalent ways of expressing the same proposition. Nothing in Fillmore's theory says that one way should be harder to understand than the other. Passive sentences are not transforms of active sentences, but rather, they have an equal footing. Research on memory for sentences provides substantial evidence in favor of Fillmore's theory. When we remember a sentence, we remember an abstract proposition of the sort described by Fillmore.

Assimilation to Propositions

Wanner (1968) conducted a sneaky experiment. His subjects reported for the experiment and were given instructions on what to do. Then, when they were ready to begin, Wanner surprised them. Rather than getting to do what they had been instructed to do, they were tested for their recognition of sentences in the instructions they had just read. Test items were of three types: (1) sentences that were exactly the same as the original; (2) sentences with different word order but exactly the same meaning; and (3) sentences with different word order that also changed the meaning. All three sentences contained exactly the same words, but in different arrangements. Subjects showed very poor ability to discriminate the second type of sentence from the original sentences. They were very good at recognizing that they had *not* seen the third type of sentence before. Thus, verbatim memory was poor, but memory for meaning was good—people remember meanings rather than exact details.

Bransford and Franks (1971) carried out an experiment that extended these findings. Their subjects were shown sentences each of which expressed some elements of a proposition. Here are some examples:

1. Rambo came to Vietnam.
2. Rambo rescued the POWs.
3. The POWs were in the jungle.
4. The POWs were hungry.

These basic elements can be combined to form two-element sentences. These combine two of the one-element sentences shown above; for example, "The hungry POWs were in the jungle." This sentence combines all the information in the third and fourth examples. Three-element sentences combine all the information from three of the simple sentences; for example, "Rambo rescued the hungry POWs in the jungle." Finally, a four-element sentence combines all four of the simple sentences: "Rambo came to Vietnam to rescue the hungry POWs in the jungle." The four-element sentence could be described in terms of a complete proposition. The one-, two-, and three-element sentences give only parts of this proposition.

Now for Bransford and Franks's experiment. Subjects were shown a series of sentences. Some were 1-element, 2-element, 3-element, or 4-element sentences of the type described above. Five minutes after all the sentences had been shown, subjects were shown another series of sentences. Their job was to say whether or not they had seen each sentence previously. They were asked also to say how sure they were of their judgments. Some of the sentences actually had been shown. Others had not, but expressed the same meanings as sentences that had been shown. The more elements the test sentence contained, the more confident people were that they had seen it. The main determinant of people's confidence ratings was how many elements a sentence contained, rather than whether they actually had seen the sentence or not. They were more confident that they had seen 4-element sentences they had not been shown, for example, than that they had seen 3-element sentences that they had in fact been shown.

Bransford and Franks's experiment suggests that people assimilate inputs to propositions that can be described in terms of Fillmore's case grammar. Given several sentences that can be combined into a single proposition, people make this combination. The components that were combined to form the proposition are forgotten promptly. Only the abstract proposition is retained, so we remember the *gist* of what is said rather than the specific sentences. If a speaker has not put all the components together, we automatically do it ourselves.

Parallel Parsing

We can figure out how to parse a nonsense sentence such as Chomsky's (1957) "Colorless green ideas sleep furiously." We can sometimes also figure out the meaning of ungrammatical sentences. "Shoot duck man" has only one plausible interpretation—"The man shoots the duck." One approach to understanding sentences is influenced by Chomsky's tranformational grammar (e.g., Frazier & Rayner, 1982). When we hear a sentence, we figure out the syntax first, and then we figure out the semantics. In other words, the syntactic analyzer comes into play first. After it has assigned parts of speech, the parsed sentence is sent to the semantic analyzer. This system does not fit the facts very well, because it does not take semantic context into account (Schank, Goldman, Rieger, & Riesback, 1973). Consider the example about "The big ones are shooting ducks." A syntactic analyzer that took no account of meaning would have to output two propositions (see Figure 9–5). In one, the verb is "are"; in the other, the verb is "are shooting." The semantic analyzer would have to pick one, but how would it determine which one to pick? Schank et al. (1973) suggest turning things around: put the semantic analyzer first. This method will not work either, however, unless one sneaks some syntactic knowledge into the semantic analyzer. The latter would output a "word heap" consisting of all possible meanings of each word. How would the syntactic analyzer even know if "duck" were a noun or a verb?

Syntactic and semantic analysis must take place at the same time (Marslen-Wilson & Tyler, 1981; Riesbeck, 1986). Waltz and Pollack (1985) suggest how simultaneous analysis could be accomplished. Their scheme involves spreading activation and lateral inhibition in both the syntactic and

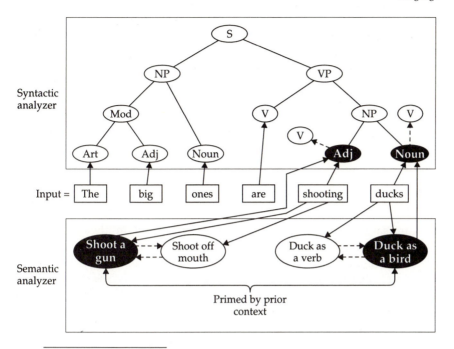

F I G U R E   9 – 6   Parallel parsing of "The big ones are shooting ducks," where prior context has indicated that the big ducks are doing the shooting. Solid lines indicate excitation; dashed lines indicate inhibition. With no prior context, "shooting" would probably be interpreted as a verb.

the semantic analyzers. The two analyzers are massively interconnected; what happens in one of them almost instantly influences what happens in the other. Waltz and Pollack's idea is that different senses of a word are coded by different nodes (see Figure 9–6). These nodes inhibit each other in the semantic analyzer. They also activate the appropriate nodes in the syntactic analyzer. Some of the words in the shooting duck sentence have several meanings: *duck* can mean "a bird that quacks," and it can also be a verb meaning "to stoop down quickly." The nodes coding these meanings inhibit each other. *Shoot* can mean "shoot with a gun," or it can also mean "start talking." The nodes coding these meanings also inhibit each other. Because the rest of the words are not so ambiguous, they don't appear in the figure. Depending on prior context, we may get the pattern of activation shown in Figure 9–6.

Here is a sentence that might take one aback: "The astronomer married the star." Because of the strong association between "astronomer" and "star" as a celestial body, the sentence at first makes no sense. Lateral inhibition comes to the rescue. The node coding "marry" activates the nodes coding "animate" and "human being." These nodes inhibit the node coding "star" as a celestial body and activate the node coding "star" as a movie star. The correct interpretation—the astronomer married the movie star—wins the competition. Waltz and Pollack (1985) did computer simulations showing that a neural network at first misinterprets sentences like this one, then, after activation and inhibition reverberate, settles on the correct interpretation.

LANGUAGE DISORDERS

BROCA'S APHASIA

We can learn a lot about language from people in whom the language circuits are damaged. There are two main types of aphasia. People with *Broca's aphasia* have a problem with syntax (Broca, 1861; Jakobson, 1956). Patients suffering from this disorder have trouble with function words, such as prepositions (e.g., *on*, *in*), pronouns (e.g., *he*, *she*), and connectives (e.g., *and*, *but*). Function words are those that allow us to express the cases of propositions and the relationships between phrases. People with Broca's aphasia have little difficulty producing or understanding nouns. Here is an example (quoted by Geschwind, 1979) of such a patient's response to a question about a dental appointment: "Yes . . . Monday . . . Dad and Dick . . . Wednesday nine o'clock . . . ten o'clock . . . doctor . . . and . . . teeth." This kind of speech is a "word heap"—the nouns are all there, but the syntax is missing. The content words are not strung together with function words into a complete sentence. Most of the function words indicating cases are missing. Patients with Broca's aphasia can understand speech if it is semantically unambiguous; for example, they can understand "The man shot the duck," but they would misunderstand "The duck shot the man."

WERNICKE'S APHASIA

The type of aphasia discovered by Wernicke (1874) is just the opposite of Broca's aphasia; here, the problem is with semantics rather than with syntax (Jakobson, 1956). The speech of a patient with Wernicke's aphasia sounds normal as long as one does not listen to what is being said—that is, there is no problem with syntax or intonation. The problem is that what is said makes no sense. Patients may use the wrong words or neologisms. Geschwind (1979) quotes this sample from a patient asked to describe a picture of boys stealing cookies while their mother's back was turned: "Mother is away here working her work to get her better, but when she's looking the two boys looking in the other part. She's working another time." Jakobson (1956) describes a patient whose content words consisted mainly of only two made-up nouns, *seriat* and *feriat*. When asked his occupation (blacksmith), he responded, "I am a feriat. Work at a seriat." The examiner replied, "You mean an anvil?" "That's right," the patient said, "a seriat." When this patient read a printed text, he pronounced every word as "seriat." Patients with Wernicke's aphasia have a thought disorder as well as a language disorder. The semantic analyzer has apparently been destroyed (Zurif, Caramazza, Meyerson, & Galvin, 1974). In a way, this is fortunate, because in severe cases the patient does not even realize that anything is wrong.

WHAT APHASIA TELLS US

Broca's area is in the left frontal lobe of the brain, just beneath the motor area; Wernicke's area is in the left temporal lobe, just behind the primary auditory receiving area. Their positions are shown in Figure 9–7. As you can see, the two areas are connected by a bundle of fibers called the *arcuate fasciculus*. On the basis of findings concerning damage to Wernicke's and Broca's areas, Wernicke (1874) proposed a theory of speech that is still widely accepted.

Wernicke's area contains the semantic analyzer and the speech analyzer. When we speak, we select a set of meanings from the semantic ana-

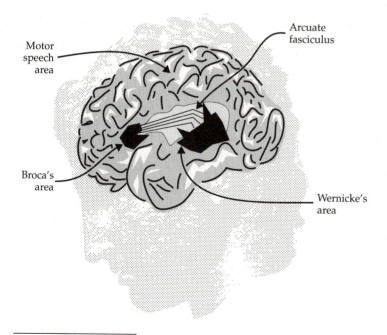

Motor speech area

Arcuate fasciculus

Broca's area

Wernicke's area

F I G U R E   9 – 7   Locations of Wernicke's area and Broca's area. (From "Language and the Brain," by Norman Geschwind. Copyright © 1972 by *Scientific American*, Inc. All rights reserved. Reprinted by permission.)

lyzer. The meanings are coded in the form of a proposition—for example, *speak (John, Mary, aphasia, past)*. Wernicke did not put it in exactly these terms, because case grammar had not yet been devised; this is the author's reinterpretation of his theory (Martindale, 1977). The point is that the elements of the sentence are not arranged as words in a sequential string. After the proposition has been selected, meanings are associated with morphemes. From Wernicke's area, information about these elements is sent to Broca'a area via the *arcuate fasciculus*. Broca's area arranges the elements into a sequential string—for example, "John spoke to Mary about aphasia." When the proposition is arranged in this way, the cases are expressed in various ways. The past tense is expressed by using *spoke* rather than *speak*. The object and the recipient are expressed by the addition of the function words *to* and *about*. Finally, all the elements are arranged into a sequential string. It is incorrect to think about these elements as words; they are not words until they are spoken. Broca's area passes information about the elements to the motor speech area, the part of the motor cortex that controls the mouth, tongue, and vocal cords. This area moves the speech apparatus, and the elements are expressed as words. When these words are heard by someone else, they go first to the auditory receiving area. From there, they are passed to Wernicke's area, where they excite activity in the spoken-word and semantic analyzers. Broca's area is also involved, so that syntax can be decoded simultaneously.

In Broca's aphasia, Broca's area is damaged, but Wernicke's area is intact. A semantically meaningful proposition can be generated and passed to Broca's area via the *arcuate fasciculus*; however, when it arrives, it cannot be decoded and strung together because Broca's area is damaged. Because Wernicke's area is intact, the patient can still understand some words. Understanding a word involves passing information from the auditory receiving area to the speech analyzer to the semantic analyzer. We have an opposite state of affairs in Wernicke's aphasia. Understanding of spoken words is poor: information about the word cannot get from the auditory cortex to the semantic analyzer because Wernicke's area is damaged. The patient's speech is semantically deviant. The propositions sent to Broca's area are not right in the first place, because they are formed by the damaged semantic analyzer. Because Broca's area is working normally, it strings together what it receives, but it receives gibberish.

LANGUAGE ACQUISITION
IS LANGUAGE ABILITY INNATE?

The hypothesis that language is innate was tested in what was probably the first psychology experiment. An ancient Egyptian pharaoh wanted to see whether a child raised without ever hearing language would speak Egyptian or Greek when it began to speak. He caused a newborn child to be raised in such a way that his curiosity would be satisfied. The child never said anything. Nobody thinks that language is innate in the way the pharaoh did; however, Chomsky (1986) does argue that linguistic *capacity* is innate. His claim is that language is a uniquely human ability. We are born with the capacity to learn language—not one specific language, but any language.

There are several reasons for saying that linguistic capacity is innate. At a deep level, Chomsky points out that all languages share universal properties. All languages have a natural order for subject (S), verb (V), and object (O). For example, English is a SVO language. There are six possible orders in which S, V, and O can be arranged, but two of these—OVS and OSV—are not used in any language (Greenberg, 1963). Chomsky's argument is that our innate language capacity makes languages of this type impossible. All languages put an adjective next to the noun it modifies. English puts it in front of the noun, and French after. Consider the sentence "The nice man killed the mean duck." It would be *possible* to have a language where the adjective modifying the subject (man) was next to the object (duck) and vice versa, but no such language exists. Using an artificial language, Anderson (1985) showed that people cannot learn such languages.

Infants are born with the ability to discriminate all the phonemes used in all languages (Eimas, 1985). After we learn a language, we loose this ability, and it is difficult, if not impossible, to regain it. Unless you had heard Arabic as a child, it is almost impossible for you to learn to discriminate or produce its two /k/ sounds. If you have grown up in the part of America where *Mary, merry,* and *marry* are pronounced identically, it is almost impossible for you to hear the differences when you enter the regions of the country where people claim they pronounce these words completely differently. If you raise your children in these parts of the country, though, they will hear and pronounce the three words differently.

FIRST WORDS

Even if a child is born with the innate capacity to learn language, one must talk to it, or it won't learn. In all cultures, people speak to infants in a special way (Brown, 1973). Pitch is raised, speech is simplified and slowed down, and there is a lot of repetition. This special speech accounts in part for why children produce baby talk: that is exactly what they are taught. For its part, the infant does not do much at first. Around six months, it starts to babble. At one year, it produces sounds that (with some imagination) sound like speech. Babies first produce vowels; their first consonants are almost always /m/ and /p/. In most languages the child eventually says something vaguely resembling "mama" or "papa"—words that are quite reinforcing to parents.

The parents now want to teach the infant other words. They point at objects and name the objects. Soon enough, the child learns the words, much as a dog becomes conditioned. The child is not exactly sure to what the words refer, so it shows a lot of generalization (Rescorla, 1980). There is no way for the child to know if *dog* refers to the specific thing in front of it, or to all dogs, or to all things with four legs, or what. Discrimination training is called for, although the child continues to overgeneralize for quite a while. Eventually, it gets things straight.

First Syntax

Around the age of two, the child begins to learn that words can be put together in a meaningful way rather than randomly. Reasonably enough, it starts simply by putting two words together (Brown, 1973). One way of looking at the child's first syntax is that there is a small class of *pivot words* (e.g., *go, my*) and a large, open class of *content words* (e.g., *Daddy, doggie, transcendentalism*). The exact meaning of the child's sentences is not clear: "Daddy go" may mean "Daddy is going," "Daddy has gone," "Daddy will go," "Daddy should go," and so on.

This original syntax expands quickly so that the child can soon produce Subject-Verb-Object sentences such as, "Daddy go work." In some sense, the child learns that there are rules that apply to large classes of words—which leads to a setback. The first verbs a child learns are high-frequency ones, most of which are irregular. The child learns the past tense correctly. The next verbs learned are mostly regular ones in which the past tense is formed by adding *-ed*. The child overgeneralizes this rule (Ervin, 1964; Kuczaj, 1977). Whereas the child used to know that the past tense of "go" is "went," it now thinks that the past tense is "goed."

Rumelhart and McClelland (1986a) have shown that the child's acquisition of the past tense can be modeled in neural-network terms. The child does not learn explicit rules. If it did, it would ask embarrassing questions about the precise rules for forming the past pluperfect. Learning the past tense of high-frequency irregular verbs consists of establishing a set of connection strengths. If a network is then bombarded with many regular verbs, it does the same thing a child does: it regresses and regularizes the past tense. What is really happening is that the connection strengths are being adjusted to handle all of the new "*-ed*" past tenses. After the weights have been adjusted to handle them, some minor weight changes allow the network to relearn the past tense of irregular verbs. The same process occurs with plurals. Connection strengths have to be learned for the huge number of regular nouns: input *dog*, and *dogs* comes out. Only then can the connection strengths be adjusted to take care of the exceptions: input *mouse* and get *mice* as the output, or input *sheep* and get the same thing out. The weights are adjusted to take care of the most frequent forms first. It never occurs to the child that the plural of *dog* should be *deeg*, but it almost always occurs to the child that the plural of *mouse* should be *mouses*.

SUMMARY AND CONCLUSIONS

Language is a unique human ability. Animals can communicate with one another, but they do so with isolated signs so that nothing very complicated can be communicated. Language allows people to string signs together to communicate extremely complex messages. Without it, we would not have civilization. Knowledge could not be passed on, and possibilities and ideas could not be communicated. Language is composed of three parts. Semantics is about what words mean, syntax is about how words are combined to communicate meaning, and phonology concerns how the words are spoken. The grammar of a language is a description of the rules of phonology, syntax, and semantics. It is impossible to formulate a complete grammar of any language because the rules are so numerous and so complex. We know literally millions of rules about English grammar, but most of us can describe verbally only a few of these rules. We know the rules implicitly, through the strengths of the connections among the cognitive units dealing with language.

Speech is easy to hear if one understands the language being spoken. The stream of speech is more or less continuous. Top-down effects break it up into distinct words so that we perceive pauses between words even though they are not really there. Sentences are analyzed phrase by phrase. Syntactic analysis consists of abstracting the underlying propositions from these phrases. Semantic and syntactic analysis go on simultaneously, because both meaning and syntax are context dependent: nouns can be verbs, and verbs can be nouns. Both are used metaphorically much more commonly than we realize. Lakoff argues that if we took all the metaphors out of language, there would not be much of anything left. Language disorders shed light on what happens in normal language. In Broca's aphasia, localized brain damage causes loss of syntactic ability; in Wernicke's aphasia, semantic knowledge is destroyed, and the patient loses the ability to understand the meanings of words.

Children go through several stages in the acquisition of language. First, they learn individual words, then they have to figure out what they mean. There is no way for the child to know if "doggie" means a specific dog, all dogs, all organisms, or what. Before the child has this completely straight, it discovers syntax. This discovery presents no problems until the child's neural network also discovers that language has some regularities. These, too, are at first overgeneralized.

Thinking

WHAT IS THINKING?

We have been talking about thoughts for the last several chapters. When we study attention or short-term memory, we focus on brief periods of time. Thinking could be defined as what happens in attention and short-term memory across a stretch of time. There are several types of thinking. As Hobbes (1642) put it,

> This Trayne of Thoughts, or Mental Discourse, is of two sorts. The first is Unguided, without Designe, and inconstant . . . : In which case the thoughts are said to wander, and seem impertinent one to another, as in a Dream . . . . And yet in this wild ranging of the mind, a man may of times perceive the way of it, and the dependence of one thought upon another . . . . The second is more constant; as being regulated by some desire, and designe. (p. 9)

Wundt (1896) called the second type of thinking *intellectual*. Intellectual thinking has a purpose or goal. To reach this goal, thinking takes reality into account and performs logical operations on representations of reality. Wundt called the first type of thinking *associative*. Associative thinking has no goal; one idea just leads to another. The only "logic" of mental sequencing is the connection strengths among cognitive units. Intellectual and associative thinking define poles of a continuum. When we solve a logic problem, we are engaging in intellectual thinking. In a state of reverie, where one idea drifts aimlessly to another, we are engaging in associative thinking. Fantasies, in which we show or tell ourselves stories, are somewhere between these two poles. We can think of intellectual thinking as what occurs across time in the focus of attention. Though we often take little note of it, there is a parallel sequence of associative thinking in the fringes of awareness (Neisser, 1967). When our attention lapses, we take more note of the rambling associations that have been passing through our minds all along.

DEDUCTIVE REASONING

How Logicians Think

Logic is a subdivision of philosophy and mathematics rather than of psychology. It is not about how people actually think. Of course, we all want to think logically, but that is using the term in a somewhat different sense. Deductive logic is about rules that let us prove a statement true or false when we are given other statements; the other statements are called *premises*. The statement that gets proved is the *conclusion*. One needs to know about these rules if he needs to prove things.

Conditional Logic

Conditional logic is about *if . . . then* statements; for example:

If A, then B	*If you take off your clothes, then you will be naked*
A exists	*You took off your clothes*
B exists	Therefore, you are naked

This kind of deduction is called *modus ponens*: if *A* causes *B*, then if *A* exists, it will cause *B*. If *B* has been caused, it exists. Most people have no problem with this type of reasoning (Rips & Marcus, 1977). Let us have another look at logic:

If A, then B	*If God exists, then there are blue roses*
B does not exist	*There are no blue roses*
A does not exist	Therefore, God does not exist

What say you? In fact, this *is* a valid conclusion. This kind of deduction is called *modus tollens*. People have a *lot* of trouble with this type of reasoning (Anderson, 1985). They are likely to say that nothing can definitely be concluded from this syllogism. A more concrete example will make it easy to see why we can conclude something.

If A, then B	*If* you kill a lawyer, then she will die
B does not exist	*The lawyer is not dead*
A does not exist	Therefore, you did not kill her

Here is a way to remember how to use *modus tollens.* If you are accused of killing someone, bring the person to court with you and demonstrate that the person is not dead. The case may eventually be thrown out of court on this technicality. Our legal system is bizarre, but there is some logic to it.

REPRESENTATION OF THE PROBLEM

Unless they have taken a course on logic, people do not do very well at solving most logic problems (Anderson, 1985). What cognitive units in what analyzers can people use to solve logic problems? The answer is not at all clear, because we don't have a syllogism analyzer. One must use some nodes in an analyzer usually devoted to other purposes. Guyote and Sternberg (1981) argue that people may try to construct a miniworld in solving logic problems. Say the first premise is that "Some generals are ballet dancers." The person forms a visual image of some generals, some of whom are dressed in tutus. Let us say that the next premise is that "Some ballet dancers carry knives." That is easy enough to picture. If the conclusion is that "Some generals carry knives," the visual image may or may not show the correct answer. Another strategy would be to use semantic memory. If a premise were "Some *A*'s are *B*'s," a person might convert this to "Some ducks are mallards" and hope that things would fall into place.

People are generally not at all good at using *modus tollens,* which involves determining that something is or isn't the case because something else is *not* the case. Anderson (1985) points out that we are not used to thinking about what is *not* the case. You have a node that codes turkey. If turkey is coded by a dipole, the off-unit codes not-turkey. Usually, though, an off-unit comes on only briefly when its companion on-unit goes off. That makes off-units generally unavailable for use in thinking. In everyday life, it may occur to you that your roommate is a turkey. If not, you don't have the insight that your roommate is a not-turkey. You think of something your roommate *is*: "My roommate is a considerate person," for example. It is easy for people to notice the presence of something, because the presence of something is coded by an on-unit. It is obvious that I refer to ducks more than do most authors. What words do I use *less* frequently than other authors? That's very hard to assess.

PROBLEM SOLVING
DEFINITION

A problem involves changing a state of affairs so it matches a goal. All intellectual thought is aimed at problem solving. We have some goal, and we execute a procedure that is supposed to change the initial state into the goal state. Executing such a procedure is precisely the purpose of action units or TOTE modules. Most of the problems we solve are so straightforward that we don't think of them as problems at all. Technically, even getting out of the bed in the morning involves problem solving. Because you know perfectly well how to solve this problem, the difficulty usually has to do with motivation. It is more interesting to study problems that do not have obvious solutions. The solution may not be obvious because the problem is a new one, so that one has to figure out some new procedures.

Problem solving consists of several steps. First, one must form an internal representation of what the problem is—if you don't know the goal, you can't determine how to reach it. The point is to reduce the difference between an actual state of affairs and the goal state. In the case of a complex problem, it may not be possible to reach the goal in a straightforward way, and the problem must be broken down into subproblems. Then, each of these problems is solved by difference reduction between the goal state and the initial state (Newell & Simon, 1972).

REPRESENTING THE PROBLEM

The ease with which you can solve a problem often depends on your mental representation of it. Here is a math problem that deals with squaring integers (whole numbers). If you square two integers and add them together, can the sum be the square of an integer if the first two numbers are equal to each other? *What?* A verbal representation is not at all optimal. It would help to put the question into an equation. Is this possible: $A^2 = B^2 + C^2$, where $B = C$, and A, B, and C are integers? Actually, this representation is not the best one. If $B = C$, let's put that in the equation:

$$A^2 = B^2 + B^2$$

Here's an even better representation:

$$A^2 = 2B^2$$

Here is a better one yet:

$$\sqrt{A^2} = \sqrt{2B^2}$$

Why so? Take the square roots and remember that $\sqrt{X \times Y} = \sqrt{X} \times \sqrt{Y}$.

$$A = \sqrt{2 \times B}$$

Now, 2 is *not* an integer, so $\sqrt{2} \times B$ is not an integer, so A cannot be an integer. Whether the solution was obvious or puzzling has to do with how the problem was represented.

DIFFERENCE REDUCTION

Newell and Simon (1972) suggest that problems are often solved by breaking them down into subgoals. The subgoals are arranged so as to reduce the difference between the initial state and the goal state. The Tower of Hanoi problem provides an example of this way of solving problems; a simple

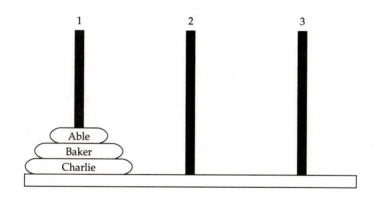

F I G U R E   1 0 – 1   The Tower of Hanoi. The three disks must be moved from Peg 1 to Peg 3 following the rules described in the text.

version appears in Figure 10–1. There are three disks—Able, Baker, and Charlie—and three pegs—1, 2, and 3. The goal is to get the tower of disks from Peg 1 to Peg 3. This would be easy enough except for the rules: a disk can be moved to any other peg, only one disk can be moved at a time, and a larger disk can never be placed on a smaller disk.

The goal is clear, but we cannot achieve it at once. The problem has to be broken down into subgoals. Have a go at it. Here is what you do: Able to 3 (2 would do, but let's say 3), Baker to 2, and Able to 2. Now move Charlie to 3. That is a major difference reduction, because Charlie is now at the goal. The rest is a piece of cake: Able to 1, and Baker to 3, where we want it to be. The final solution is left to the reader.

CREATIVE PROBLEM SOLVING

DEFINITION

We reserve the term *creativity* for solution of ill-defined problems. If a problem could be solved by something even resembling an already known procedure, we would not say the solution was creative (Amabile, 1983). A creative idea is one that is original and appropriate for the situation in which it occurs. Original means the idea is novel—no one has had it before. To say that an idea must be appropriate allows us to differentiate between what is creative and what is bizarre or ridiculous.

CREATIVITY AND ANALOGY

Creative ideas are always novel combinations of preexisting elements. As French mathematician Henri Poincaré (1913) put it, "To create consists of making new combinations of associative elements which are useful." Creative ideas, he went on to say, "reveal to us unsuspected kinships between other facts well known but wrongly believed to be strangers to one another. Among chosen combinations the most fertile will often be those formed of elements drawn from domains which are far apart." The assembly line Henry Ford invented to manufacture cars is a good example of a creative idea. The idea was based on an analogy: assembly lines had been used for a long time in butchering plants, and one of Ford's executives reasoned that if you can take apart animals with an assembly line, you can put together automobiles with one (Weisberg, 1986).

ANALOGIES AND CONCEPTS

Henry Ford's idea about assembly lines involved an analogy between animal carcasses and automobiles, but on a more abstract or conceptual level, it involved an identity: use an assembly line to perform operations on a product. If one thinks in terms of abstractions, many things that seem totally different on the surface are the same thing. Langley, Simon, Bradshaw, and Zytkow (1987) describe several "creative" computer programs. If they are given some data, the programs use a few simple heuristics (rules of thumb) to discover scientific laws! For example, one program discovered Kepler's Third Law of planetary motion, which states that the ratio of the cube of a planet's distance from the sun to the square of the period of the planet is constant: $D^3/P^2 = k$. How could a program—or Kepler—figure that out? With three simple heuristics: (1) if the values of two things increase or decrease together, take their ratio; (2) if one thing increases as another decreases, take their product; and (3) if the value of a term is always about the same, then ignore details and assume that it is a constant. Give the program the relevant data, and it comes up with Kepler's law.

The further a planet is from the sun, the longer its period (time to go around the sun). Therefore, the program takes a ratio, D/P. Now, D/P decreases as D decreases. Therefore, the program computes the product, $D \times D/P = D^2/P$. D^2/P decreases as D/P increases, so it computes the product: $D/P \times D^2/P = D^3/P^2$. That remains constant no matter what D and P are. Therefore, $D^3/P^2 = k$, which is Kepler's law. The heuristics work no matter what you are dealing with; that is, they work on other things besides planets. Boyle's Law is that, for a gas, pressure (P) is inversely related to volume (V): $PV = k$. The program discovers that law in one pass through the data; for the data Boyle used, the value of PV ranged from 28.7 to 40.0. Forget the trees and look at the forest: PV is somewhat the same—it is not all over the place from one to 50 billion, so we call it a constant.

STAGES OF THE CREATIVE PROCESS

How do obviously creative people come up with creative ideas? One way to approach this question is to look at the recollections of such people. Wallas (1926) has suggested that four successive stages commonly occur in the creative process: preparation, incubation, illumination, and verification. Helmholtz (1896) was the first to describe the first three stages in the context of a discussion of the origin of his own ideas. At first, he worked intensively on a problem, but often came up with no solution—this is the stage of *preparation*. During this stage, the elements known or presumed to be relevant to the problem are thought about or learned. When there was no progress, Helmholtz set the problem aside—the period of *incubation*. Often with no apparent cause, a solution finally occurred to him—*illumination*. It is in the illumination or inspiration stage that the creative analogy occurs to the thinker. The creative analogy consists of the simultaneous juxtaposition of two or more mental elements in the focus of attention. These elements may have been entered into memory during the preparation stage, but as often as not, some seemingly irrelevant element provides the key to the creative solution. Following inspiration is the *verification* stage. During this stage, the creative idea is subjected to critical scrutiny. Does it make sense? Is it useful? The verification stage also involves expressing the idea or taking some action on the basis of it. For the scientist, action may involve designing and executing an experiment to test the idea. A poet will have to fit the idea into a form that follows the rules of the genre in which he or she works.

INCUBATION, EFFORTLESS INSPIRATION, AND PRIMARY MEMORY

A period of incubation followed by effortless illumination or inspiration is common in creative production. Creative ideas do not arise from purely logical, intellectual thought for either scientists or artists. Ghiselin (1952) concluded from a study of creative people's self-reports that "production by a process of purely conscious calculation seems never to occur." This is a strong statement, but investigators have concluded the same thing for quite a while. Plato held that "it is not by wisdom that poets create their works but by a certain natural power and inspiration like soothsayers and prophets, who say many fine things but who understand nothing of what they say."

Perhaps creative people just think of ideas more or less at random and keep the good ones. Campbell (1960) has proposed that this may be all there is to creativity, which is not completely implausible. Everyone thinks all the time; if creative people have a lot of diverse mental elements, they have a better chance of thinking of a useful combination purely by chance. But whereas this concept of creative thinking suggests they would tend to have many ridiculous ideas and a few good ones, this is not the case. Poincaré (1913, pp. 386–387) was emphatic that creative people tend not to do this at all; they only think of good ideas. Not every single one is right, but off-the-wall ideas tend not to occur to them.

Mendelsohn (1976) hypothesized that creativity arises from defocused attention: "The greater the attentional capacity, the more likely the combinatorial leap which is generally described as the hallmark of creativity." To

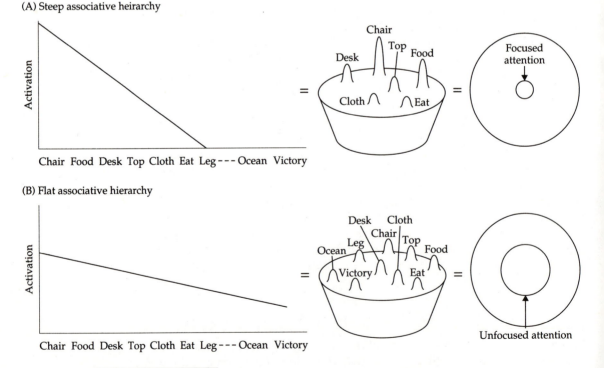

F I G U R E   1 0 – 2 Lack of creativity (A) and creativity (B) in terms of associative gradients, activation of cognitive units, and focus of attention.

be aware of a creative idea, one must obviously attend to the elements to be combined. If one could attend to only two things at the same time, one could discover only one possible analogy at a time. If one could attend to four things at once, six possible analogies could be discovered, and so on. In fact, there is quite a lot of evidence that creative people have less focused attention than uncreative people (Dykes & McGhie, 1976). Mednick (1962) said the same thing in another way; his hypothesis was that creative people have *flat associative gradients*. In the terms we have been using, this notion means that many cognitive units can be activated (but not *highly* activated) at the same time—but this is the same thing as defocused attention (see Chapter 6). It would really be better to think in terms of primary memory: creative people can keep more nodes simultaneously activated than can uncreative people (Martindale, 1981, 1989). The similarity between Mendelsohn's and Mednick's theories is shown in Figure 10–2. Recall that attention is related to the arousal system. High arousal focuses attention, and low arousal defocuses it. When they are engaged in creative thought, creative people do show lower levels of arousal than uncreative people (Martindale & Hasenfus, 1978).

Now we can make sense of the preparation-incubation-inspiration sequence. During preparation, attention is too focused, and one attends to ideas thought to be relevant to the problem. The difficulty is that the solution lies in ideas one thinks are *irrelevant*. During incubation, the nodes coding the problem remain partially activated on the fringe of awareness. As the creator goes about his or her business, many nodes are activated. One of these nodes may be connected to the nodes coding the problem, which will become activated and leap into attention. This process is inspiration—the discovery of the creative analogy. The discovery would not have occurred if the nodes coding the problem were not already partially activated. The more nodes that can be simultaneously activated (that is, the more creative the person), the more likely it is that inspiration will occur, because more paths among more nodes can be simultaneously activated. Campbell's (1960) idea about quasi-random combination of mental elements suggests that we think of inspiration as an idea in the focus of awareness "pulling" a primed idea into consciousness. Our experiences are not random, but they *may* be random with respect to the problem we are trying to solve.

INDUCTIVE REASONING

INDUCTION AND SCIENTIFIC REASONING

When one comes up with a creative scientific idea, the idea must be tested. Testing involves some inductive reasoning. Deductive logic involves going from the general to the specific—one has a general or major premise and a minor premise that is usually more specific. If the premises are true, one can *prove* that some conclusion does or does not follow. Inductive logic turns this around—one moves from the specific to the general. From observations, one draws a conclusion; for example:

Premise: I dropped something.
Conclusion: It will fall to the ground.

How can we conclude that? We have inferred the conclusion from past experience. What justifies drawing conclusions from past experience? Inductive reasoning rests upon the assumption that nature is uniform (Mill, 1846; Reichenbach, 1949). If something has always happened in the past, it will probably happen in the future; if it always happens in one place, it will probably happen in another place. This assumption is itself an inference based upon past experience. Inductive reasoning does not allow us to *prove* anything, it merely allows a conclusion that is *probable*. The conclusion may be highly probable, but it can never be certain.

Inductions are often missing a major premise. We can turn an induction into a syllogism by supplying a major premise (Mill, 1846). Unfortunately, supplying a premise causes another problem: one can never be certain that one has chosen the right major premise. For example:

Possible major premises: Objects seek their proper level. (Aristotle)

                             Large objects attract small objects. (Newton)

                             It's too complicated to explain in a sentence, but dropped stuff falls. (Einstein)

Minor premise: *I dropped an object.*

Conclusion: It will move toward the earth.

At the moment, people who specialize in dropping things prefer Einstein's premise. We cannot be certain that a better one will not be thought of in the future.

If this sounds like science, there is a good reason: science is based mainly on inductive reasoning. When a scientific hypothesis is tested, it is usually embedded in a large set of premises. On the basis of all the premises, you deduce a conclusion, then check to see if the conclusion is true. Even if it is true, that does not prove your theory—it just makes it more probable. If the conclusion is false, we say that your theory has been *falsified* (Popper, 1972).

HYPOTHESIS TESTING AND CONFIRMATION BIAS

According to Popper (1972), one should test scientific hypotheses by trying to falsify them. If the hypothesis is *not* falsified, that provides evidence in its favor. Scientists often tend not to test hypotheses in this way; rather, they try to accumulate as much evidence as possible to confirm the hypothesis.

Of course, if the hypothesis is wrong, it won't be possible to confirm it, and it will be falsified whether or not one sets out to do so. Popper's point is that a hypothesis may have considerable evidence in its favor, but if one does not actively try to falsify it, one may never find out that there is a simpler or better hypothesis to account for all the data.

An AK47 is an efficient and lethal gun. You undoubtedly have no use for one, but if you came into possession of an AK47, you could sell it. One hypothesis about the purpose of life is that it is to accumulate money. If you hold this hypothesis, here is a problem that should interest you. Suppose there are four cards:

$$\boxed{A} \quad \boxed{K} \quad \boxed{4} \quad \boxed{7}$$

Someone with an extra AK47 poses this problem: if a card has a vowel on one side, then it has an even number on the other side. You are to turn over only those cards that need to be turned over to confirm that this rule is correct. If you turn over the correct cards, you get the AK47. If you make a mistake, you get nothing. Which cards should you turn over?

If you are like most people, you have only a 4% chance of walking away with the gun in hand (Wason & Johnson-Laird, 1972). There are several mistakes you can make. According to 46% of subjects, the A card and the 4 card should be turned over. Another 33% think only the A card needs to be turned over. Here is what you must do: turn over the A card and the 7 card. The K card and the 4 card are irrelevant, because the rule doesn't say anything about them. You have to turn over the A card. If it has an even number, that *confirms* the rule. You also have to turn over the 7 card. If it has a vowel on the other side, that would *falsify* the rule. It would show that the rule is wrong. Most people exhibit what is called *confirmation bias*, meaning that they seek evidence that confirms a hypothesis but fail to seek evidence that could disconfirm or falsify the hypothesis. That is why most people don't think the 7 card has to be turned over.

I expect the problem here is the same as we ran into when we discussed the mistakes people make on deductive logic problems. We are accustomed to thinking positively, about what *is* rather than about what *is not*. Furthermore, we have no analyzer devoted to abstract logic. If the problem is changed to a concrete or practical one, most people solve it correctly (Cosmides, 1989; Griggs & Cox, 1982). For example, if the rule is that only people over 21 can drink beer and the cards show ages on one side and what a person is drinking on the other, the majority of subjects turn over the correct cards to determine if the rule is being followed.

CHOICE AND DECISION MAKING

In real life, confirmation bias is held in check by brute facts. We are constantly testing hypotheses. Every time we turn the key in our car, we are testing the hypothesis that the motor will start. If our hypothesis is falsified, we are faced with another cognitive task: we have to decide whether to call a mechanic or buy a new car. Of course, we do not usually buy a new car the first time our car fails to start. We fix the old one. After a number of cycles through this process, the odds begin to shift. A car is supposed to get us from one point to another without the constant help of a mechanic. At some point, we decide to cut out the middleman and buy a new car. We are relying upon Mill's assumption of the uniformity of nature. If the car kept breaking down in the past, it will continue to do so in the future. Every time you decide to fix your car—or to do anything at all—you make a choice. How do you make choices? If you decide to buy a new car, how do you choose which one to buy?

STRATEGIES OF CHOICE

Additive Strategy

When you decide to buy a car, you have many cars to judge on a variety of attributes. Below I list some automobiles and their attributes:

	Automobile			
	Yugo	Rolls-Royce	BMW	Trans Am
Price	10	0	2	6
Ease of locking keys in car	1	10	9	3
Gas mileage	5	0	3	4
Acceleration	1	8	9	7
Attractiveness of tinted glass	0	10	5	6
Attractiveness of eagle on front hood	0	0	0	10
Score	17	28	28	36

You could use an *additive strategy* by rating the desirability of each car on each attribute, totaling the scores, and buy the car with the highest number. In this case, you should buy the car with the eagle painted on the hood. This is not how we make decisions, though. One problem here is that we didn't weight the attributes. Price should probably be weighted more heavily than whether one can mistakenly lock the keys inside the car.

We don't use an additive strategy when we buy a car for several reasons. One is that there are *costs* involved in making a choice. One has to go around and collect all the information, and that takes time, because cars come with a bewildering array of options. Do you want a sunroof, tapedeck, tires, engine? Even if you aren't paid a salary, your time is of value to you. You don't have time for all the bother and hassle. Besides the costs of time, there are also mental costs. We can only keep seven or so items in mind at once. If we figured out the ratings for the first attribute in our list, we would promptly forget them when we moved on to the second attribute. We would have to write them down. But hardly anyone writes them down, because we probably don't make choices in an additive way.

Short-Cut Strategies

One way to cut through the costs of decision making is what Simon (1979) called *satisficing*. Rather than use the additive strategy, one buys the first car that is above some cutoff on all relevant criteria. Most of us don't do exactly that, though; we look at a few cars, and then we *satisfice*—we pick one that passes all the cuts. We may set out to buy a Ford and come home with a Toyota, because the only Fords we could find were painted in pink polka dots. The only car that had all the attributes we wanted happened to be a Toyota.

Tversky (1972) suggests that we may use a strategy called *elimination by aspects*. We don't choose; rather, one item wins by default. Tversky's notion is that we consider one aspect at a time. Perhaps tinted glass comes to mind first—if we want it, any car that doesn't have it is off the list. Country of origin may occur next; if you want to support your local economy, you throw all the foreign cars off the list. You keep doing this until only one car is left. Of course, if you did this in the wrong order, that car might be an expensive Cadillac. But we *don't* go through the process that way—the most important aspects are likely to be coded by stronger cognitive units and will automatically come to mind first. Price usually comes to mind early rather than late, and as the price of a new Cadillac is pretty high, we will experience an attentional reset so that the Cadillac-node is inhibited and units coding other automobiles remote from it are activated.

CHOOSING SOMETHING SIMILAR

When we set out to buy a car, we sometimes know exactly what we want until we see the price tag, then decide that we will have to settle for something else that is similar. Computing similarity is heavily dependent on context (Tversky, 1977). Say you have your heart set on a Corvette, but it costs too much. Finding something similar depends upon what else is around. Let us consider how similar a Corvette and a Trans Am are on this car lot:

Corvette

Trans Am   Volvo   Buick

They're pretty similar; it wouldn't be so bad to have a Trans Am. Let's reconsider this on another car lot:

Corvette

Trans Am   Porsche   Maserati

Now the Corvette and the Trans Am don't seem nearly so similar. Tversky (1977) got this kind of result when he had people judge similarity of countries rather than of cars. How similar is Cuba to Russia? Just pick a number. How similar is Russia to Cuba? Pick another number. The results don't add up—most people said that Cuba is more similar to Russia than Russia is to Cuba (Tversky, 1977). The similarity *should* be the same no matter how we ask the question, but it isn't.

How can we explain this oddity? Nodes coding similar items are close to one another and laterally inhibit each other, so perhaps we judge similarity on the basis of amount of inhibition. If the nodes coding two stimuli are of equal strength, similarity judgments should be symmetrical, as shown in

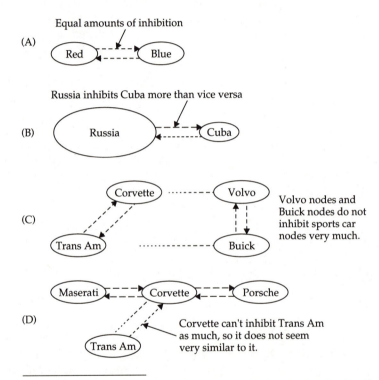

F I G U R E   1 0 – 3   Inferring similarity from inhibition. Similarity is symmetric if lateral inhibition is equal (A), but asymmetric if lateral inhibition is unequal (B). As shown in (C) and (D), similarity is influenced by context because the presence of other items will influence the amount of lateral inhibition.

Figure 10–3(a). How similar is red to blue? How similar is blue to red? It doesn't much matter how we ask; for perceptual stimuli, judged similarities are usually symmetrical (Tversky & Gati, 1982); there is no reason to expect the nodes coding red and blue to differ in strength. For conceptual judgments, on the other hand, similarity is usually asymmetric. Take Russia and Cuba (Figure 10–3[b]): Russia is salient, so the node coding it should be strong and can inhibit the node coding Cuba. A great deal of inhibition arriving at the Cuba node tells us that Cuba is quite similar to Russia. To most of us, Cuba is not so salient, so its node doesn't as strongly inhibit the node coding Russia; thus we conclude that Russia is not very similar to Cuba.

What about Corvettes? Figure 10–3(c) shows what may occur. Volvos and Buicks aren't similar to sports cars. The Corvette node and the Trans Am node can inhibit each other. Maseratis and Porsches are sports cars, and many of us would consider them more similar to a Corvette than to a Trans Am, so their nodes inhibit the Corvette node (Figure 10–3[d]). The Corvette node thus cannot inhibit the Trans Am node as much now. Therefore, the two do not seem to be very similar. Keep in mind, this is not the way Tversky would explain the effect.

EXPECTED VALUE AND EXPECTED UTILITY

All choices involve risk. There is little apparent risk in buying a new car with a warranty—the warranty covers virtually anything that could go wrong with the car for something like the first 5000 miles or so. We know our problems will begin after the 5001st mile. To estimate the value of the car, we need to estimate the probability that something will go wrong and how much it will cost to repair. These are difficult things to estimate, so let's estimate something easier. You may want to insure the car to cover the costs in case you accidentally run over someone's prized landscaping. How much should you pay for insurance?

We need to calculate the expected value, $E(V)$, of the insurance. Here is the formula:

$$E(V) = P(W) \times V(W) - P(L) \times V(L)$$

$P(W)$ is the probability of a win—you win if you *don't* have an accident. Serious accidents are not all that likely; say that $P(W) = .9999$—that is, chances are 9,999 out of 10,000 that you *won't* have a serious accident next year. That leaves .0001 or 1 out of 10,000 for the probability of a loss, $P(L)$—the probability that you will have an accident. Now, the value of a win, $V(W)$, can be computed exactly: $V(W) = \$0$. When was the last time you got paid for *not* having an accident? Let's say that the value of a loss, $V(L)$, is – \$500,000, which should cover replacement costs for any landscaping and several Rolls-Royces parked nearby. Now, we tote up the expected value:

$$E(V) = .9999 \times \$0 - .0001 \times (-\$500,000) = \$50$$

Two questions spring to mind. First, why is your insurance so much higher than this? Although we have used made-up numbers as an example and the probability of an accident is not quite as low as our figure, rest assured that you are paying a lot more for your insurance than its expected value.

Insurance companies are not charitable institutions; they have to make a profit, and they have to pay their employees.

Second, even if our odds are a little off, the probability of a loss is very small. Why not just chance it and skip the insurance? There are two reasons: one has to do with how you estimate probabilities, which we shall get to later; the other is that in most states, you don't have a choice—you *have* to buy the insurance. The state does not want poor people running into Ferraris and coming up a hundred thousand dollars short when they have to pay for the damages, or even bumping into your fender and coming up $500 short.

Some poor people like lotteries. Many states are very obliging; they provide lotteries as a public service. It is a handy way for the state to make some money while "helping" its poorer citizens. Say a lottery ticket costs $1, and if you win, you get $500,000. Not bad—depending upon the probability that you will win. Let us say you have one chance in a million. Now we can compute the expected value of the ticket:

$$E(V) = \$500,000 \times .000001 - \$0 \times .99999 = 50¢$$

This is not a good investment. Why pay $1.00 for something that is worth only 50¢? Most people won't—they don't know the formula, but they know you are likely to lose when you gamble unless you cheat or own the casino.

Expected Utility

One reason that people gamble is that they compute expected *utility* rather than expected value. People seek pleasure or reinforcement or happiness. We call this *utility*. There is not a one-to-one correspondence between dollars and utility. What is the formula for expected happiness or expected utility? It is the same as that for expected value except that we compute it with subjectively estimated probabilities of wins and losses and subjective rather than dollar-denominated values. Let us think first about subjective value.

The Psychophysics of Money and Happiness

Assume that the value of something is a function of how activated the cognitive units coding it are (Grossberg & Gutowski, 1987; Martindale & Moore, 1988). Consider money or happiness—more money should produce more activation. We know what activation functions look like (one is shown in Figure 10–4). So far as money and happiness are concerned, the function cannot be linear. There is an upper limit on how activated a cognitive unit can be, just as there is an upper limit on how happy one can be. If you play the lottery and win $2,000,000, will you be twice as happy as if you had won $1,000,000? That is unlikely. The $1,000,000 already gets you to the top of the curve. Another way to read Figure 10–4 is in terms of how much money one already has. Let's say one already has a million dollars. What does gaining $100 mean? Not much, because the person is on the flat part of the curve.

F I G U R E   1 0 – 4
The subjective value of money.

If one has nothing much, the $100 means a lot: that person is on the linear part of the curve. What about the flat part of the curve near zero? How far it extends will vary from person to person. What is a penny worth? About nothing. Say I bet you $1.26 on something and lose, but have only $1.25. Are you going to hound me for the extra penny? No, $1.25 is quite close enough.

The Future Is Not Worth Much

Think about someone who does not make much money. After all expenses are paid, he could perhaps save $365 per year. Does he? Probably not. Perhaps he buys a $1 lottery ticket every day. If the person were to put the money in the bank, he would have $3650 plus interest after ten years. He could buy a Yugo, but he knows as well as you do that Yugos will probably cost $10,000 in ten years. He is *never* going to be able to buy a new car. This is sad, but plenty of people are in this position. The person has no hope. Well, he does have one hope: the lottery ticket may pay off and he will be rich. Objectively, the ticket is not worth the price, but subjectively it may be. When the person buys the ticket, there is a brief moment of hope. The probability of "winning" this moment of happiness is certain. In fact, the person may wonder why the state charges so little for this ticket to certain happiness.

If our hypothetical person cut some corners, he could probably save more. He could quit smoking, or he could walk to work rather than taking a bus. Then he could save enough to buy a car. Why doesn't he do so? We have a strong tendency to prefer a small immediate gain over a large delayed gain (Rachlin, 1989; Rachlin, Logue, Gibbon, & Frankel, 1986). This is true of animals in Skinner boxes and of people making choices. It is just as true of rich people as of poor people. One reason was pointed out by J. P. Morgan, who was as rich as anyone needs to be: "In the long run, we are all dead."

Would you like to be a millionaire? Would you accept this offer to become one? You must stay in a sealed room for 20 years. You can have about anything you want to entertain yourself, but no visitors are allowed— you can't see any human beings for 20 years. You won't see anything living, since no pets are allowed, either. You won't see the sun or stars, because the room is sealed. After 20 years you get 20 million dollars tax-free. If there is inflation, the difference will be made up. You can leave the room any time you want, but if you leave early, you don't get any money. Interested? Probably not many people would do this even if we doubled the stakes. How about this? Same deal, but you only have to stay a week. Do it, and you get $1000. This offer sounds much more attractive—a lot of people would be interested in it. You would be paid $142.86 a day to sit around, read books, or watch TV. But this is not much. Your pay with the 20-million-dollar deal would be about $2,739 per day. You are not as interested in money as you thought you were.

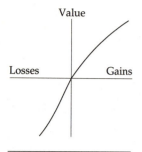

Value

Losses   Gains

F I G U R E   1 0 – 5
The subjective value of gains and loses. (From D. Kahneman and A. Tversky [1984]. Choices, values, and frames. *American Psychologist, 39,* p. 342. Copyright © American Psychological Association. Reprinted by permission.)

The Value of Gains and Losses

Have you ever lost a $20 bill? That really hurts, doesn't it? Have you ever found $20? That is merely rather nice. Most people would agree that it hurts more to loose $20 than it feels good to find $20. Tversky and Kahneman (1981) argue that the value of gains and losses can be diagramed as shown in Figure 10–5. The curve means that, at least up to a point, it hurts more to lose *X* than it makes one happy to gain *X*. On the upper right, the curve flattens out: the more one already has, the less *X* means. One can only get so happy. The curve on the lower left flattens out, too—one can only get so unhappy. Suppose you have $10,000 to your name and invest it all in the Persian Gulf Cruise Line Company. Their ship sinks, so you lose all your money. That hurts. Say you were the only person in the world who had invested. (This is certainly conceivable, given how dangerous the Persian Gulf is.) You are stuck as the sole owner of the company that, incidentally, has debts of $20 million. Does that hurt any more? No. You don't have the money, and you can only lose what you have. You go bankrupt. For all you care, the debt could be $20 billion.

Why does the curve in Figure 10–5 look the way it does? Grossberg and Gutowski (1987) argue that the emotion produced by a gain is proportional to the on-response of the dipole that codes an event, and the emotion produced by a loss is proportional to the off-response of the dipole coding the event. An off-response is usually greater than an on-response. The shape of the preference function shown in Figure 10–5 has implications for our attitude toward risk in making choices. Which would you prefer—(A) a sure gain of $240 or (B) a 25% chance to gain $1000 and a 75% chance to gain nothing?

Kahneman and Tversky (1984) found that 84% of people prefer (A), whereas only 16% prefer (B). Here is another choice: (A) a sure loss of $750 or (B) 75% chance to lose $1000 and a 25% chance to lose nothing.

Kahneman and Tversky (1984) found that, in this case, only 13% of people prefer (A), and 87% prefer (B). As you can see, our attitude toward risk depends upon whether gain or loss is involved. In the case of gains, we are *risk aversive:* we want to take the money and run. In the case of loses, we are *risk seeking:* we would rather take our chances than face a sure loss.

One reason for this preference may have to do with attention (Grossberg & Gutowski, 1987). In the first problem, considering (A) means turning on the on-unit of a dipole. When you shift your attention from (A), the off-unit comes on. The off-unit codes a *loss* of $240, which is unpleasant. Now your attention is on (B). Objectively, the expected value of (B), at $250, is greater than that of (A). The negative emotion left over from (A), however, subtracts from the emotion produced by (B). This effect would still be true if one considered (B) first. The point is that the affect produced by not-(A) and (B) is more negative than the affect produced by not-(B) and (A). In the second problem, the emotion produced by the on-unit coding (A) is negative. When you turn your attention from (A), the off-unit (coding a sure *gain* of $750) comes on and produces *positive* affect. This positive affect is added to the positive affect produced by (B), where there is a chance of losing nothing. Thus, (B) is chosen.

Framing and Choice

How something is stated can have a major effect on our choices. We have been chatting about expensive cars and people going bankrupt to avoid paying off $20-billion debts. We all have our dreams, but in your heart you know it's pretty unlikely that you'll ever be sitting in the back seat of a Rolls-Royce limousine talking to your banker in Zurich on one of your cellular phones. Cheer up—"The paths of glory lead but to the grave." Feel better? You really shouldn't. Where do you think the other paths lead? The way I framed the statement highlighted a connection between glory and death, which inhibited your knowledge that in the long run we are *all* dead.

Framing effects show up in making choices. Here is a Kahneman and Tversky (1984) problem that lets you pretend that you are the president:

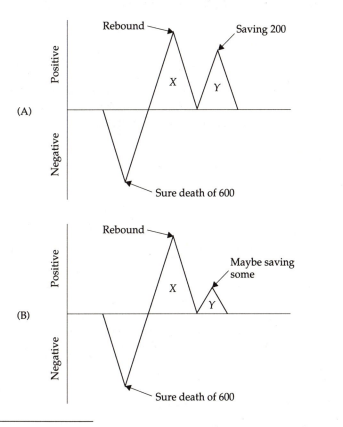

F I G U R E   1 0 – 6   In comparing alternatives, we choose the alternative that produces the most positive activation. Because X + Y are larger in (A) than in (B), we choose alternative (A).

Imagine that the United States is preparing for the outbreak of an unusual Asian disease, which is expected to kill 600 people. Two alternative programs to combat the disease have been proposed. Assume the exact scientific estimate of the consequences are as follows:

If Program A is adopted, 200 people will be saved.

If Program B is adopted, there is a 1/3 probability that 600 people will be saved, and a 2/3 probability that no people will be saved.

Most people prefer Program A. Why? To assess Program A, one has to compare it to something. The most obvious thing to compare it to is the certain death of 600 people, which is terrible. The rebound of the dipole when you turn to Program A is positive (see Figure 10–6[a]). As shown, Program A is also positive, and the positive affect adds up. Program B can be compared either to the certain death of 600 people or the certain saving of 200. In either case, there will not be as much positive affect as there was for program A (Grossberg & Gutowski, 1987). The alternatives are shown in Figure 10–6.

SUBJECTIVE PROBABILITY

Another reason for the choices people make has to do with the way we estimate probability. We do it incorrectly, but at least we do it consistently incorrectly. People tend to *overestimate* the probability of low-probability events,

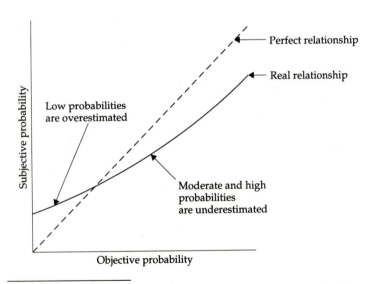

F I G U R E   1 0 – 7 Relationship between objective and subjective probability.

and they tend to *underestimate* the probability of more probable events (Kahneman & Tversky, 1984). This tendency is shown in Figure 10–7.

Subjective estimation of probabilities provides another explanation for some of the choices described in the previous section. Recall the $1 lottery ticket. Its objective expected value is 50¢. Even if it is printed on the ticket that "Your chance of winning is 1 in a million," many people don't believe it. If someone believes that his personal chances of winning are actually 2 in a million, then the ticket really is worth $1 to him. Even if you did not have to, you would probably insure your car. The probability of having an accident is low, but people overestimate low probabilities. The objective probability of an accident may be 1 in 10,000, whereas the subjective probability may come out closer to 1 in 1000. If so, the insurance appears to be worth the money. We have to estimate probabilities all the time. Cars, for example, do not come with tags that say "The probability that this vehicle will break in the next three years is .15063." We have to estimate the probability by means of two main methods: *availability* and *representativeness* (Kahneman & Tversky, 1973).

Availability

You do not usually go to the library and look up statistics to estimate probabilities. As you go about your daily business, your brain automatically stores information about all kinds of events. When you need to estimate a probability, you call on your long-term memory—that is, you recall some relevant instances and tally up the frequencies. This method often does give you a pretty accurate ballpark figure. How probable is it that there will be a tornado in your state next month? If you are not completely sure of exactly what counts as a tornado, it is safe to guess that the probability must be pretty low. If you live in Kansas, you know that the answer depends upon what next month is. In either case, your probability estimate will be fairly accurate.

Even if you are not sure exactly how to define a tornado, you know that tornadoes are dangerous. They kill a lot of poeple. Are more people killed by tornadoes or by asthma? We don't seem to hear much about death by asthma, but every summer the news reports many deaths from tornadoes—so the answer must be tornadoes (Slovic, Fischhoff, & Lichtenstein, 1976). In fact, death from asthma is 20 times more likely. How about the deadly scourge of botulism versus asthma? About 40% of people think that botulism is a more likely cause of death, whereas death from asthma is really 920 times more likely than death from botulism. The reason for these incorrect estimates is probably media coverage (Slovic et al., 1976). Tornadoes and botulism are rare, discrete events that happen in one place, so they get a lot of news coverage. Deaths from asthma are unrelated events that occur throughout the year and throughout the country and thus do not get media coverage.

Some items in memory are more accessible than others. Are there more words in the English language that begin with *K* or that have *K* as their third letter? Most people think there are more that begin with *K* (Tversky & Kahneman, 1973). Why? Well, we can think of lots of words that start with *K*, but we can't think of very many that have *K* as their third letter. That is because of the way our memory for words is organized, though; actually, about three times more words have *K* as their third letter. Tversky and Kahneman (1973) had people read the names of equal numbers of famous men and women, then asked about the proportion of males and females on the list. In one condition in which the women were more famous than the men, people greatly overestimated the frequency of women on the list. In another condition, the men were more famous, and subjects now overestimated the frequency of men. To answer the question, people must have recalled the list and done a rough count; because they remembered more of the more famous names, they incorrectly estimated the frequencies.

Grossberg and Gutowski (1987) note that low-probability events are novel or surprising and thus cause an attentional reset. Their mental representations therefore become more activated than nodes coding more usual events. If two events are compared in short-term memory, the node coding the low-frequency event is too activated, and the node coding the high-frequency event is not activated enough. Thus, the ratio of the two frequencies gets miscalculated. High activation in short-term memory causes long-term memory connections to be strengthened. Because of the strengthening, low-frequency events get more "space" in long-term memory than they deserve.

Representativeness

Another method for judging probabilities involves representativeness or similarity. We judge an event to be probable if it appears representative of what we think an event of its type should look like (Kahneman & Tversky, 1982). Which sequence of births of boys (B) and girls (G) is more probable: GGGBBB or GBBGBG? We know that the probability of a boy or a girl is random. The second sequence looks more random, so most people say it is more likely. Both sequences, however, are equally likely. Each birth is an independent event, and the baby does not know the sex of those that came before. The sequence GGGBBB is not very likely compared to *all other* possible sequences added together, but the same is equally true of the *specific* sequence GBBGBG.

This quite honest mistake is called the *gambler's fallacy*. A gambler may get the notion that the longer a string of losses becomes, the more likely it is that his luck will turn. If you are flipping coins and betting on heads, it will seem from the sequence TTTTTTTTTT that the next one has *got* to come up heads. Unfortunately, the coin doesn't know its history or your plight. The odds for the next flip are constant at 50:50. Intuitively, these odds do not strike us as right. But we are comparing the specific sequence with all other possible sequences, and that is the wrong comparison. The specific sequence TTHTHHHTTH is just as unlikely; however, it doesn't stand out and grasp our attention and thus doesn't lead us into the gambler's fallacy. People may generalize the gambler's fallacy to other games of chance such as lotteries. The fact that you lost on your last 1000 lottery tickets does not change your odds on the next lottery ticket.

SUMMARY AND CONCLUSIONS

There are two types of thinking. Associative thought occurs in the fringes of awareness, and intellectual thought occupies the focus of attention. Intellectual thought is goal-oriented. It uses various methods to reach a conclusion or make a choice; for example, deductive reasoning allows us to prove conclusions given that certain premises are true. People are quite good at using what is called *modus ponens*, which involves deducing that something exists because something else exists. People are especially poor at using what is called *modus tollens*, which involves deducing that one thing does not exist because something dependent on it does not exist, probably because we are not used to thinking about what is *not* the case. Many mistakes in logic occur because people do not have a cognitive module devoted specifically to formal logic, so they fall back on commonsense heuristics that should work. The problem is that sometimes they hurt rather than help. People are better at concrete problem solving than at formal logic, at least if problems are well defined or straightforward.

Creative problem solving involves finding a novel solution to a difficult and ill-defined problem. Creativity usually involves perception of an analogy. To become aware of the analogy requires that the relevant cognitive units be activated at the same time. The best way for this activation to occur is to be in a low state of arousal, where attention is broad or defocused. In such a state, many cognitive units can be activated at the same time. Inductive reasoning is used in both science and everyday life. On the basis of past experience, we infer—rather than prove—that something is likely to happen. One problem people have with inductive reasoning is *confirmation bias.* Once we have an idea, we tend to check to see if it is right, but we often omit tests that might falsify our hypothesis—that is, we don't check to see if our idea might be wrong.

Intellectual thinking is also used in making choices. When we make a choice, we have to figure out the utility of our choice and also the risk involved in it. Because we are not computers, we don't do this in a mechanical way. Subjective utility is not related to objective value in a linear way. Making money is nice; however, the more we have, the less it means to have even more of it. Losing money is downright awful. Most of us *like* to make money, but we *hate* to lose it, which makes us aversive to risks when gains are concerned but risk-seeking when losses are concerned.

To figure out the particular risks in making a choice, we have to estimate probabilities. People are fairly good at this, but we tend to overestimate low-probability events and underestimate events of high probability because we use two heuristics to judge probabilities. The availability heuristic means that we think of instances and make a rough frequency count. Low-probability events tend to stand out in memory, so we think that they are more probable than they are. The representativeness heuristic involves a judgment of how probable an event is based upon how representative it seems. If we are flipping coins, a long string of heads looks very unrepresentative, or nonrandom. We may mistakenly think that the next flip is likely to be a tail, but unfortunately the coin doesn't think this way.

References

Alba, J. W., & Hasher, L. (1983). Is memory schematic? *Psychological Bulletin, 93*, 203–231.

Amabile, T. M. (1983). *The social psychology of creativity.* New York: Springer-Verlag.

Anderson, J. A., Silverstein, J. W., Ritz, S. A., & Jones, R. S. (1977). Distinctive features, categorical perception, and probability learning: Some applications of a neural model. *Psychological Review, 84*, 413–451.

Anderson, J. R. (1985). *Cognitive psychology and its implications.* New York: W. H. Freeman.

Andrews, S. (1989). Frequency and neighborhood effects on lexical access: Activation or search? *Journal of Experimental Psychology: Learning, Memory, and Cognition, 15*, 802–814.

Arbib, M. A. (1972). *The metaphorical brain: An introduction to cybernetics as artificial intelligence and brain theory.* New York: Wiley.

Asch, S. E. (1958). The metaphor: A psychological inquiry. In R. Tagiuri and

L. Petrulo (Eds.), *Person perception and interpersonal behavior.* Stanford, CA: Stanford University Press.

Ashby, W. R., von Foerster, H., & Walker, C. C. (1962). Instability of pulse activity in a net with threshold. *Nature, 196,* 561–562.

Averbach, E., & Coriell, A. S. (1961). Short-term memory in vision. *The Bell System Technical Journal, 40,* 309–328.

Bahrick, H. (1984). Semantic memory content in permastore: Fifty years of memory for Spanish learned in school. *Journal of Experimental Psychology: General, 113,* 1–29.

Barnes, J. M., & Underwood, B. J. (1959). "Fate" of first-list associations in transfer theory. *Journal of Experimental Psychology, 58,* 97–105.

Bartlett, F. C. (1932). *Remembering.* Cambridge: Cambridge University Press.

Bates, E. (1979). *Emergence of symbols.* New York: Academic Press.

Battig, W. F., & Montague, W. E. (1969). Category norms for verbal items in 56 categories: A replication and extension of the Connecticut category norms. *Journal of Experimental Psychology Monographs, 80* (3, Pt. 2).

Beck, J. (1982). Textural segmentation. In J. Beck (Ed.), *Organization and representation.* Hillsdale, NJ: Erlbaum.

Békésy, G. von (1967). *Sensory inhibition.* Princeton, NJ: Princeton University Press.

Bentin, S., & Moscovitch, M. (1988). The time course of repetition effects for words and unfamiliar faces. *Journal of Experimental Psychology: General, 117,* 148–160.

Berlyne, D. E. (1960). *Conflict, arousal, and curiosity.* New York: McGraw-Hill.

Berlyne, D. E. (1971). *Aesthetics and psychobiology.* New York: Appleton-Century-Crofts.

Beurle, R. L. (1956). Properties of a mass of cells capable of regenerating pulses. *Philosophical Transactions of the Royal Society, B, 240,* 55–94.

Biederman, I. (1985). Human image understanding: Recent research and a theory. *Computer Vision, Graphics, and Image Processing, 32,* 29–73.

Blakemore, C. B. (1970). The representation of three-dimensional visual space in the cat's striate cortex. *Journal of Physiology, 209,* 155–178.

Blum, G. (1961). *A model of the mind.* New York: Wiley.

Bolles, R. C. (1975). Learning, motivation, and cognition. In W. K. Estes (Ed.), *Handbook of learning and cognitive processes, Vol. 1.* Hillsdale, NJ: Erlbaum.

Bornstein, M. H., Kessen, W., & Weiskopf, S. (1976). Color vision and hue categorization in young human infants. *Journal of Experimental Psychology: Human Perception and Performance, 2,* 115–129.

Boswell, J. (1791). *Life of Johnson.* New York: Oxford University Press, 1953.

Bower, G. H. (1981). Mood and memory. *American Psychologist, 36,* 129–148.

Bransford, J. D., & Franks, J. J. (1971). The abstraction of linguistic ideas. *Cognitive Psychology, 2,* 331–350.

Bransford, J. D., & Johnson, M. K. (1973). Considerations of some problems in comprehension. In W. G. Chase (Ed.), *Visual information processing.* New York: Academic Press.

Brewer, W. F., & Lichtenstein, E. H. (1982). Event schemas, story schemas, and story grammars. In J. Long & A. D. Baddeley (Eds.), *Attention and performance IX*. Hillsdale, NJ: Erlbaum.

Broadbent, D. E. (1958). *Perception and communication*. New York: Pergamon.

Broadhurst, P. L. (1959). The interaction of task difficulty and motivation: The Yerkes-Dodson Law reviewed. *Acta Psychologica, 16*, 321–338.

Broca, A., & Sulzer, D. (1902). La sensation lumineuse en fonction de temps. *Journal de Physiologie et de Pathologie Générale, 4*, 632–640.

Broca, P. (1861). Remarques sur la siège de la faculté du langage articulé suivies d'une observation d'aphémie. *Bulletin de la Société Anatomique de Paris, 36*, 330–357.

Brown, A. S. (1981). Inhibition in cued retrieval. *Journal of Experimental Psychology: Human Learning and Memory, 7*, 204–215.

Brown, C. R., & Rubinstein, H. (1961). Test of response bias explanation of word-frequency effect. *Science, 133*, 280–281.

Brown, J. (1958). Some tests of the decay theory of immediate memory. *Quarterly Journal of Experimental Psychology, 10*, 12–21.

Brown, R. (1973). *A first language: The early stages*. Cambridge, MA: Harvard University Press.

Bruce, C., Desimone, R., & Gross, C. G. (1981). Visual properties of neurons in a polysensory area in superior temporal sulcus of the macaque. *Journal of Neurophysiology, 46*, 369–384.

Bruce, V., & Valentine, T. (1985). Identity priming in the recognition of familiar faces. *British Journal of Psychology, 76*, 373–383.

Bruner, J. S., & Potter, M. C. (1964). Interference in visual recognition. *Science, 144*, 424–425.

Bybee, J. L., & Slobin, D. I. (1982). Rules and schemes in the development and use of the English past tense. *Language, 58*, 265–289.

Campbell, D. T. (1960). Blind variation and selective retention in creative thought as in other knowledge processes. *Psychological Review, 67*, 380–400.

Carpenter, R. H. S., & Blakemore, C. (1973). Interactions between orientations in human vision. *Experimental Brain Research, 18*, 287–303.

Castaneda, C. (1971). *A separate reality: Further conversations with Don Juan*. New York: Simon & Schuster.

Cherry, E. C. (1953). Some experiments on the recognition of speech with one and with two ears. *Journal of the Acoustical Society of America, 25*, 975–979.

Chomsky, N. (1957). *Syntactic structures*. The Hague: Mouton.

Chomsky, N. (1959). Review of *Verbal Behavior* by B. F. Skinner. *Language, 35*, 26–58.

Chomsky, N. (1986). *Knowledge of language: Its nature, origins, and use*. New York: Praeger.

Chomsky, N., & Halle, M. (1968). *The sound pattern of English*. New York: Harper & Row.

Clarke, R., & Morton, J. (1983). Cross modality facilitation in tachistoscopic word recognition. *Quarterly Journal of Experimental Psychology, 35*, 79–96.

Cole, M., & Perez-Cruet, J. (1964). Prosopangnosia. *Neuropsychologia, 2,* 237–246.

Collins, A. M., & Loftus, E. F. (1975). A spreading activation theory of semantic processing. *Psychological Review, 82,* 407–428.

Collins, A. M., & Quillian, M. R. (1969). Retrieval time from semantic memory. *Journal of Verbal Learning and Verbal Behavior, 8,* 240–247.

Cosmides, L. (1989). The logic of social exchange: Has natural selection shaped how humans reason? *Cognition, 39,* 187–276.

Craik, F. I. M., & Lockhart, R. S. (1972). Levels of processing: A framework for memory research. *Journal of Verbal Learning and Verbal Behavior, 11,* 671–684.

Crick, F. H. C., & Asanuma, C. (1986). Certain aspects of the anatomy and physiology of the cerebral cortex. In J. L. McClelland & D. E. Rumelhart (Eds.), *Parallel distributed processing, Vol. 2.* Cambridge, MA: MIT Press.

Crowder, R. G. (1978). Mechanisms of auditory backward masking in the stimulus suffix effect. *Psychological Review, 85,* 502–524.

Crowder, R. G., & Morton, J. (1969). Precategorical acoustic storage (PAS). *Perception and Psychophysics, 5,* 365–373.

Dallett, K. M. (1965). "Primary memory": The effects of redundancy upon digit repetition. *Psychonomic Science, 3,* 237–238.

Daniels, A. (1895). Memory, afterimage, and attention. *American Journal of Psychology, 6,* 558–564.

Deutsch, D. (1969). Music recognition. *Psychological Review, 76,* 300–307.

Deutsch, D. (1970). Tones and numbers: Specificity of interference in short-term memory. *Science, 168,* 1604–1605.

Deutsch, D. (1972). Mapping of interactions in the pitch memory store. *Science, 175,* 1020–1022.

Deutsch, D., & Feroe, J. (1975). Disinhibition in pitch memory. *Perception and Psychophysics, 17,* 320–324.

Deutsch, J. A., & Deutsch, D. (1963). Attention: Some theoretical considerations. *Psychological Review, 70,* 80–90.

Dodd, D. H., & White, R. M. (1980). *Cognition: Mental structures and processes.* Boston: Allyn & Bacon.

Dooling, D. J., & Christianson, R. E. (1977). Episodic and semantic aspects of memory for prose. *Journal of Experimental Psychology: Human Learning and Memory, 3,* 428–436.

Dykes, M., & McGhie, A. (1976). A comparative study of attentional strategies of schizophrenic and highly creative normal subjects. *British Journal of Psychiatry, 128,* 50–56.

Easterbrook, J. A. (1959). The effect of emotion on cue utilization and the organization of behavior. *Psychological Review, 66,* 183–201.

Egan, J. P., Carterette, E. C., & Thwing, E. J. (1954). Some factors affecting multi-channel listening. *Journal of the Acoustical Society of America, 26,* 774–782.

Eich, J., Weingartner, H., Stillman, R. C., & Gillin, J. C. (1975). State-dependent accessibility of retrieval cues in the retention of a categorized list. *Journal of Verbal Learning and Verbal Behavior, 14,* 408–417.

Eimas, P. D. (1985). The perception of speech in early infancy. *Scientific American, 252,* 46–52.

Eimas, P. D., & Corbit, J. D. (1973). Selective adaptation of linguistic feature detectors. *Cognitive Psychology, 4,* 99–109.

Epstein, R., Lanza, R. P., & Skinner, B. F. (1980). "Self-awareness" in the pigeon. *Science, 212,* 695–696.

Erdmann, B., & Dodge, R. (1898). *Psychologische Untersuchungen über das Lesen auf experimenteller Grundlage.* Halle, Germany: M. Niemeyer.

Erickson, R. P. (1984). On the neural bases of behavior. *American Scientist, 72,* 233–241.

Ervin, S. (1964). Imitation and structural change in children's language. In E. Lenneberg (Ed.), *New directions in the study of language.* Cambridge, MA: MIT Press.

Estes, W. K. (1972). An associative basis for coding and organization in memory. In A. W. Melton and E. Martin (Eds.), *Coding processes in human memory.* Washington, DC: Winston.

Estes, W. K. (1985). Some common aspects of models for learning and memory in lower animals and man. In L. Nilsson & T. Archer (Eds.), *Perspectives in learning and memory.* Hillsdale, NJ: Erlbaum.

Estes, W. K., & Taylor, H. A. (1964). A detection method and probabilistic models for assessing information processing from brief visual displays. *Proceedings of the National Academy of Sciences, 52,* 446–454.

Fechner, G. T. (1860). *Elemente der Psychophysik.* Leipzig: Breitkopf und Härtel.

Feldman, J. A., & Ballard, D. H. (1982). Connectionist models and their properties. *Cognitive Science, 6,* 205–254.

Fillmore, C. J. (1968). Toward a modern theory of case. In D. A. Reibel & S. A. Schane (Eds.), *Modern studies in English.* Englewood Cliffs, NJ: Prentice-Hall.

Finke, R. A. (1980). Levels of equivalence in imagery and perception. *Psychological Review, 87,* 113–132.

Finke, R. A., & Kosslyn, S. M. (1980). Mental imagery acuity in the peripheral visual field. *Journal of Experimental Psychology: Human Perception and Performance, 6,* 126–139.

Flexner, A. J., & Tulving, E. (1978). Retrieval independence in recognition and recall. *Psychological Review, 85,* 153–171.

Fodor, J. A. (1983). *The modularity of mind.* Cambridge, MA: MIT Press.

Fodor, J. A., & Bever, T. G. (1965). The psychological reality of linguistic segments. *Journal of Verbal Learning and Verbal Behavior, 4,* 414–420.

Fodor, J. A., Bever, T. G., & Garrett, M. F. (1974). *The psychology of language.* New York: McGraw-Hill.

Fodor, J. A., & Pylyshyn, Z. W. (1988). Connectionism and cognitive architecture: A critical analysis. *Cognition, 28,* 3–71.

Forster, K. I. (1987). Form priming with masked primes: The best match hypothesis. In M. Coltheart (Ed.), *Attention and performance XII.* Hillsdale, NJ: Erlbaum.

Frazier, L., & Rayner, K. (1982). Making and correcting errors during sentence comprehension: Eye movements in the analysis of structurally ambiguous sentences. *Cognitive Psychology, 14,* 178–210.

Friedman, M. J., & Reynolds, J. H. (1967). Retroactive inhibition as a function of response-class similarity. *Journal of Experimental Psychology, 74,* 351–355.

Frisch, K. von (1967). *The dance language and orientation of bees.* Cambridge, MA: Harvard University Press.

Ganong, W. F. (1980). Phonetic categorization in auditory word perception. *Journal of Experimental Psychology: Human Perception and Performance, 6,* 110–125.

Gardner, G. T. (1973). Evidence for independent parallel channels in tachistoscopic perception. *Cognitive Psychology, 4,* 130–155.

Gardner, R. A., & Gardner, B. T. (1969). Teaching sign language to a chimpanzee. *Science, 165,* 664–672.

Geschwind, N. (1972). Language and the brain. *Scientific American, 226*(4), 76–83.

Geschwind, N. (1979). Specialization of the human brain. *Scientific American, 241*(3), 180–199.

Ghiselin, B. (Ed.) (1952). *The creative process.* Berkeley: University of California Press.

Gibson, J. J., & Radner, M. (1937). Adaptation, aftereffect and contrast in the perception of tilted lines: I. Quantitative studies. *Journal of Experimental Psychology, 20,* 453–467.

Ginsburg, A. P. (1986). Spatial filtering and visual form perception. In K. Boff, L. Kaufman, & J. P. Thomas (Eds.), *Handbook of perception and human performance, Vol. 2.* New York: Wiley.

Glanzer, M., & Cunitz, A. R. (1966). Two storage mechanisms in free recall. *Journal of Verbal Learning and Verbal Behavior, 5,* 351–360.

Glass, A. L., & Holyoak, K. J. (1975). Alternative conceptions of semantic memory. *Cognition, 3,* 313–339.

Glass, A. L., Holyoak, K. J., & O'Dell, C. (1974). Production frequency and the verification of quantified statements. *Journal of Verbal Learning and Verbal Behavior, 13,* 237–254.

Gleitman, H. (1955). Place learning without prior performance. *Journal of Comparative and Physiological Psychology, 48,* 77–79.

Glenn, G. C. (1978). The role of episodic structure and of story length in children's recall of simple stories. *Journal of Verbal Learning and Verbal Behavior, 17,* 229–247.

Gluck, M. A., & Bower, G. H. (1988). From conditioning to category learning: An adaptive network model. *Psychological Review, 117,* 227–247.

Godden, D. R., & Baddeley, A. D. (1975). Context-dependent memory in two natural environments: On land and under water. *British Journal of Psychology, 66,* 325–331.

Graf, P., & Schachter, D. L. (1987). Selective effects of interference on implicit and explicit memory for new associations. *Journal of Experimental Psychology: Learning, Memory, and Cognition, 13,* 45–53.

Greenberg, J. H. (1963). Some universals of grammar with particular reference to the order of meaningful elements. In J. H. Greenberg (Ed.), *Universals of language.* Cambridge, MA: MIT Press.

Griggs, R. A., & Cox, J. R. (1982). The elusive thematic-materials effects in Wason's selection task. *British Journal of Psychology, 73,* 407–420.

Gross, C. G. (1973). Inferotemporal cortex and vision. *Progress in physiological psychology, Vol. 5.* New York: Academic Press.

Grossberg, S. (1969). Some networks that can learn, remember, and reproduce any number of complicated space-time patterns: I. *Journal of Mathematics and Mechanics, 19,* 53–91.

Grossberg, S. (1975). A neural model of attention, reinforcement, and discrimination learning. *International Review of Neurobiology, 18,* 263–327.

Grossberg, S. (1978a). A theory of human memory: Self-organization and performance of sensory-motor codes, maps, and plans. *Progress in Theoretical Biology, 5,* 233–374.

Grossberg, S. (1978b). Behavioral contrast in short-term memory: Serial binary models or parallel continuous memory models? *Journal of Mathematical Psychology, 17,* 199–219.

Grossberg, S. (1980). How does the brain build a cognitive code? *Psychological Review, 87,* 1–51.

Grossberg, S. (Ed.). (1987). *The adaptive brain, II: Vision, speech, language, and motor control.* Amsterdam: Elsevier/North-Holland.

Grossberg, S. (Ed.). (1988a). *Neural networks and natural intelligence.* Cambridge, MA: MIT Press.

Grossberg, S. (1988b). Nonlinear neural networks: Principles, mechanisms, and architectures. *Neural Networks, 1,* 17–62.

Grossberg, S., & Gutowski, W. (1987). Neural dynamics of decision under risk: Affective balance and cognitive-emotional interactions. *Psychological Review, 94,* 300–318.

Grossberg, S., & Levine, D. S. (1987). Neural dynamics of attentionally modulated Pavlovian conditioning: Blocking, inter-stimulus interval, and secondary reinforcement. *Applied Optics, 26,* 5015–5030.

Grossberg, S., & Schmajuk, N. A. (1987). Neural dynamics of attentionally-modulated Pavlovian conditioning: Conditional reinforcement, inhibition, and opponent processing. *Psychobiology, 15,* 195–240.

Grossberg, S., & Stone, G. O. (1986). Neural dynamics of word recognition and recall: Attentional priming, learning, and resonance. *Psychological Review, 93,* 46–74.

Gruenewald, P. J., & Lockhead, G. R. (1980). The free recall of category examples. *Journal of Experimental Psychology: Human Learning and Memory, 6,* 225–240.

Guyote, M. J., & Sternberg, R. S. (1981). A transitive-chain theory of syllogistic reasoning. *Cognitive Psychology, 13,* 461–525.

Haber, R. N. (1983). The impending demise of the icon: A critique of the concept of iconic storage in visual information processing. *Behavioral and*

Brain Sciences, 6, 1–54.

Hamilton, W. (1859). *Lectures on metaphysics and logic.* Edinburgh: Blackwood.

Hanson, H. M. (1959). Effects of discrimination training on stimulus generalization. *Journal of Experimental Psychology, 58,* 321–334.

Hasher, L., & Zacks, R. T. (1979). Automatic processing of fundamental information: The case of frequency of occurrence. *American Psychologist, 39,* 1372–1388.

Hebb, D. O. (1949). *The organization of behavior.* New York: Wiley.

Hebb, D. O. (1955). Drives and the C. N. S. (Conceptual Nervous System). *Psychological Review, 62,* 243–253.

Hécaen, H., & Ajuriaguerra, J. de (1956). Agnosie visuelle pour les objets inanimés par lésion unilatéral gauche. *Revue Neurologique, 94,* 222–233.

Hellström, A. (1985). The time-order error and its relatives: Mirrors of cognitive processes in comparing. *Psychological Bulletin, 97,* 35–61.

Helmholtz, H. von (1866). *Handbuch der physiologischen Optik.* Hamburg: Voss.

Helmholtz, H. von (1896). *Vorträge und Reden.* Brunswick: Friedrich Vieweg und Sohn.

Henderson, L. (1985). Toward a psychology of morphemes. In A. W. Ellis (Ed.), *Progress in the psychology of language, Vol. 1.* London: Erlbaum.

Heyd, V. (1954). *Language reform in modern Turkey.* Jerusalem: Israel Oriental Society.

Hintzman, D. L. (1986). "Schema abstraction" in a multiple-trace memory model. *Psychological Review, 93,* 411–428.

Hirst, W. (1986). The psychology of attention. In J. E. LeDoux & W. Hirst (Eds.), *Mind and brain: Dialogues in cognitive neuroscience.* Cambridge: Cambridge University Press.

Hobbes, T. (1642). *Leviathan.* New York: Liberal Arts Press, 1958.

Hobbs, J. R. (1983). Metaphor interpretation as selective inferencing: Cognitive processes in understanding metaphor (Part 1). *Empirical Studies of the Arts, 1,* 17–33.

Hockett, C. F. (1960). The origin of speech. *Scientific American, 203,* 89–96.

Hoffman, H. S., & Ison, J. R. (1980). Reflex modification in the domain of startle: I. Some empirical findings and their implications for how the nervous system processes sensory input. *Psychological Review, 87,* 175–189.

Hoffman, J. E. (1986). The psychology of perception. In J. E. LeDoux & W. Hirst (Eds.), *Mind and brain: Dialogues in cognitive neuroscience.* Cambridge: Cambridge University Press.

Holender, D. (1986). Semantic activation without conscious identification in dichotic listening, paraforeal listening, and visual masking: A survey and appraisal. *Behavioral and Brian Sciences, 9,* 1–66.

Holyoak, K. J., & Glass, A. L. (1975). The role of contradictions and counter-examples. *Journal of Verbal Learning and Verbal Behavior, 14,* 215–239.

Horwich, R. H. (1972). *The ontogeny of social behavior in the gray squirrel (Sciurus carolinensis).* Berlin: Verlag Paul Parey.

Howarth, C. F., & Ellis, K. (1961). The relative intelligibility threshold for one's own and other people's names. *Quarterly Journal of Experimental Psychology, 13,* 236–240.

Howes, D. H., & Solomon, R. L. (1951). Visual duration threshold as a function of word-probability. *Journal of Experimental Psychology, 41,* 401–410.

Hubel, D. H. (1988). *Eye, brain, and vision.* New York: W. H. Freeman.

Hubel, D. H., & Wiesel, T. N. (1965). Receptive fields and functional architecture in two nonstriate visual areas (18 and 19) of the cat. *Journal of Neurophysiology, 28,* 229–289.

Hull, C. L. (1943). *Principles of behavior.* New York: Appleton-Century-Crofts.

Jakobson, R. (1956). Two aspects of language and two types of aphasic disturbance. In R. Jakobson & M. Halle, *Fundamentals of language.* The Hague: Morton.

Jakobson, R., Fant, G., & Halle, M. (1963). *Preliminaries to speech analysis.* Cambridge, MA: MIT Press.

James, W. (1890). *The principles of psychology.* New York: Holt, Rinehart & Winston.

James, W. (1892). *Psychology, briefer course.* New York: Henry Holt & Co.

Jameson, F. (1972). *The prison-house of language: A critical account of structuralism and Russian formalism.* Princeton, NJ: Princeton University Press.

Jarvella, R. J. (1970). Effects of syntax on running memory span for connected discourse. *Psychonomic Science, 19,* 235–236.

Jarvella, R. J. (1971). Syntactic processing of connected speech. *Journal of Verbal Learning and Verbal Behavior, 10,* 409–416.

Jenkins, J. G., & Dallenbach, K. M. (1924). Oblivescence during sleep and waking. *American Journal of Psychology, 35,* 605–612.

Jevons, W. S. (1871). The power of numerical discrimination. *Nature, 3,* 281–282.

Johnston, J. C., & McClelland, J. L. (1974). Perception of letters in words: Seek not and ye shall find. *Science, 184,* 1192–1194.

Johnston, W. A., & Dark, V. J. (1986). Selective attention. *Annual Review of Psychology, 37,* 43–76.

Juszyck, P. W. (1986). Speech perception. In K. Boff, L. Kaufman, & J. P. Thomas (Eds.), *Handbook of perception and human performance, Vol. 2.* New York: Wiley.

Kahneman, D. (1973). *Attention and effort.* Englewood Cliffs, NJ: Prentice-Hall.

Kahneman, D., & Tversky, A. (1973). On the psychology of prediction. *Psychological Review, 80,* 237–251.

Kahneman, D., & Tversky, A. (1982). On the study of statistical intuitions. In D. Kahneman, P. Slovic, & A. Tversky (Eds.), *Judgements under uncertainty: Heuristics and biases.* Cambridge: Cambridge University Press.

Kahneman, D., & Tversky, A. (1984). Choices, values and frames. *American Psychologist, 39,* 341–350.

Kamin, L. J. (1969). Predictability, surprise, attention, and conditioning. In

B. A. Campbell & R. M. Church (Eds.), *Punishment and aversive behavior.* New York: Appleton-Century-Crofts.

Kellogg, W. N., & Kellogg, L. A. (1933). *The ape and the child.* New York: McGraw-Hill.

Keppel, G., & Underwood, B. J. (1962). Proactive inhibition in short-term retention of single items. *Journal of Verbal Learning and Verbal Behavior, 1,* 153–161.

Kinchla, R. A. (1980). The measurement of attention. In R. S. Wickerson (Ed.), *Attention and performance.* Hillsdale, NJ: Erlbaum.

Köhler, W. (1923). Zur Analyse des Sukzessivvergleichs und der Zeitfehler. *Psychologische Forschung, 4,* 115–175.

Kohonen, T. (1989). Speech recognition based on topology-preserving neural maps. In I. Aleksander (Ed.), *Neural computing architectures: The design of brain-like machines.* Cambridge, MA: MIT Press.

Konorski, J. (1967). *Integrative activity of the brain.* Chicago: University of Chicago Press.

Kosslyn, S. M. (1976). Can imagery be distinguished from other forms of internal representation? Evidence from studies of information retrieval times. *Memory & Cognition, 4,* 291–297.

Kroll, N., Parks, T., Parkinson, S., Bieber, S., & Johnson, A. (1970). Short-term memory while shadowing: Recall of visually and of aurally presented letters. *Journal of Experimental Psychology, 85,* 220–224.

Kuczaj, S. A. (1977). The acquisition of regular and irregular past tense forms. *Journal of Verbal Learning and Verbal Behavior, 16,* 589–600.

Külpe, O. (1912). The modern psychology of thinking. In J. M. Mandler & G. Mandler (Eds.), *Thinking: From association to gestalt.* New York: Wiley, 1964.

Lakoff, G. (1987). *Women, fire, and dangerous things: What categories reveal about the mind.* Chicago: University of Chicago Press.

Lakoff, G., & Johnson, M. (1980). *Metaphors we live by.* Chicago: University of Chicago Press.

Lamb, S. M. (1966). Linguistic structure and the production and decoding of discourse. In E. C. Carterette (Ed.), *Brain function, Vol. 3.* Berkeley: University of California Press.

Langley, P., Simon, H. A., Bradshaw, G. L., & Zytkow, J. M. (1987). *Scientific discovery: Computational explorations of the creative process.* Cambridge, MA: MIT Press.

Lashley, K. (1958). Cerebral organization and behavior. In F. A. Beach et al. (Eds.), *The neuropsychology of Lashley: Selected papers of K. S. Lashley.* New York: McGraw-Hill, 1960.

Lass, R. (1984). *Phonology: An introduction to basic concepts.* Cambridge: Cambridge University Press.

Lenneberg, E. (1967). *Biological foundations of language.* New York: Wiley.

Lettvin, J. Y., Maturana, H. R., McCulloch, W. S., & Pitts, W. H. (1959). What the frog's eye tells the frog's brain. *Proceedings of the Institute of Radio Engineers, 47,* 1940–1951.

Levy, W. B. (1985). Associative changes at the synapse: LTP in the hippocampus. In W. B. Levy, J. Anderson, & S. Lehmkuhle (Eds.), *Synaptic modification, neuron selectivity and nervous system organization*. Hillsdale, NJ: Erlbaum.

Liberman, A. M. (1982). On finding that speech is special. *American Psychologist, 37*, 148–167.

Liberman, A. M., Harris, K. S., Hoffman, H. S., & Griffith, B. C. (1957). The discrimination of speech sounds within and across phoneme boundaries. *Journal of Experimental Psychology, 54*, 358–368.

Lindsay, P. H., & Norman, D. A. (1977). *Human information processing: An introduction to psychology*. New York: Academic Press.

Lindsley, D. B. (1957). Psychophysiology and motivation. In M. R. Jones (Ed.), *Nebraska symposium on motivation, Vol. 5*. Lincoln: University of Nebraska Press.

Lindsley, D. B., Bowden, J., & Magoun, H. W. (1949). Effect upon EEG of acute injury to the brain stem activating system. *Electroencephalography and Clinical Neurophysiology, 1*, 475–486.

Livingstone, M. S., & Hubel, D. H. (1984). Anatomy and physiology of a color system in the primate visual cortex. *Journal of Neuroscience, 4*, 309–386.

Loftus, E. F. (1979). *Eyewitness testimony*. Cambridge, MA: Harvard University Press.

Loftus, E. F., & Loftus, G. R. (1980). On the permanence of stored information in the human brain. *American Psychologist, 35*, 409–420.

Loftus, E. F., Miller, D. G., & Burns, H. J. (1978). Semantic integration of verbal information into a visual memory. *Journal of Experimental Psychology: Human Learning and Memory, 4*, 19–31.

Lynn, R. (1966). *Attention, arousal and the orienting reaction*. Oxford: Pergamon.

MacFarlane, D. A. (1930). The role of kinesthesis in maze learning. *University of California Publications in Psychology, 4*, 277–305.

Mach, E. (1865). Über die Wirkung der räumlichen Vertheilung des Lichtreizes auf die Netzhaut. *Sitzungsberichte mathematisch-naturwissenschaftlichen der Kaiserlichen Akademie der Wissenschaft, 52*, 303–322.

Magnussen, S., & Kurtenbach, W. (1980). Adapting to two orientations: Disinhibition in a visual aftereffect. *Science, 207*, 908–909.

Mandler, J. M., & Johnson, N. S. (1977). Remembrance of things parsed: Story structure and recall. *Cognitive Psychology, 9*, 111–151.

Marcel, A. J. (1983). Conscious and unconscious perception: Experiments on visual masking and word recognition. *Cognitive Psychology, 15*, 197–237.

Marrocco, R. T. (1986). A neurobiological view of the psychology of perception. In J. E. LeDoux & W. Hirst (Eds.), *Mind and brain: Dialogues in cognitive neuroscience*. Cambridge: Cambridge University Press.

Marslen-Wilson, W. D., & Tyler, L. K. (1981). Central processes in speech understanding. *Philosophical Transactions of the Royal Society, London B, 295*, 317–332.

Martindale, A. E., & Martindale, C. (1988). Metaphorical equivalence of elements and temperaments: Empirical studies of Bachelard's theory of imagination. *Journal of Personality and Social Psychology, 55*, 836–848.

Martindale, C. (1977). Syntactic and semantic correlates of verbal ties in Gilles de la Tourette's syndrome: A quantitative case study. *Brain and Language, 4*, 231–247.

Martindale, C. (1980). Subselves: The internal representation of situational and personal dispositions. In L. Wheeler (Ed.), *Annual review of personality and social psychology, Vol. 1.* Newbury Park, CA: Sage Publications.

Martindale, C. (1981). *Cognition and consciousness.* Pacific Grove, CA: Brooks/Cole.

Martindale, C. (1989). Personality, situation, and creativity. In J. A. Glover, R. R. Ronning, & C. R. Reynolds (Eds.), *Handbook of creativity.* New York: Plenum.

Martindale, C., & Hasenfus, N. (1978). EEG differences as a function of creativity, stage of the creative process, and effort to be original. *Biological Psychology, 6*, 157–167.

Martindale, C., & Moore, K. (1988). Priming, prototypicality, and preference. *Journal of Experimental Psychology: Human Perception and Performance, 14*, 661–670.

Massaro, D. (1988). Some criticisms of models of human performance. *Journal of Memory and Language, 27*, 213–234.

McClelland, J. L. (1981). Retrieving general and specific knowledge from stored knowledge of specifics. *Proceedings of the Third Annual Conference of the Cognitive Science Society*, 170–172.

McClelland, J. L., & Elman, J. L. (1986). The TRACE model of speech perception. *Cognitive Psychology, 18*, 1–86.

McClelland, J. L., & Rumelhart, D. E. (1985). Distributed memory and the representation of general and specific information. *Journal of Experimental Psychology: General, 114*, 159–188.

McClelland, J. L., & Rumelhart, D. E. (Eds.). (1986). *Parallel distributed processing, Vol. 2.* Cambridge, MA: MIT Press.

McGeoch, J. A. (1942). *The psychology of human learning.* New York: Longmans.

McKay, D. G. (1973). Aspects of the theory of comprehension, memory and attention. *Quarterly Journal of Experimental Psychology, 25*, 22–40.

McKoon, G., Ratcliff, R., & Dell, G. S. (1985). The role of semantic information in episodic retrieval. *Journal of Experimental Psychology: Learning, Memory and Cognition, 11*, 742–751.

Mednick, S. A. (1962). The associative basis of the creative process. *Psychological Review, 69*, 220–232.

Melton, A. W., & Irwin, J. M. (1940). The influence of degrees of interpolated learning on retroactive inhibition and overt transfer of specific responses. *American Journal of Psychology, 53*, 175–203.

Mendelsohn, G. A. (1976). Associative and attentional processes in creative performance. *Journal of Personality, 44*, 341–369.

Meyer, D. E., Schvaneveldt, R. W., & Ruddy, M. G. (1974). Functions of graphemic and phonemic codes in visual word-recognition. *Memory & Cognition, 2*, 309–321.

Mill, J. S. (1846). *A system of logic, ratiocinative and inductive.* New York: Harper & Brothers.

Miller, G. A. (1956). The magical number seven, plus or minus two: Some limits on our capacity to process information. *Psychological Review, 63*, 81–97.

Miller, G. A. (1965). Some preliminaries to psycholinguistics, *American Psychologist, 20*, 15–20.

Miller, G. A., Galanter, E., & Pribram, K. H. (1960). *Plans and the structure of behavior.* New York: Holt, Rinehart & Winston.

Minsky, M. (1986). *The society of mind.* New York: Simon and Schuster.

Minsky, M., & Papert, S. (1969). *Perceptrons.* Cambridge, MA: MIT Press.

Mitchell, D. B. (1989). How many memory systems? Evidence from aging. *Journal of Experimental Psychology: Learning, Memory, and Cognition, 15*, 31–49.

Mitchell, D. B., & Brown, A. A. (1988). Persistent repetition priming in picture naming and its dissociation from recognition. *Journal of Experimental Psychology: Learning, Memory, and Cognition, 14*, 213–222.

Monsell, S., Doyle, M. C., & Haggard, P. N. (1989). Effects of frequency on visual word recognition tasks: Where are they? *Journal of Experimental Psychology: General, 118*, 43–71.

Moray, N. (1959). Attention in dichotic listening: Affective cues and the influence of instructions. *Quarterly Journal of Experimental Psychology, 11*, 56–60.

Moruzzi, G., & Magoun, H. W. (1949). Brain stem reticular formation and activation of the EEG. *Electroencephalography and Clinical Neurophysiology, 1*, 455–473.

Moyer, R. S. (1973). Comparing objects in memory: Evidence suggesting an internal psychophysics. *Perception and Psychophysics, 13*, 180–184.

Murdock, B. B. (1962). The serial position effect of free recall. *Journal of Experimental Psychology, 64*, 482–488.

Murray, H. A. (1938). *Explorations in personality: A clinical and experimental study of fifty men of college age.* New York: Oxford University Press.

Nakayama, K. (1985). Biological image motion processing: A review. *Vision Research, 25*, 625–660.

Neisser, U. (1967). *Cognitive psychology.* New York: Appleton-Century-Crofts.

Nelson, J. I., & Frost, B. J. (1978). Orientation-selective inhibition from beyond the classic visual receptive field. *Brain Research, 139*, 359–365.

Newell, A., & Simon, H. A. (1972). *Human problem solving.* Englewood Cliffs, NJ: Prentice-Hall.

Nickerson, R. S., & Adams, M. J. (1979). Long-term memory for a common object. *Cognitive Psychology, 11*, 287–307.

Norman, D. A. (1968). Toward a theory of memory and attention. *Psychological Review, 75*, 522–536.

Norman, D. A. (1969). Memory while shadowing. *Quarterly Journal of Experimental Psychology, 21*, 85–93.

Norman, D. A., & Bobrow, D. G. (1976). On the role of active memory processes in perception and cognition. In C. N. Cofer (Ed.), *The structure of human memory.* San Francisco: Freeman.

Paap, K. R., Newsome, S. L., McDonald, J. E., & Schvaneveldt, R. W. (1982). An activation-verification model for letter and word recognition: The word superiority effect. *Psychological Review, 89,* 573–594.

Paivio, A. (1975). Neomentalism. *Canadian Journal of Psychology, 29,* 263–291.

Parkin, A. J. (1984). Levels of processing, content, and facilitation of pronunciation. *Acta Psychologia, 55,* 19–29.

Pavlov, I. (1927). *Conditional reflexes.* London: Oxford University Press.

Pearce, J. M., & Hall, G. (1980). A model of Pavlovian learning: Variations in the effectiveness of conditioned but not unconditioned stimulus. *Psychological Review, 87,* 532–552.

Peterson, L. R., & Peterson, M. J. (1959). Short-term retention of individual verbal items. *Journal of Experimental Psychology, 58,* 193–198.

Peterson, L. R., Rawlings, L., & Cohen, C. (1977). The internal construction of spatial patterns. In G. H. Bower (Ed.), *The psychology of learning and motivation.* New York: Academic Press.

Pillsbury, W. B. (1897). A study in apperception. *American Journal of Psychology, 8,* 315–393.

Pinker, S. (1984). *Language learnability and language development.* Cambridge, MA: Harvard University Press.

Podgorny, P., & Shepard, R. N. (1978). Functional representations common to visual perception and imagination. *Journal of Experimental Psychology: Human Perception and Performance, 4,* 21–35.

Poincaré, H. (1913). *The foundations of science.* Lancaster, PA: Science Press.

Polf, J. O. (1976). The word superiority effect: A speed-accuracy analysis and test of a decoding hypothesis. Doctoral dissertation, University of Oregon.

Pollack, I., & Pickett, J. M. (1964). Intelligibility of excerpts from fluent speech: Auditory vs. structural context. *Journal of Verbal Learning and Verbal Behavior, 3,* 79–84.

Pomerantz, J. (1981). Perceptual organization in information processing. In M. Kubovy & J. Pomerantz (Eds.), *Perceptual organization.* Hillsdale, NJ: Erlbaum.

Popper, K. R. (1972). *Objective knowledge.* Oxford: Oxford University Press.

Posner, M. I. (1969). Abstraction and the process of recognition. In G. H. Bower (Ed.), *Advances in learning.* New York: Academic Press.

Posner, M. I. (1980). Orienting of attention. *Quarterly Journal of Experimental Psychology, 32,* 3–25.

Posner, M. I. (1986). Overview: Information processing. In K. Boff, L. Kaufman, & J. P. Thomas (Eds.), *Handbook of perception and human performance, Vol. 2.* New York: Wiley.

Posner, M. I., & Boies, S. J. (1971). Components of attention. *Psychological Review, 78,* 391–408.

Posner, M. I., & Snyder, C. R. R. (1975). Attention and cognitive control. In

R. Solso (Ed.), *Cognition and information processing: Third Loyola Symposium.* New York: Winston.

Postman, L., & Stark, K. (1969). Role of response availability in transfer and interference. *Journal of Experimental Psychology, 79,* 168–177.

Postman, L., Stark, K., & Fraser, J. (1968). Temporal changes in interference. *Journal of Verbal Learning and Verbal Behavior, 7,* 672–694.

Premack, D., & Premack, A. J. (1983). *The mind of an ape.* New York: Norton.

Pritchard, R. M. (1961). Stabilized images on the retina. *Scientific American, 204*(6), 72–78.

Pritchard, R. M., Heron, W., & Hebb, D. O. (1960). Visual perception approached by the method of stabilized images. *Canadian Journal of Psychology, 14,* 67–77.

Rachlin, H. (1989). *Judgment, decision, and choice.* New York: W. H. Freeman.

Rachlin, H., Logue, A. W., Gibbon, J., & Frankel, M. (1986). Cognition and behavior in studies of choice. *Psychological Review, 93,* 33–45.

Rashevsky, N. (1948). *Mathematical biophysics.* Chicago: University of Chicago Press.

Ratliff, F. (1965). *Mach bands: Quantitative studies on neural networks in the retina.* San Francisco: Holden-Day.

Reber, A. S. (1989). Implicit learning and trait knowledge. *Journal of Experimental Psychology: General, 118,* 219–235.

Reder, L. M. (1982). Plausibility judgment versus fact retrieval: Alternative strategies for sentence verification. *Psychological Review, 89,* 250–280.

Reichenbach, H. (1949). *Theory of probability.* Berkeley: University of California Press.

Reicher, G. M. (1969). Perceptual recognition as a function of meaningfulness of stimulus material. *Journal of Experimental Psychology, 81,* 274–280.

Reitman, J. S. (1971). Mechanisms of forgetting in short-term memory. *Cognitive Psychology, 2,* 185–195.

Reitman, J. S. (1974). Without surreptitious rehearsal, information in short-term memory decays. *Journal of Verbal Learning and Verbal Behavior, 13,* 365–377.

Rescorla, L. A. (1980). Overextension in early language development. *Journal of Child Language, 7,* 321–335.

Rescorla, R. A. (1988). Pavlovian conditioning: It's not what you think it is. *American Psychologist, 43,* 151–160.

Rescorla, R. A., & Wagner, A. R. (1972). A theory of Pavlovian conditioning: Variations in the effectiveness of reinforcement and nonreinforcement. In A. H. Black & W. F. Prokasy (Eds.), *Classical conditioning II: Current research and theory.* New York: Appleton-Century-Crofts.

Restorff, H. von (1933). Über die Wirkung von Bereichsbildungen im Spurenfeld. *Psychologie Forschung, 18,* 242–299.

Ribot, T. (1911). *The psychology of the emotions.* New York: Walter Scott.

Riesbeck, C. K. (1986). From conceptual analyzer to direct memory access parsing: An overview. In N. E. Sharkey (Ed.), *Advances in cognitive science.*

New York: Wiley.

Rips, L. J., & Marcus, S. L. (1977). Supposition and the analysis of conditional sentences. In M. A. Just & P. A. Carpenter (Eds.), *Cognitive processes in comprehension.* Hillsdale, NJ: Erlbaum.

Robinson, D. L., & Peterson, S. E. (1984). Posterior parietal cortex of the awake monkey: Visual responses and their modulation by behavior. In F. Reinoso-Suarez & C. Ajmone-Marsan (Eds.), *Cortical integration: Basic, archicortical, and cortical association levels of neural integration, Vol. 2.* New York: Raven.

Robson, J. G. (1975). Receptive fields: Neural representation of the spatial and intensive attributes of the visual image. In E. C. Carterette & M. P. Friedman (Eds.), *Handbook of perception, Vol. 5.* New York: Academic Press.

Rock, I. (1983). *The logic of perception.* Cambridge, MA: MIT Press.

Roediger, H. L. (1973). Inhibition in recall from cuing with recall targets. *Journal of Verbal Learning and Verbal Behavior, 12,* 644–657.

Roediger, H. L., & Blaxton, T. A. (1987). Retrieval modes produce dissociations in memory for surface information. In D. S. Gorstein & R. R. Hoffman (Eds.), *Memory and cognitive processes: The Ebbinghaus centennial conference.* Hillsdale, NJ: Erlbaum.

Rosch, E. (1973). On the internal structure of perceptual and semantic categories. In T. E. Moore (Ed.), *Cognitive development and the acquisition of language.* New York: Academic Press.

Rosch, E. (1975). Cognitive representations of semantic categories. *Journal of Experimental Psychology, 104,* 192–233.

Rosch, E., Simpson, C., & Miller, R. S. (1976). Structural bases of typicality effects. *Journal of Experimental Psychology: Human Perception and Performance, 2,* 491–502.

Rosenblatt, F. (1962). *Principles of neurodynamics.* New York: Spartan.

Rumelhart, D. E., & McClelland, J. L. (1982). An interactive activation model of context effects in letter perception: Part 2. The contextual enhancement effect and some tests and extensions of the model. *Psychological Review, 89,* 60–94.

Rumelhart, D. E., & McClelland, J. L. (1986a). On learning the past tense of English verbs. In J. L. McClelland & D. E. Rumelhart (Eds.), *Parallel distributed processing: Explorations in the microstructure of cognition, Vol. 2.* Cambridge, MA: MIT Press.

Rumelhart, D. E., & McClelland, J. L. (Eds.) (1986b). *Parallel distributed processing, Vol. 1.* Cambridge, MA: MIT Press.

Rumelhart, D. E., Hinton, G., & McClelland, J. L. (1986). A general framework for parallel distributed processing. In D. Rumelhart & J. L. McClelland (Eds.), *Parallel distributed processing, Vol. 1.* Cambridge, MA: MIT Press.

Rundus, D. (1971). Analysis of rehearsal processes in free recall. *Journal of Experimental Psychology, 89,* 63–77.

Rychlak, J. F. (1987). Can the strength of past associations account for the direction of thought? *Journal of Mind and Behavior, 8,* 185–193.

Sacks, O. W. (1985). *The man who mistook his wife for a hat and other clinical tales.* New York: Summit Books.

Samuel, A. G. (1981). Phonemic restoration: Insights from a new methodology. *Journal of Experimental Psychology: General, 110,* 474–494.

Schab, F. R., & Crowder, R. G. (1988). The role of succession in temporal cognition: Is the time-order error a recency effect in memory? *Perception and Psychophysics, 44,* 233–242.

Schachter, D. L. (1987). Implicit memory: History and current status. *Journal of Experimental Psychology: Learning, Memory, and Cognition, 13,* 501–518.

Schank, R., & Abelson, R. (1977). *Scripts, plans, goals and understanding.* Hillsdale, NJ: Erlbaum.

Schank, R., Goldman, N., Rieger, C., & Riesback, C. (1973). MARGIE: Memory, analysis, response generation and inference in English. *Proceedings of the Second International Joint Conference on Artificial Intelligence.* Stanford University, Stanford, CA.

Sebeok, T. A. (1984). Personal communication.

Sekuler, R. (1975). Visual motion perception. In E. C. Carterette & M. P. Friedman (Eds.), *Handbook of perception, Vol. 5.* New York: Academic Press.

Sekuler, R., & Blake, R. (1985). *Perception.* New York: Knopf.

Sekuler, R., & Ganz, L. (1963). A new aftereffect of seen movement with a stabilized visual image. *Science, 139,* 419–420.

Selfridge, O. G. (1959). Pandemonium: A paradigm for learning. In D. V. Blake & A. M. Uttley (Eds.), *Proceedings of the symposium on the mechanization of thought processes.* London: H. M. Stationery Office.

Shallice, T. (1978). The dominant action system: An information-processing approach to consciousness. In K. S. Pope & J. L. Singer (Eds.), *The stream of consciousness: Scientific investigations into the flow of human experience.* New York: Plenum.

Shepard, R. N., & Metzler, J. (1971). Mental rotation of three-dimensional objects. *Science, 171,* 701–703.

Shiffrin, R. M., & Schneider, W. (1977). Controlled and automatic human information processing: II. Perceptual learning, automatic attending and a general theory. *Psychological Review, 84,* 127–190.

Shimamura, A. P., & Squire, L. R. (1989). Impaired priming of new associations in amnesia. *Journal of Experimental Psychology: Learning, Memory, and Cognition, 15,* 721–728.

Sillito, A. M. (1979). Inhibitory mechanisms influencing complex cell orientation selectivity and their modification at high resting discharge levels. *Journal of Physiology, 289,* 33–53.

Simon, H. A. (1974). How big is a chunk? *Science, 183,* 482–488.

Simon, H. A. (1979). *Models of thought.* New Haven, CT: Yale University Press.

Simpson, G. B. (1984). Lexical ambiguity and its role in models of word recognition. *Psychological Bulletin, 96,* 316–340.

Singer, W. (1983). Neuronal activity as a shaping factor in the self-organization of neuron assemblies. In E. Basar, H. Flohr, H. Haken, & A. J. Mandell (Eds.),

Synergetics of the brain. New York: Springer-Verlag.

Skinner, B. F. (1975). The steep and thorny way to a science of behavior. *American Psychologist, 30,* 42–49.

Slamecka, N. J. (1969). Testing for associative storage in multitrial free recall. *Journal of Experimental Psychology, 81,* 557–560.

Slovic, P., Fischhoff, B., & Lichtenstein, S. (1976). Behavioral decision theory. *Annual Review of Psychology, 28,* 1–39.

Smith, S. M., Glenberg, A., & Bjork, R. A. (1978). Environmental context and human memory. *Memory & Cognition, 6,* 342–353.

Smolensky, P. (1988). On the proper treatment of connectionism. *Behavioral and Brain Sciences, 11,* 1–74.

Sokolov, E. N. (1963). *Perception and the conditioned reflex.* New York: Macmillan.

Solomon, R. L., & Corbit, J. D. (1974). An opponent process theory of motivation, I: Temporal dynamics of affect. *Psychological Review, 81,* 119–145.

Spence, K. W. (1956). *Behavior theory and conditioning.* New Haven, CT: Yale University Press.

Sperling, G. (1960). The information available in brief visual presentations. *Psychological Monographs, 74* (Serial No. 11).

Sperling, G. (1984). A unified theory of attention and signal detection. In R. Parasuramen & D. R. Davies (Eds.), *Varieties of attention.* Orlando, FL: Academic Press.

Spieth, W., Curtis, J. F., & Webster, J. C. (1954). Responding to one of two simultaneous messages. *Journal of the Acoustical Society of America, 26,* 391–396.

Squire, L. R. (1982). The neuropsychology of human memory. *Annual Review of Neuroscience, 5,* 241–273.

Staddon, J. E. R. (1983). *Adaptive behavior and learning.* Cambridge: Cambridge University Press.

Sternberg, S. (1966). High-speed scanning in human memory. *Science, 153,* 652–654.

Stone, G. O., & Van Orden, G. C. (1989). Are words represented by nodes? *Memory & Cognition, 17,* 511–524.

Streufert, S. (1969). Increasing failure and response rate in complex decision making. *Journal of Experimental Social Psychology, 5,* 310–323.

Sulin, R. A., & Dooling, D. J. (1974). Intrusion of a thematic idea in retention of prose. *Journal of Experimental Psychology, 103,* 255–262.

Svenko, B., Jerneic, A., & Kulenovic, A. (1983). A contribution to the investigation of time-sharing ability. *Ergonomics, 26,* 151–160.

Swinney, D. A. (1979). Lexical access during sentence comprehension: (Re)consideration of context effects. *Journal of Verbal Learning and Verbal Behavior, 18,* 645–659.

Tartter, V. C. (1986). *Language processes.* New York: Holt, Rinehart & Winston.

Thomson, D. M., & Tulving, E. (1970). Associative encoding retrieval: Weak and strong cues. *Journal of Experimental Psychology, 86,* 255–262.

Thorndike, E. L. (1911). *Animal intelligence: Experimental studies.* New York: Macmillan.

Thorndyke, P. W. (1977). Cognitive structures in comprehension and memory of narrative discourse. *Cognitive Psychology, 9,* 77–110.

Tinbergen, N. (1951). *The study of instinct.* Oxford: Oxford University Press.

Titchener, E. B. (1910). *A text-book of psychology.* New York: Macmillan.

Todorov, T. (1971). The two principles of narrative. *Diacritics, 1,* 37–44.

Tolhurst, D. J. (1973). Separate channels for the analysis of the shape and the movement of a moving visual stimulus. *Journal of Physiology, 231,* 385–402.

Tolman, E. C., & Honzik, C. H. (1930). Introduction and removal of reward, and maze performance in rats. *University of California Publishings in Psychology, 4,* 257–275.

Tootell, R. B., Silverman, M., & DeValois, R. L. (1981). Spatial frequency columns in primary visual cortex. *Science, 214,* 813–815.

Treisman, A. M. (1969). Strategies and models of selective attention. *Psychological Review, 76,* 282–299.

Treisman, A. M., & Gormican, S. (1988). Feature analysis in early vision: Evidence from search asymmetries. *Psychological Review, 95,* 15–48.

Treisman, A. M., & Riley, J. G. A. (1969). Is selective attention selective perception or selective response? A further test. *Journal of Experimental Psychology, 79,* 27–34.

Treisman, A. M., & Schmidt, H. (1982). Illusory conjunctions in the perception of objects. *Cognitive Psychology, 14,* 107–141.

Tulving, E. (1985). How many memory systems are there? *American Psychologist, 40,* 385–398.

Tulving, E., & Thomson, D. M. (1973). Encoding specificity and retrieval processes in episodic memory. *Psychological Review, 80,* 352–373.

Turkkan, J. S. (1989). Classical conditioning: The new hegemony. *Behavioral and Brain Sciences, 12,* 121–179.

Turvey, M. T. (1973). On peripheral and central processes in vision: Inferences from an information processing analysis of masking with patterned stimuli. *Psychological Review, 80,* 1–52.

Tversky, A. (1972). Elimination by aspects: A theory of choice. *Psychological Review, 79,* 281–299.

Tversky, A. (1977). Features of similarity. *Psychological Review, 84,* 327–352.

Tversky, A., & Gati, I. (1982). Similarity, separability, and the triangle inequality. *Psychological Review, 89,* 123–154.

Tversky, A., & Kahneman, D. (1973). Availability: A heuristic for judging frequency. *Cognitive Psychology, 5,* 207–232.

Tversky, A., & Kahneman, D. (1981). The framing of decisions and the psychology of choice. *Science, 211,* 453–458.

Underwood, B. J. (1948). Retroactive and proactive inhibition after five and forty-eight hours. *Journal of Experimental Psychology, 38,* 29–38.

Ungerleider, L. G., & Mishkin, M. (1982). Two cortical visual systems. In D. J. Ingle, M. A. Goodale, & R. J. W. Mansfield (Eds.), *Analysis of visual behavior.* Cambridge, MA: MIT Press.

Wallas, G. (1926). *The art of thought.* New York: Harcourt Brace Jovanovich.

Walley, R. E., & Weiden, T. D. (1973). Lateral inhibition and cognitive masking: A neuropsychological theory of attention. *Psychological Review, 80,* 284–302.

Waltz, D. L., & Pollack, J. B. (1985). Massively parallel parsing. *Cognitive Science, 9,* 51–74.

Wanner, E. (1968). On remembering, forgetting, and understanding sentences: A study of the deep structure hypothesis. Doctoral dissertation, Harvard University.

Warren, R. M., & Warren, R. P. (1970). Auditory illusions and confusions. *Scientific American, 223,* 30–36.

Wason, P. C., & Johnson-Laird, P. N. (1972). *Psychology of reasoning.* London: B. T. Batsford.

Watkins, M. J., & Kerkar, S. P. (1985). Recall of a twice-presented item without recall of either memory for events: Generic memory for events. *Journal of Memory and Language, 24,* 666–678.

Watson, J. B. (1913). Psychology as the behaviorist views it. *Psychological Review, 20,* 158–177.

Weinburg, H. I., Wadsworth, J., & Baron, R. S. (1983). Demand and the impact of leading questions on eyewitness testimony. *Memory and Cognition, 11,* 101–104.

Weisberg, R. W. (1986). *Creativity: Genius and other myths.* New York: Freeman.

Weisstein, N., & Harris, C. S. (1974). Visual detection of line segments: An object superiority effect. *Science, 186,* 752–755.

Wernicke, C. (1874). *Der aphasische Symptomen-Complex.* Breslau: Franck & Weigert.

Wertheimer, M. (1912). Experimentelle Untersuchungen über das Sehen von Bewegung. *Zeitschrift für Psychologie, 61,* 161–265.

Wickelgren, W. A. (1976). Memory storage dynamics. In W. K. Estes (Ed.), *Handbook of learning and cognitive processes, Vol. 4.* Hillsdale, NJ: Erlbaum.

Wickelgren, W. A. (1977). *Learning and memory.* Englewood Cliffs, NJ: Prentice-Hall.

Wickelgren, W. A. (1979a). Chunking and consolidation: A theoretical synthesis of semantic networks, configuring in conditioning, S-R versus cognitive learning, normal forgetting, the amnesic syndrome, and the hippocampal arousal system. *Psychological Review, 86,* 44–60.

Wickelgren, W. A. (1979b). *Cognitive psychology.* Englewood Cliffs, NJ: Prentice-Hall.

Wickelgren, W. A., & Corbett, A. T. (1977). Associative interference and retrieval dynamics in yes-no recall and recognition. *Journal of Experimental Psychology: Human Learning and Memory, 3,* 189–202.

Wickelgren, W. A., & Norman, D. A. (1966). Strength models and serial position in short-term recognition memory. *Journal of Mathematical Psychology, 3,* 316–347.

Wickens, C. D. (1984a). *Engineering psychology and human performance.* Columbus, OH: Merrill.

Wickens, C. D. (1984b). Processing resources in attention. In R. Parasuraman & D. R. Davies (Eds.), *Varieties of attention.* Orlando, FL: Academic Press.

Wickens, D. D. (1973). Some characteristics of word encoding. *Memory and Cognition, 1,* 485–490.

Williams, A., & Weisstein, N. (1978). Line segments are perceived better in a coherent context than alone: An object-line effect in visual perception. *Memory and Cognition, 6,* 85–90.

Wilson, E. O. (1975). *Sociobiology: The new synthesis.* Cambridge, MA: Harvard University Press.

Wilson, H. R., & Cowan, J. D. (1972). Excitatory and inhibitory interactions in localized populations of model neurons. *Biophysical Journal, 12,* 1–24.

Wood, F., Taylor, B., Penney, R., & Stump, B. (1980). Regional cerebral blood flow response to recognition memory versus semantic classification tasks. *Brain and Language, 9,* 113–122.

Wundt, W. (1896). *Lectures on human and animal psychology.* New York: Macmillan.

Yaroush, R., Sullivan, M. J., & Ekstrand, B. R. (1971). The effect of sleep on memory. II: Differential effects of the first and second half of the night. *Journal of Experimental Psychology, 88,* 361–366.

Yerkes, R. M., & Dodson, J. D. (1908). The relation of strength of stimulus to rapidity of habit formation. *Journal of Comparative and Neurological Psychology, 18,* 459–482.

Zechmeister, E. B., & Nyberg, S. E. (1982). *Human memory: An introduction to research and theory.* Pacific Grove, CA: Brooks/Cole.

Zeki, S. M. (1974). Functional organization of a visual area in the posterior bank of the superior temporal sulcus of the rhesus monkey. *Journal of Physiology, 236,* 549–573.

Zeki, S. M. (1978). Uniformity and diversity of structure and function in rhesus monkey pre-striate visual cortex. *Journal of Physiology, 277,* 273–290.

Zurif, E. B., Caramazza, A., Meyerson, R., & Galvin, J. (1974). Semantic feature representations for normal and aphonic language. *Brain and Language, 1,* 167–187.

Author Index

Subject Index